PROCLAIM THE
GOOD NEWS

PROCLAIM THE GOOD NEWS

A Short History of the Church Missionary Society

Jocelyn Murray

HODDER AND STOUGHTON
LONDON SYDNEY AUCKLAND TORONTO

British Library Cataloguing in Publication Data

Murray, Jocelyn
   Proclaim the good news: a short history of
the Church Missionary Society.—(Hodder
Christian paperbacks)
   1. Church Missionary Society—History
   I. Title
266'.3   BV2500

   ISBN 0 340 34501 2

Hodder and Stoughton Editorial Office: 47 Bedford Square, London WC1B 3DP.

To

Rosemary

and

Jean

FOREWORD

The Church Missionary Society has been fortunate in its historiographers. Eugene Stock's four stout volumes told the story from its inception up to the First World War. Canon Gordon Hewitt's two volumes, under the general title of *The Problems of Success*, were a worthy sequel. But it is not everyone who has the time, or indeed the inclination, to study the story in such detail. And it is a story which should be widely known.

Jocelyn Murray has now made this possible and many will be grateful to her. She has given us, in readable form, a summary which brings before us a galaxy of men and women who were not disobedient to the heavenly vision and, counting not their lives dear to them, went out to spread the Gospel in a wide variety of ways. There are stories of martyrs here, of great leaders like Henry Venn and Max Warren, of ventures and triumphs, of sin and failure. We need to look back and see how the CMS story began and what ensued from its beginnings. We need to appreciate what revival in Africa has given to the world and to appraise the daring of India in matters of church unity and of revised liturgy. A reading of this book will rebuke us for our insularity and help us to lift up our eyes and look on wider fields. Europe and America need the ministry, the insights, the discoveries of Asia and Africa, of China and Japan.

The Epilogue should be read with special care. Why should we jettison the time-honoured word *missionary* and replace it with *mission partners*? Why, rather, should we *not* do so? A new concept of missionary endeavour is rapidly emerging, the implementation of which calls for the abandonment of certain old patterns and well-loved phraseology, while at the same time those engaged on that endeavour hold fast to the essential Christian message with total devotion.

I wish this book well. It does not make comfortable reading, but it will prick many a conscience and stab awake many a mind.

DONALD COGGAN

ACKNOWLEDGEMENTS

It is always difficult to make proper acknowledgement, especially when the subject is one that has included much of one's life, and therefore the number of those who have directly or indirectly given help and information is almost unlimited. I must ask those who for reason of space I cannot name to pardon me.

My first debt to the New Zealand Church Missionary Society and to my CMS colleagues in Kenya underlies the whole effort. I must thank my present community family, and especially Liz, Ellie and Will, for the help and life support they have given me. A number of former missionaries have given me counsel and information, as also have former members of headquarters staff: Archbishop Leslie Brown, Archbishop C. J. Patterson, Bishop Lesslie Newbigin, Bishop Bengt Sundkler, Jennifer Carey, Paul Hunt, Elliott Kendall, Bernard Nicholls, former CMS community relations secretary; Rev. David Chaplin of Partnership for World Mission. I have been greatly helped by Wilbert Shenk, whose book on Henry Venn has illuminated much.

Many working today within 157 Waterloo Road have given practical help as well as information, and have taken time to read sections and make suggestions. I must thank Susan Musgrave, who started the process off, and Mary Endersbee, who has helped to finish it. Jesse Hillman, in charge of the Communications Division, has helped with information on Egypt and East Africa, as well as in his present capacity. The present general secretary, Canon Simon Barrington-Ward, and Glynne Evans, executive assistant in his department, have taken time in their very busy lives to read and make suggestions. Simon Barrow, Joan Burton and Andrew Morton have given me help and support. For all these people, and many others, I am deeply grateful. Dilwyn's help with typing, and in other ways, has been much appreciated.[1]

But my deepest debt is to the two friends to whom the book is dedicated. Rosemary Keen, archivist, and Jean Woods, librarian, have given me every possible help and support as they have in the past to many others. The original idea for the book came from them. I want to record again my thanks not only for the knowledge they have put at my disposal, but also for the spirit in which it has been done, and their love.

JOCELYN MURRAY
Highgate
November 1984

---

[1]Special thanks to Leny for her help with the index.

LIST OF ABBREVIATIONS

AACC	All Africa Conference of Churches
BCMS	Bible Churchmen's Missionary Society
BFBS	British and Foreign Bible Society
BMS	Baptist Missionary Society
C&CCS	Commonwealth and Continental Church Society
CBMS	Conference of British Missionary Societies (Conference of Missionary Societies of Great Britain and Ireland)
CEZMS	Church of England Zenana Missionary Society
CIBC	Church of India, Burma and Ceylon
CICCU	Cambridge Inter-Collegiate Christian Union
CIM	China Inland Mission
CMA	Church Missionary Association
CSI	Church of South India
CSM	Church of Scotland Mission
DWME	Division of World Mission and Evangelism
FES	Female Education Society (Society for Promoting Female Education)
IBEAC	Imperial British East Africa Company
IMC	International Missionary Council
KAU	Kenya African Union
KCA	Kikuyu Central Association
LMS	London Missionary Society
MRI	Mutual Responsibility and Interdependence (in the body of Christ)
NSW	New South Wales
OMF	Overseas Missionary Fellowship

PECUSA	Protestant Episcopal Church USA
PWM	Partnership for World Mission
SAMS	South American Missionary Society
SIUC	South India United Church
SPCK	Society for Promoting Christian Knowledge
SPG	Society for the Propagation of the Gospel (in Foreign Parts)
UMCA	Universities' Mission to Central Africa
USPG	United Society for the Propagation of the Gospel
WCC	World Council of Churches
ZBMM	Zenana Bible and Medical Mission

CONTENTS

Map   xiv
Introduction   1
 1 The Church Principle   7
 2 The First Missionaries at Work   19
 3 A Great Missionary Administrator   37
 4 India: Bishop Wilson and his Successors,
      1832–1876   59
 5 New Work in the New Worlds   79
 6 The First Century   97
 7 New Fields, New Developments   114
 8 Oriental Ups and Downs   140
 9 Taking Stock: CMS at the Centenary
      and After   163
10 Retreat and Advance 1918–1942   176
11 New Partners in War and Peace   196
12 Max Warren's Prophetic Vision   207
13 Tensions in Africa   235
14 Growing Partnership in Changing Circumstances   259
Epilogue   285
Select Bibliography   293
Index   295

CHURCH MISSIONARY SOCIETY
Fields of work from 1804

North-West Pacific
(British Columbia)
1857

Canada
(Manitoba)
1822

West Indies
1826-61

West Africa
(Sierra Leone)
1804

Nige
185

Nigeria
(Yoruba Mission)
1844

Persia
(Iran)
1869

e

Malta
1811

gypt
826
founded mission)
899

Palestine
1849

India
1813

China
1844

Japan
1875

Sudan
1899

Uganda
1877

Abyssinia
(Ethiopia)
1830-41

Ceylon
(Sri Lanka)
1818

Malaya
1951

uanda
urundi
1921

East Africa
(Kenya)
1844

nganyika
Tanzania)
1878

Mauritius
1856

South Africa
1837-43

New Zealand
(1809) 1814

INTRODUCTION

In 1799 a small group of laymen and clergymen of the Church of England met together and founded a society soon to be known as the Church Missionary Society. At first called The Society for Missions to Africa and the East, its purpose was to enable the Established Church to send missionaries to "the Continent of Africa, or other parts of the heathen world."

This was the last year of a century in which religion had come increasingly under attack, and the Church often seemed powerless to defend itself, let alone to take the offensive. It was, moreover, a time of war. Across the Channel, in France, the fall of the Bastille in 1789 marked the beginning of the French Revolution. From 1793 Britain was at war with revolutionary and Napoleonic France, and it was a time of economic difficulties, of food shortages, and of fear and uncertainty. The country's leadership was less than inspiring; the sick old king had been on the throne for almost forty years; his large family was unpopular.

The Church of England was not likely to do much, officially, to promote missions to those of other faiths, or of no faith. The so-called Deists were attacking supernatural Christianity, and the Scottish philosopher David Hume went even further in advocating outright scepticism. Even bishops in the Church despaired, and Bishop Butler had refused to accept the primacy because he could see no hope of saving the Church. Many of the parish clergy and, even more, the higher clergy, were slack and self-seeking, holding plural livings and doing little in any of them except to collect the tithes. Church-going

1

was not even fashionable; morals and ethics were little influenced by Christian teaching.

Almost one hundred years earlier another missionary society had been inaugurated within the Church of England: the Society for the Propagation of the Gospel (SPG). With its slightly earlier sister-society, the Society for Promoting Christian Knowledge (SPCK), there had at least been an attempt to teach, evangelise and shepherd British settlers overseas, and the non-Christians they lived among. But by the end of the 18th century zeal and enthusiasm were low.

Nevertheless, the Spirit of God was not limited by the deficiencies of the established Church. The Bible was read; within families and in some churches there was teaching which led to active spiritual life. Within the Church of England three men were ordained in the 1730s who were to be apostles of a new movement in the land. The brothers John and Charles Wesley, and George Whitefield, all ordained around 1736, went to the American colony of Georgia, where they encountered at first hand the difficulties of missionary work, even among their fellow Englishmen and women. Coming back as a failure to England, John Wesley in 1738 went to the Moravian meeting in Aldersgate Street, in the City of London, where he felt his heart "strangely warmed" within him, and he received the assurance of God's forgiveness which he had lacked. Within a comparatively short time these three men were to begin the itinerant preaching throughout Britain which was to lead to revival. The Moravians of Germany who played a part in John Wesley's conversion influenced others, and the "Great Awakening" in Britain was paralleled on the Continent, especially in Germany and in Switzerland. Seminaries were set up to train young men who, touched by the revival, wished to serve in the ministry, and one of the first was in Basel. In Britain the universities of Oxford and Cambridge saw young men of religious enthusiasm offering for ordination. At Cambridge the leading personality and the great influence on the students was Charles Simeon, Fellow of King's College and Rector of Holy Trinity Church. At Oxford, John Wesley and his friends had as students formed a "Methodist Society", and his later followers formed Methodist Societies which did not, however, form a distinct denomination outside of the Church of England until after John Wesley's death as a very old man in 1791.

But independently of the Wesley brothers and George Whitefield there were, within the Church of England, a number of men who were becoming known as "Evangelicals". Some of the same influences – such as that of the Moravians – came to bear on both groups, but there was surprisingly little contact. It needs to be understood that these Evangelicals were not merely a section of the Methodist revival who remained within the Church of England, but, as Stephen Neill has written, part of "a distinct movement, with its own marked characteristics, which have continued to be the characteristics of the Evangelical wing of the Church of England till the present day" (*Anglicanism*, p. 190).

It was the men of this Evangelical wing of the established Church, having much in common with the Methodists, yet resolved to remain loyal to the Establishment, who were to be the founders and early supporters of the Church Missionary Society. Charles Simeon, Henry Venn, William Romaine, John Berridge, John Newton, William Grimshaw – these were a few of the leading figures.

Along with the thanksgiving for their own salvation, these men, now active in preaching the Gospel to their country-men, began also to be conscious of the needs of those in other countries who were outside the Church of Christ. The 18th century Enlightenment extended to exploration and brought a new consciousness of the wider world, and in Britain the journeys of Captain James Cook and his publications were of great influence. The new world of the Pacific was opening up; at the same time British influence was expanding in India.

Explorers were travelling in Africa. And although before the end of the century Britain had lost most of her colonies in North America, trading links remained, and in time these led to the connection established through the slave trade, which slowly came to the attention of Christians.

So, with these factors active, it is not surprising that in the last decade of the 18th century missionary societies were founded by British Christians who were looking outward to the whole world where Christ was not yet preached. The first, in 1792, was the Baptist Missionary Society, inspired by the cobbler William Carey who was himself to be the pioneer in eastern India. Next, in 1795, came the London Missionary Society, originally interdenominational, whose earliest missionaries went to the Pacific, and who sent pioneers also to China and southern Africa. Third, in 1799, came the Church Missionary Society.

It arose out of an Anglican discussion society, the Eclectic Society, which had, more than once, discussed "foreign missions". In April 1799 the Society met at an inn in Aldersgate Street, not far from the place where John Wesley had worshipped with the Moravians. They discussed on this occasion "What methods can we use more effectually to promote the knowledge of the Gospel among the Heathen?" They warmly acknowledged the existence of the two older societies, but saw that there was room, and that there was a need, for a society with a wider remit. So they resolved together to found a new society which came to be known as the Church Missionary Society. The founders were few in number and were without much influence in Church or State. But they believed that they were acting according to God's guidance. This book sets out to tell the story of what they accomplished, and how they went about it. It is the story of a voluntary society of the Church of England which has been, under God, a midwife bringing into birth a world-wide community of Churches.

The author comes to write this book out of a background

in which the Church Missionary Society has been of major importance. Brought up in a British dominion where the Gospel was first preached through CMS agency, she later worked with the CMS in Africa.

This obviously makes complete impartiality impossible, and indeed she would argue that it is a quality which never completely exists. But she has tried to take into account a wide range of views, and especially those of national Christians in the Churches which have grown out of the CMS endeavour. In particular the partnership of CMS missionaries with local Christians, in almost every area where they went, is noteworthy. As the Society comes near its second centenary, and its role, in a changing world, is likewise changing, that joint mission is continuing.

1 THE CHURCH PRINCIPLE

1799 to 1813: foundation and very early developments

". . . the Church-principle, not the high-Church principle." At the meeting which set up the Church Missionary Society (12 April 1799), John Venn, Rector of Clapham, laid down guide-lines for such a society coming out of the established Church. His last word was that the Society must be founded on the "Church-principle, not the high-Church principle" and he added that if clergy could not be found to go out as missionaries, then laymen should be sent.

Two points need clarifying here. First, it needs to be stressed that his use of the term "high-Church" did not then mean what it came to mean later under the influence of the Tractarians and the Anglo-Catholic party. But secondly, in a positive sense, it indicated clearly both the important principles which have continued to guide CMS over almost two centuries of great social, political and religious change, and also the divergences from the other, existing, missionary societies which made the founders believe that their new organisation was necessary.

Thus, unlike the London Missionary Society and other, denominational, societies, it was to be loyal to the leadership of bishops and to the Book of Common Prayer, a part of the "Church of England established by law". But it was also to be a society not wholly dominated by the clergy, one which emphasised the role of laymen and laywomen in the missionary enterprise. Over the years it has been criticised from both sides, both for what it has done and for what it has left undone. Anglicans have seen it as too "free"; non-Anglicans as too much tied to the Church of England, too "Establishment". Like its mother-Church, the Church Missionary Society has chosen the difficult middle path. But it is still seeking to follow these early principles.

It was in fact the determination to do nothing without at least informing the leaders of the Church of England which held up the real beginnings of the Society for over a year. At the founding meeting it was decided to send a deputation to the Archbishop of Canterbury, the Bishop of London (in whose diocese they were meeting) and to the Bishop of Durham (chairman of the missionary committee of the SPCK) with a copy of the rules adopted and "a respectful letter". William Wilberforce, a Member of Parliament, was asked to see the Archbishop, but it was not until July 1800 that he was able to make a report. None of the bishops were exactly enthusiastic about the new project. But they had no decided objections, and were willing to watch the endeavour "with candour". The founding fathers were realistic enough to expect no more, and resolved to "proceed in their great design with all the activity possible".

They had finally chosen a name – "the Society for Missions to Africa and the East", but they were soon known as the *Church* Missionary Society. However, this nickname did not become official until 1812.

To function, a missionary society needs money, personnel and a sphere of work – a field, as CMS jargon used to describe it. Money was not an immediate problem. But men to send, and a place to send them, presented a problem. Needless to say, at this date it was men and men only who could be contemplated as missionaries. Despite their wide contacts the members of the committee had no really practical suggestions. A vocation to overseas mission work was not yet a possibility for English Christians. Indeed, it was to be one of the main tasks of this new society to awaken such a vocation. But one suitable candidate did offer – a brilliant young Cambridge man who was a protégé of the great Charles Simeon. Henry Martyn is sometimes spoken of as if he had been the first CMS missionary, but despite his offer, he never became, formally, a missionary of any society. He was obliged to withdraw for financial reasons, and he went to India as a chaplain of the British East India Company. Only in that way could he in that period go to India, where he was a pioneer for the later, official missionaries, especially in his translation work. It was to be a number of years before any other university-educated clergyman offered himself for service overseas.

Meanwhile a first solution to the problem of who to send came from an unexpected quarter. At the end of the 18th century all the missionaries working in south India under the SPCK were German or Danish by nationality, and in Lutheran orders. Once again, German Lutherans came to the rescue of an English missionary society. One of the seminaries established in the wake of the Pietist revival in Germany was in Berlin, and the CMS committee got in touch with its directors. During 1802 two students from the Berlin Seminary were interviewed in London (with difficulty, as neither spoke English), accepted, given a little training at Clapham and a chance to learn English, sent back to Germany for Lutheran ordination and, on 31 January 1804, dismissed for service in West Africa. How much English they then knew is not clear, but one of them, Peter Hartwig, had progressed sufficiently to become engaged to Sarah Windsor, who had been governess in the Venn family, and they were married before sailing.

So the first missionaries of this very English society were German Lutherans. Many gave long, devoted and skilled service, and their record in language and translation work is particularly striking. The main problem added was that of training and of ordination. At first no English bishop would ordain a candidate for service overseas unless he could first "serve his title" in an English curacy. This was difficult in the case of the Germans. But no English clergymen were offering themselves. The first English-born missionaries were not sent out until 1809, and they were what was then called "Christian artizans" [sic] who were destined for New Zealand. No ordained Anglican clergyman went out until 1815. From that time on the proportion of English to German missionaries gradually became more balanced. In 1824, after twenty-five years of existence, exactly one hundred men had been sent out. Of these, almost one third were English laymen, almost one third were English clergymen, and just over one third were Germans, mostly in Lutheran orders. Fifty-four of these missionaries were still on the rolls at the end of 1824; many, as we shall see, had died at their posts.

But if we look at the situation at the end of 1813 we find that precisely fifteen had been sent out. Twelve were German and all had gone to West Africa. Three English laymen had set out for New Zealand, although they were then still waiting in New South Wales. Of the twelve Germans four had died before the end of this period, and the wives of four had also died.

The first field chosen was West Africa, and in particular the area which was shortly to become the colony of Sierra Leone. This choice of field was predictable because of the impossibility of entering India at that time, and because several of the men involved with the CMS were Abolitionists involved in the fight against the slave trade, and interested in repatriating former slaves to Africa. For this purpose the Sierra Leone Company had been formed, and naturally they wished for a Christian witness among the settlers. These early settlers were mainly freed slaves from England, Nova Scotia and Jamaica who had been deposited there, and the venture had been fraught with great difficulties and discouragement. From the beginning chaplains had been sent to serve the settlers and the Company officials. Many of the settlers, especially those from Nova Scotia, were already devout Christians, mainly Methodist and Baptist.

The first two men who had been "dismissed for service" in January 1804 arrived in Freetown after fifty-seven days sailing; "only four times longer than the fortnight occupied today" comments the CMS historian of 1899. The second party was delayed, stranded and forced to change ships, and they were seven months en route. Of these first five one died within two years; one (the man who had married the Venn governess) "turned out badly . . . engaged in the slave trade", and had to be dismissed. The other three survived for long service, as it was reckoned at that time, and died at their posts. One, Nyländer, worked for nineteen years, and we shall meet him again.

The turning point in Sierra Leone came when it became the haven to which "liberated Africans" (sometimes called "recaptives") were sent after being rescued at sea by British naval patrols. In 1807 Parliament finally voted for the abolition of the slave trade, and from 1808 slaves rescued by British cruisers from illegal slave ships were set down in Freetown. The population thus grew by several thousands in a few years. Unlike the Nova Scotians these people were neither educated, nor Christian, nor trained for life in the colony. The missionaries were needed more than ever. Early in 1808 the administration of the settlement was transferred from the Sierra Leone Company to the British Government. The new inhabitants were settled in townships around Freetown itself, and the missionaries became the pastors, schoolmasters and indeed the civil authorities in these towns.

The other field contemplated by the end of 1813 was New Zealand, brought to the attention of the London committee by the Rev. Samuel Marsden, a protégé of Charles Simeon and Henry Venn, who was chaplain to the convict settlement in New South Wales. The three English "artizans" who had been sent out could not get permission to go further than New South Wales. It was not until 1814 that they reached

New Zealand in company with Samuel Marsden, who preached the first sermon on New Zealand soil.

These various activities were directed in a fairly informal manner by a secretary who initially worked from his own home. The first was the Rev. Thomas Scott; from 1802 to 1824 it was the Rev. Josiah Pratt. He also worked from his home until 1813, when a house was rented in Salisbury Square. Committee meetings were held in a city rectory. From the beginning there was a General Committee and Committees of Accounts and of Correspondence, which would be equivalent to modern committees of finance, candidates and overseas affairs. The main yearly public activity, in the fashion of the time, was the Annual Sermon, preached at a city church. The Annual Sermons were (and still are) printed and distributed. The other public activity was the Dismissal meeting, arranged as necessary, when those leaving for overseas service were farewelled. A charge was delivered to the new missionaries, who were given time to reply. But in the early years few of the German missionaries knew enough English to reply. The very first Dismissal, when Renner and Hartwig were farewelled for Sierra Leone, took place at the New London Tavern, Cheapside, on 31 January 1804. At the Annual Sermon and at the Dismissals collections for the funds of the Society were taken, which were initially the source of much of the income.

But of the apparatus of a missionary society as we know it, little then existed. Mail took months to come and go, so link letters were not in vogue; regular leave periods for furloughs (as they were then called) were unknown. Those missionaries who came back were usually unwell, and often dying. Stories of converts were as yet lacking. But, at least after the first few years, the Annual Sermons were crowded, and interest was maintained through pamphlets and the occasional public meetings.

In 1812 and 1813 the organisation began to take on what would appear to us a more familiar form. After the offices in

Salisbury Square were leased, an assistant secretary began work. In 1812 a president was appointed for the first time – a distinguished naval officer, Admiral Lord Gambier. The rules of the society were revised, and Church dignitaries began to take a more active interest. That was important for the stability and growth of the Society in that period.

Home and abroad, 1813 to 1840

The Church Missionary Society in England
In 1814 the Annual Sermon was preached by a leading evangelical churchman, who was shortly to become the first bishop definitely associated with the CMS. This was the Dean of Wells, the Rev. and Hon. Dudley Ryder, who in 1815 became the Bishop of Gloucester. His elevation was important as the voluntary society sought to establish and maintain acceptance with the leaders of the established Church.

In 1815 Edward Bickersteth became formally associated with the CMS. A solicitor in Norwich, he was ordained and sent out on a special mission by the Society – to visit Sierra Leone to advise, counsel and report back. Up to that time no missionary had returned in health to make a report, and mail was slow, infrequent and unreliable. Bickersteth proved an acceptable and spiritually-alert adviser, and after his return to England he became assistant secretary, working with the Rev. Josiah Pratt, and continuing until 1830. He was involved not so much in administration as in travelling to speak for the Society and in matters involving the selection and training of missionary candidates, and in correspondence with those serving overseas.

We have constantly to remind ourselves of the novelty of overseas mission work for British Christians at this period. The very idea was not widely accepted, so practical help was slow in coming. Education was necessary, and in 1813 the

Rev. Josiah Pratt commenced a monthly paper called *The Missionary Register*, which he himself edited for twenty-five years. The paper continued up to 1855, by which time several societies had their own publications. *The Missionary Register* was never an official CMS publication, and from the beginning it faithfully reported the activities of all Protestant missions and societies. It included surveys, statistics, narratives and obituaries, reports of speeches and sermons. From 1816 it was illustrated with woodcuts and maps, and the CMS purchased some thousands of copies each month for "free distribution to its subscribers and collectors".

Collectors were becoming another important feature in the extension and consolidation of the CMS. Subscribers paid (usually) five shillings a year to become members of the Society. Money was raised by special collections in churches, but in addition it was planned to establish Church Missionary Associations whose members would undertake collection of funds from a wider group, and especially *penny-a-week* subscriptions. From twelve such pledges a shilling a week would be raised – two pounds twelve pence in a year.

The smallness of the sums involved now seem to us unbelievable. But in 1814 the annual allowance for a missionary in India was £100. The *penny-a-week* scheme in total raised useful amounts, and gave many working people the opportunity to give in a year almost the sum of the annual subscription – four shillings and fourpence – with dignity, in a way they could afford. Associations sprang up from Yorkshire to Bristol, from Wales to Devonshire, naturally in the main in parishes where the rector or vicar was a friend of the CMS. The associations also arranged meetings and often encouraged offers of missionary service. One of the very earliest associations was that of Dewsbury, Yorkshire, organised in 1813. It is interesting to note that from Dewsbury came two of the first English missionaries, William Greenwood (1815) and Benjamin Bailey (1816). A few years later Bailey's brother Joseph also became a missionary, and his sister Sarah married Thomas Dawson, another missionary from Yorkshire.

The associations encouraged, and were encouraged by, deputations. These visits were not then made by missionaries on leave, but by officials and clergy friends of the Society. Josiah Pratt himself was one of the first to be active in this role, and gradually against some opposition deputations were extended. Why was there opposition? Mainly because the use of itinerant clergy appeared to many of the parish clergy to be like the visits of itinerant evangelists working on the margin of or outside the established Church. Some of the supporters of the CMS had actually engaged in itinerant ministry in their eagerness to preach the Gospel, and parish rights were at this time very jealously guarded. Charges of "Methodism" were quickly made. Those sent out by the CMS sought to observe carefully the rules and courtesies of parish visitations, but could not entirely escape such criticisms. The greatest difficulty was when a vicar who supported the CMS was replaced by another without interest, and further contact was refused. In such cases the Society maintained its right to continue meetings, even without the support of the local incumbent, but recommended "Christian prudence and forbearance".

Other difficulties for deputationists lay in the distances involved and the hardships of travel in those days, before trains. They also encountered the opposition of bishops – at best their luke-warm approval – and on the other hand the criticism of Anglicans who wanted to support the London Missionary Society. Public meetings were not yet generally acceptable, but mission sermons were important. With the publication and widening circulation of *The Missionary Register* knowledge of a wider world and of evangelism overseas steadily increased.

The lack of interest on the part of the bishops created difficulties from the beginning, and Pratt and his colleagues tried to be careful not to offend their susceptibilities. It was not only that the support of bishops for fund-raising was needed. More serious was the problem of ordination for service overseas. Ryder's appointment in 1815 as Bishop of Gloucester was a turning-point. In 1816 he ordained several CMS candidates who left immediately for the mission field. Previous ordinands had been required to serve English curacies in order to satisfy episcopal requirements.

In 1816 Bishop Bathurst of Norwich also joined the Society, and several well-known laymen became associated. But when Bishop Ryder later was translated to the diocese of Lichfield and Coventry his successor in Gloucester forbad all sermons and collections for the CMS, despite the years of interest and support under Ryder. It was to be a very long time before the cooperation of bishops could be taken for granted.

Leadership

During the formative years the leading personality in the Society was undoubtedly the Rev. Josiah Pratt. He resigned in April 1824, after over twenty years of devoted and unpaid service. His generosity to other societies was unlimited, and is shown especially in the pages of *The Missionary Register*. He was succeeded as clerical secretary by Edward Bickersteth, who had been an assistant secretary since 1815, but the administration of the Society came largely into the hands of Dandeson Coates, assistant secretary from 1824 and from 1830 given the title of lay secretary. An efficient, zealous administrator, though of rather narrow views and sympathies, he was important in building up the machinery of the Society, but provided for some of the clerical critics of the CMS confirmation of their fears that the laity had more influence than the clergy. His ordained colleagues, Bickersteth and later William Jowett, provided the "more conciliatory element". Coates continued as lay secretary till 1846; Bickersteth as clerical secretary till 1830. And, significantly for the future of the Society, Henry Venn in 1822 moved to a charge in London and began to attend the committees regularly. In the next eighteen years he was being prepared for his future role.

The last annual report written by Pratt (1824) was somewhat gloomy. Advances were slow; converts few. In some fields sickness and death had actually brought recession. Public opinion, at least among political and ecclesiastical leaders, was if anything more opposed to missionary work. But giving had steadily increased (to £40,000 in 1824–25), meetings were well-attended and, even more important, there were now increased offers of service from British Christians.

These early mission administrators were pioneers in fundraising, in publicity, in public relations. The societies in Britain were quick to learn from one another; the CMS followed the Bible Society in organising local associations, and the SPG followed the lead of the CMS in organising district committees. In some areas they could learn from the continental seminaries in Basel and Berlin; in 1822 the principal of Basel visited London and spoke at the Anniversary Meeting. From 1818 the secretaries of the various societies in London met together regularly and doubtless they exchanged ideas on practical as well as spiritual topics.

Training missionaries for service

A continuing and pressing problem was the training of missionaries and it could only increase as more made offers. There were several areas of need. The continental candidates needed to learn English, and those who were ordained as Lutheran ministers needed the instruction which would qualify them for Anglican ordination. British candidates might need general education and some, also, ordination training. All, including ordained men from a university background, needed special instruction for their overseas posting. Initially, the CMS made use of clergy friends who took candidates into their own homes. This could only be a temporary answer while numbers were few. Later, some candidates stayed at the Salisbury Square headquarters; again, this was not a long-term solution. At this time, theological training for ordination scarcely existed within Britain; in Charles Simeon's Cambridge the ordination examination "consisted merely of the construing of a passage from the Greek New Testament", taken on the day of the ordination already fixed.

So, in 1824, the Church Missionary Institution was set up in Upper Street, Islington, near the parish church where a leading friend of the Society was Rector (this was Daniel Wilson, later Bishop of Calcutta). The Institution became the Church Missionary College, with purpose-built premises to accommodate fifty students. The first missionaries trained there went overseas in 1825; one was Samuel Gobat, the Swiss Lutheran who became Bishop in Jerusalem. In 1826 there were twenty-six students in residence. Now almost as a matter of course those put forward by the CMS for ordination were ordained by the Bishop of London. Not only had relations with him become closer, but an Act of Parliament passed in 1819 clarified the situation completely by making it legally possible to ordain men for service overseas.

The number of missionaries going out, and the proportion of British to continental candidates, was increasing steadily. In the first twenty-five years, just on a hundred men went overseas; in the next *ten* years there were as many. In the first period a third had come from the continent; this proportion now slowly fell. In addition all the Lutherans came to the Church Missionary Institution and those who were clergy received Anglican ordination. Another feature of the Society which was to be a continuing one began to emerge: from 1831 sons and daughters of serving missionaries were accepted and appointed. The first two were the orphaned daughters of Nyländer, the veteran German missionary in Sierra Leone, who had died in 1823.

2   THE FIRST MISSIONARIES AT WORK

West Africa: Sierra Leone, 1813–1840

Up to 1813 twelve missionaries, all German, and most in
Lutheran orders, had been sent to Sierra Leone. Four had
died, one had been suspended, and the wives of three had
also died. Despite the fact that British administration had (in
1808) replaced company rule, matters in the colony were
in disarray. The population now consisted of settlers and
recaptives as well as local Africans. The settlers were former
slaves from Nova Scotia and Jamaica, with some knowledge
of English and some skills, and, in many cases, already
Christians. The recaptives were Africans largely from the
western coastlands who had been freed from slave ships, and
who had no previous contacts with the European culture and
religion. The settlers had organised their own churches with
their own preachers, and there were good relationships and
constant visiting among the congregations of the different
chapels.

Most of the missionaries were in fact working outside the
colony among the Susu people in the Rio Pongas, learning
the language, translating, and running small schools. It was
depressing work with few visible results. One missionary,
Butscher, visited England in 1812, and he returned to
Freetown with three German artisans to help with practical
work. But that effort was an almost complete failure – all
three were dead before the end of 1814.

At this point the CMS committee in London sent Edward
Bickersteth out on his visit of inspection. Perhaps his most

important contact was with the new governor, Sir Charles MacCarthy. A devout Roman Catholic, and an efficient and compassionate officer, he planned with the CMS to use their personnel in a new venture. The recaptives, who had been badly neglected, were to be settled in villages or parishes, each centering on a school, and the missionary was to be head teacher, pastor, and civil administrator. The Government would give financial aid to the schools, and Government chaplains were to take over the missionaries' work among the European population. The work among the Susu had to be abandoned because of the hostility of a local chief, so soon most of the missionaries were working among the recaptives.

On the whole the scheme worked well, especially under one of the new missionaries, the Rev. William Johnson – despite his name, German – whose parish at Regent soon gained the reputation of a model village. Housing, gardens, school, market, trade and craft training helped to make a transformation, and many were baptised; something of a revival took place as early as 1817. Johnson's main difference with the governor came from his refusing to baptise as quickly as the governor wished. Düring, at Gloucester, also achieved remarkable results. But the deaths among the missionaries continued; in one terrible year, 1823, six died, and also the chaplain and his wife, and several officials. Those who died included Johnson, and Düring and his wife, who were lost at sea. In 1826, it is recorded that of seventy-nine persons sent out (including wives) in twenty-two years, only fourteen remained, most of the others having died. And in 1824, having gone back on active duty to the Gold Coast, Sir Charles MacCarthy was also dead.

During the eight years of his governorship, with the assistance of active and spiritual missionaries like Johnson and Düring, a great deal had been accomplished. It was in this period that the sawmilling of African teak had been developed and a profitable trade commenced. But MacCarthy's spending had been (to the home government) excessive, and with the rapid deaths of the next four governors, and continuing missionary deaths, it was hard to carry on at all. In 1831 the mission was touched by a very serious scandal and the last of the early pioneers, Wilhelm, died in 1834 after unbroken service from 1811. Could they – should they – continue?

In fact, though at the time they did not recognise it, one of the most important steps for the continuity and building up of the Church in Sierra Leone and in West Africa had taken place. In 1827 the CMS refounded the Christian Institution, which was to grow into Fourah Bay College. The first principal was one of the German missionaries, Hänsel, who came out already in Anglican orders. His successor was a black American Episcopal priest, Edward Jones, who had come out as a schoolmaster in 1831, and married one of Nyländer's daughters.

The first pupil on the lists of the Institution was the young Samuel Adjai Crowther, a recaptive who had already visited England, and was seen as a promising Christian leader. After his time at the Institution, Crowther joined a missionary, Weeks, at Regent Village as a teacher. The two future bishops, neither then ordained, worked together at carpentry.

By the end of the 1830s, matters in Sierra Leone were improving. From 1830 to 1840 over twenty new missionaries arrived, and though a number died or left after short terms (the English missionaries appear to have "lasted" less well than the Germans) a number of men had come who were to make long and valuable contributions. One was Henry Townsend, the future leader in the Niger Mission, who arrived in 1836 at the age of only twenty-one and served in West Africa for almost forty years. Among the Germans was Frederic Bültman who served for twenty-two years, and J. U. Graf, nineteen.

Again, we may note the immense personal sacrifice involved in the missionary calling at that time, not least for wives and dependants. Of the men who came out up to 1840, ten married twice and four married three times, the wives having died as a result of the climate or childbirth (or a combination of both). Six widows remarried other missionaries, and two were married three times. It seems that men became aware that their chances of having a long-lived wife were increased if they married a widow no longer able to bear children. Weeks, the future bishop, was twice married, and both times to the widows of deceased missionaries. We have no adequate record of the number of infant deaths. It is worth noting also that several missionaries married black women, mainly Nova Scotians, without any objections being raised. The daughters of Nyländer and his Nova Scotian wife were taken to England by the CMS for education and returned to Sierra Leone to serve as teachers for several years before they, in turn, married missionaries and shortly afterwards died.

New Zealand 1809–1842

How did such isolated islands come to be the second CMS field of work? It was neither Africa nor the East, but rather the remotest south. Prevented by legal restrictions from sending men to India and Ceylon, and given the widespread interest in the Pacific, the committee was ready to listen to the appeal of the Rev. Samuel Marsden, who was visiting England from the convict settlement at Port Jackson, New South Wales, where he was chaplain.

Marsden owed his education and ordination to friends of the CMS, for he had been sent to Cambridge by the Elland Society, founded by Henry Venn the elder "to assist godly men to study for holy orders" and he owed his chaplaincy appointment (1793) to William Wilberforce.

In New South Wales Marsden encountered natives from the islands some one thousand miles away, and recorded his impression of their intelligence. Whalers, sealers and marine adventurers were beginning to visit and even settle in New

Zealand, and there was potential for good or evil. When Marsden came back to England in 1808 and asked for missionaries, he was speaking of an area which had already come to the notice of many Christians in Britain. One reason was the journeys of Captain James Cook and the publications arising from them; the other was the missionary expedition of the LMS to islands in the Pacific – the "South Seas".

New Zealand was to be the scene of an early experiment in missionary method. Marsden advocated the view that the Maoris, who had a fearful reputation, must be "civilised" before they could be evangelised, and Pratt concurred. So the first Englishmen to be sent out were not termed missionaries, but were Christian artisans or lay settlers. Hall was a carpenter and King a shoe-maker and twine-spinner. They sailed with Marsden in 1809, but got no further than New South Wales. Marsden was frustrated for years, trying to find a vessel and to get permission for them to move to New Zealand. In fact, they did not go until joined by a third man, Thomas Kendall, a teacher who was later ordained and who did not leave England till May 1813. All three sailed for New Zealand early in 1814. Marsden finally obtained permission to visit and he preached to the assembled Maoris on a beach on Christmas Day 1814, and then left the missionaries with wives and children to carve a living out of the wilderness and to teach by life and example. Kendall made some progress with the language and started a school, but it was hard going. Their greatest difficulty was the settlement of escaped convicts and other lawless Europeans close to their site. An ordained man, the Rev. John Butler, joined them in 1818, and by 1820 Marsden reported signs of progress, but then disaster struck. In 1822 Kendall and two younger missionaries (one of them Butler's son) were found to be involved in the armed rising of Hongi, a Maori chief. The three were dismissed, and the senior Butler resigned.

But in the same year, 1822, came the first of two brothers who were to be the apostles of the Church in New Zealand.

Henry Williams had been a naval officer; his brother William, originally a surgeon, had a later university education. Both were ordained and they came with their wives and brought up large families in New Zealand. Both worked in New Zealand till their deaths, Henry's in 1867 and William's in 1876. Henry became an archdeacon; William the first Bishop of Waiapu. Sons, daughters, and sons-in-law served with the CMS and held high office in the emerging Anglican Church. The two brothers and their descendants made a great and lasting contribution to the country as well as the Church.

In 1825, the year that William Williams arrived, the first baptism took place. But progress was very slow. The situation was to be greatly complicated by the choice of New Zealand for white settlement, not originally with British government approval, but eventually with its concurrence. Edward Gibbon Wakefield sent the *Tory* and other ships with settlers to Port Nicholson (Wellington) in 1840, and in the same year, with active help from the missionaries, many Maori chiefs signed the Treaty of Waitangi. By this the chiefs conceded sovereignty to Queen Victoria in return for her protection and with their continuing rights to the land. So the stage was set for the coming of the first Bishop of New Zealand, the dauntless George Augustus Selwyn, in 1842.

India up to the arrival of Bishop Wilson

West Africa was the first CMS field of work and maintained a special place in the interest of English supporters. First slavery, and then problems of Christian marriage and polygamy, persisted to impede the growth and development of the Church in Africa.

In India it was caste which came to be seen as the perpetual problem of the Indian Church; polygamy was not an issue, though there were difficulties over child-marriage and child-betrothal and the treatment accorded to young widows who could not remarry, and became chattels in their in-laws' home. But in India, unlike Africa, the western missionaries could not delude themselves that they were preaching to people with no religion and with "primitive" social and political institutions. India was quite obviously a highly developed and complex society, literate, with adherents of major religions having priests, temples and shrines.

For the English Anglicans who wished to evangelise in India there were further problems. Prior to the mid-19th century, British rule over much of India was through the East India Company, chartered under British law. It was established in three areas – presidencies – centering on the cities of Calcutta, Madras and Bombay. Each presidency had a governor, and that of Calcutta acted as a governor-in-charge. The employees of the Company were the administrators of India, the officers of its armies and police force, and also the exporters, importers and entrepreneurs. Chaplains were provided for the Company employees, but they were forbidden to teach or preach to the Indian inhabitants. The Company feared that any threat to the traditional religions might also affect their commercial interests.

But there were some missionaries in India, mainly in enclaves under the control of other European powers, and in territories outside the Company's control. In fact, one of the older Anglican societies maintained missionaries in the Danish territory of Tranquebar, south of Madras. King Frederick IV of Denmark had sent German Lutheran missions to the trading settlement in the late 17th century, and in 1710 the SPCK had accepted financial responsibility for the mission which had expanded even to Madras. But in the early 19th century its affairs were at a low point. Still, it was a delicate matter for the CMS to think of sending its own missionaries.

Initially the way out of the dilemma came through the Company's absolute prohibition of missionary work in its territories. William Carey and his companions, the Baptist pioneers, survived by settling in another Danish enclave, and by engaging in secular employment. But the interest in India continued and was fuelled by the reports and writings of British Christians living in India, mainly chaplains and employees of the Company.

A group of the chaplains, known as the "pious chaplains", were in effect the first Anglican missionaries in many areas. They included local Indians in their ministrations, impelled especially by the fact that many English men had married or set up homes with Indian women, and so there were many children of mixed race (Eurasians), to be baptised and taught. There were also many Goan Christians, nominally Roman Catholic, from the Portuguese enclaves, who needed teaching. Two of the chaplains, David Brown and Claudius Buchanan, both former students of Charles Simeon at Cambridge, wrote influential books and reports. So did Charles Grant, a young Company official who was known as a "serious" Christian. In 1806 Henry Martyn, Simeon's "dear son", came to Calcutta. His translation work was to mean much to the Church in the future. Still the Company refused to allow missionaries entry.

But there was some hope of effecting change. The Company's charter had to come before Parliament for renewal and possible change every twenty years. This happened in 1793, and William Wilberforce, following suggestions from Brown and Grant, put forward some resolutions which would have allowed the appointment of missionaries, under safeguards. In fact, the resolutions were passed, but were never put into operation, so great was the opposition within the Company.

So as 1813 approached the friends of the CMS began to lobby. They were experienced in such matters from their work against the slave trade, and had learned from their earlier failure. So they framed their resolutions in a way that gave less offence. In June 1813 the East India Act was passed, and it included clauses which provided for the appointment of a bishop and three archdeacons for India, and which took away from the Company the absolute power of forbidding foreigners and non-Company expatriates access to its territories.

This time the provisions were put into effect. A bishop was chosen and consecrated, and he arrived in Calcutta in December 1814. Three archdeacons for the three "capitals" of Calcutta, Madras and Bombay also arrived.

At much the same time the first CMS missionaries also arrived. There were so few Germans left in Tranquebar that help was asked for, and the first two CMS men, both Germans and both in Lutheran orders, were destined for Tranquebar. One, Rhenius, in fact remained in Madras under the direction of the new CMS Corresponding Committee. In 1815 three more men arrived, including the first two ordained English missionaries. Because of the continuing difficulty over getting bishops to ordain for overseas service, they had had to serve out a period in English curacies before they could proceed overseas. Two went to north India and the third to south India.

Bishop Middleton of Calcutta worked faithfully until his death, and advances were made, but the CMS was seriously disappointed by his decisions in two areas. He would not ordain Indian converts, nor license missionaries. This second decision meant that no missionary could officiate, even temporarily, at English services. It appears that Middleton believed himself to be legally unable to act otherwise, and the CMS on its side cooperated with him as fully as possible, making generous grants to the theological institution he founded in Calcutta – Bishop's College.

After his death (July 1822) it was more than a year before his successor was selected, consecrated, and able to travel to Calcutta. This was Reginald Heber, the brilliant and universally loved parish priest, scholar and hymn-writer, already a good friend of missions and of the CMS. He ordained the first

Indian priest, Abdul Masih, converted through Henry Martyn, in November 1825, together with two others. He also licensed missionaries, any legal impediments having been removed by a new Act of Parliament. Like Middleton, Heber travelled extensively on episcopal visitations, no light thing in an India without railways. Early in 1826 he left for Madras where, already, the question of caste among Christians had arisen. The earlier missionaries had not made caste an issue; newcomers took a less tolerant line and a division had arisen in Madras and Tranquebar. Heber was reluctant to take sides quickly, and was making enquiries from missionaries and Indian Christians as he travelled, took confirmation services and kept on with other work in difficult conditions. Early in April, after taking a confirmation service at Trichinopoly he was found dead in his bath. He had been in India less than two years and six months, but his gracious and saintly personality was not soon forgotten.

The next two bishops appointed to Calcutta survived for even shorter periods. Bishop John Thomas James arrived in January 1828 and died in August of the same year; Bishop John Matthias Turner arrived in December 1829 and died in July 1831. So no great hopes were held out for the long episcopate of the fifth bishop, who was already fifty-four when he set foot in Calcutta. But in fact he stayed for over twenty-five years and died in India in his eightieth year. He was Daniel Wilson, Rector of St. Mary's Islington and a close friend of the CMS.

In the period from the coming of the first CMS missionaries up to the end of 1832, when Bishop Wilson arrived, fifty-eight men had been sent to India. Twenty-eight of these had died or resigned by that date. The death-rate was nothing like that in Sierra Leone, but early deaths did occur. Twenty-two of the missionaries were from the continent, mainly from the Basel Institute, and in Lutheran orders, but from 1825, after Bishop Heber's arrival, such men invariably received Anglican ordination in India. A small number were Eurasian (part Indian), one of the first men ordained by Heber being the Eurasian, William Bowley.

In many ways the work of the first CMS missionaries was not pioneering, but was building on the work of the "pious chaplains" and others who, quietly and even illegally, had been preaching by word and by example. The Muslim, Sheikh Salih, who was baptised by Daniel Corrie (one of the "pious chaplains") in 1811 as Abdul Masih – "Servant of Christ" – was the first Indian employed by the CMS as an agent. He went to Agra with Corrie and within two years over fifty adults had been baptised. Abdul Masih also treated illnesses and was known as the Christian *hakim* (doctor). So, in a pattern to be widely repeated, a national Christian and the Scriptures (Henry Martyn's Urdu translation) preceded the coming of the official missionaries, and there was a small Christian community waiting for them.

J. C. Schnarre and C. T. E. Rhenius, the first missionaries sent by the CMS, arrived in Madras early in 1814, some months before the first bishop got to Calcutta. It had been intended that both should go to Tranquebar, to the Danish mission whose veteran missionary, Dr. John, old and blind, had just died. In the end only Schnarre went to Tranquebar; the newly-founded CMS corresponding committee in Madras kept Rhenius there. Schnarre died in 1820; in the same year Rhenius was moved to Palamcotta, where a conscientious Company chaplain, James Hough, was trying to teach and shepherd numerous low-caste Christians. These people had asked for baptism with a minimum of knowledge; Hough started English and Tamil schools and had a church built, but obviously could not cope, and was also liable for transfer at any time. Rhenius was joined by another German Lutheran, Bernard Schmid, and together they built up the Palamcotta congregation which was to be so important a part of the future Anglican church of Tinnevelly.

The next two arrivals, Englishmen, had been delayed

because of the necessity to serve curacies after their ordination. William Greenwood went to Chunar in north India, and Thomas Norton to Allepie in south India. They were followed by others, German and English, whose activities were directed and supervised by corresponding committees in Calcutta, Madras and, later, Bombay. At a time when it might take a year to get a reply to a letter, these committees were necessary, important and powerful. In addition to other duties (including disbursing allowances from England) they raised money locally for church buildings, schools, and the payment of local agents. Chaplains and officials were the backbone of the committee – some of the laymen having had years of experience in India. Schools were started or continued, translations undertaken and scriptures printed. The earliest Indian agents were termed "readers" and they were just that – they literally read aloud the translated scriptures. Later such readers became catechists. Girls' education began in a small way.

But the corresponding committees, useful and necessary as they were, became also a potential source of conflict as the bishop and archdeacons became established. Some of the German Lutherans especially resented the committee's control and, never having received Anglican ordination, did not consider themselves under the bishop's authority either.

Ceylon 1818–1832

The great island lying at the southern tip of India (now Sri Lanka) had been a Portuguese and then a Dutch possession. It came under British rule only in 1796. Roman Catholicism entered with the Portuguese and Reformed Protestantism with the Dutch. Under the Dutch it was to some extent forced on the people, as baptised Christians were given preference in government service. Though the Dutch East India Company tried to teach and educate those who had been baptised, most of the "Christians" were still Buddhist or Hindu in belief and practice.

It was not until 1817 that Ceylon was placed under the jurisdiction of the Bishop of Calcutta, and the senior chaplain, the Rev. and Hon. T. J. Twistleton, was made Archdeacon. Bishop Middleton visited in 1821, by which time four CMS missionaries were installed in three different locations. A Tamil catechist from India, Christian David, had studied at Bishop's College and was considered suitable for ordination but the bishop, because of his legal scruples, felt unable to proceed. David was finally ordained by Bishop Heber in 1825.

Eleven CMS missionaries had been sent to Ceylon up to 1832, and eight were still working there at that date. Archdeacon Twistleton had asked for English missionaries only, in Anglican orders, and no German Lutherans ever went to Ceylon. It was to be complicated enough, even so, to reconcile the views of the evangelical missionary clergy with those of the chaplains, and Ceylon was in the future to prove a test case.

Able as most of these missionaries were, Ceylon remained a difficult field. "*Pure* [emphasis added] Buddhists and Hindus are tenfold more accessible than the thousands of [these] relapsed and false professors of Christianity," wrote a missionary at the time of Ceylon's jubilee in 1868. But a steady work continued.

The Eastern Mission from 1815

After West Africa and New Zealand, and at the same time that India was becoming a field, another area was being opened. In the same year that the first CMS missionaries went to India, another Anglican clergyman sailed, this time for Malta. He was the Rev. William Jowett, the first university graduate to be sent out by the Society. For many years friends of the CMS had advocated work in the area of the Eastern Churches, with the hope and belief that through those Churches entry could be gained to the Muslims living in the same lands.

In 1811, a Roman Catholic resident of Malta had written to the CMS appealing for missionaries to Malta. He had heard of the Bible Society and wanted the Scriptures taught. In 1812 the committee responded favourably, but it was not until 1815 that Jowett was able to go. He was commissioned to collect information on the general religious conditions of the region, and "to enquire as to the best methods of 'propagating Christian knowledge'". Under a treaty evangelistic work was not allowed in Malta itself, but the distribution of scriptures, and translations if necessary, were to be a prime activity.

Jowett was joined by two other missionaries, both also graduates, and the three travelled extensively, despite very difficult conditions, among the islands and on the mainland. They wrote a good deal, and Jowett in 1820 published *Christian Researches in the Mediterranean*, which aroused great interest. For a number of reasons this region was high in the interest of many British Christians. There was the association with the life of Christ and of the Apostolic Church; there was the attraction of eastern Christianity and the hope of its reformation; there was the challenge of Islam; and there was also a growing interest in prophecy, in which knowledge of the ancient places was of importance. The CMS from the beginning emphasised their opposition to mere proselytism from the Eastern Churches. It was hoped that by the translation and distribution of scriptures the Eastern Church would reform itself, and that such a reformed Church would prove an ally in the evangelisation of non-Christians, and especially Muslims.

This was the hope and aim in several areas during the 19th century, and by and large these hopes were to be disappointed. Turkey, Greece, Palestine, Ethiopia, Egypt, and the

Syrian Church of south India – in all of them work began, hopes rose, but were soon dashed by opposition from within or without. Few traces now remain of the work then begun.

Malta, as well as being the base for the travellers, was the site of a printing press which, during its years of operation (it was closed down in 1842) poured out "scriptures and tracts by the thousand in Maltese, Italian, modern Greek and Arabic". Much of the Bible was produced in Maltese, a language related to Arabic, and a version of the New Testament translated into modern Greek by an archimandrite of Constantinople was published. A translation in Amharic of the Ethiopic Bible was acquired and in part published. A feature shared by most of the Eastern Churches was the use of a liturgical language not understood by the laity, and therefore these two vernacular Bibles were a great advance. It had been Jowett who located the Amharic translation and negotiated its purchase.

In 1825 the first group of CMS missionaries, all continental Lutherans (who had been among the first students at the CMS Institution, Islington) went to Egypt. Here also they hoped to recall an Eastern Church – in this case the Coptic Orthodox Church – to a Biblical faith, but not to convert them to another Church. Both the Pope and the Sultan of Turkey – Commander of the Faithful – issued edicts against the circulation and reading of vernacular scriptures. The CMS a little later sent missionaries to the city of Smyrna and to the island of Syra (both, of course, under Turkish rule) and to Constantinople itself. Several of the missionaries who went to Egypt used it as a stepping-stone to Abyssinia, as Ethiopia was generally known, seen as the mysterious land of Prester John. Here they were able to use the Amharic scriptures already translated and printed. But no workers were able to stay long, even despite their willingness to make sacrifices. The workers in Egypt also remained few; one, Lieder, carried on till his death in 1865. But when the CMS returned to Egypt later, it was virtually to make a fresh start.

South India: the Syrian Church

Even greater hopes had been pinned on the reformation of
the Syrian Church of south India. Though not completely
unknown, English Christians had been scarcely aware of it
until they read about it in Claudius Buchanan's *Christian
Researches in Asia* (1811). Buchanan had visited the churches
of Travancore and met the head of the Church, and was
especially impressed by the need to provide scriptures in
Malayalam (the local vernacular) since liturgy and scriptures
were all read in Syriac. The head of the Church, Mar
Dionysios, was genuinely interested, and himself translated
the Gospels into Malayalam. Buchanan's request for CMS
missionaries was backed up by the English Resident in
Travancore, Colonel Munro, a devout evangelical Christian.
So in 1815 Thomas Norton was diverted to Allepie in
Travancore, and three other missionaries joined him. At first
all went well; some taught in the Syrian College founded by
Colonel Munro at Cottayam and seemed welcome. They
genuinely sought to encourage change from within, but perhaps did not recognise the complexities of the situation.
There had been pressures in the past from the Portuguese
and from Roman Catholic missionaries to make changes;
there was the relationship with the patriarch of Antioch;
there were power struggles among the leaders. These finally
overwhelmed the missionaries. Despite their attempt to work
quietly and make few demands, their connections with the
ruling power put them into a role of superiority. Eventually,
also, some of the newer missionaries became tired of using
indirect influence and came to feel that they should openly
denounce "Syrian errors", and naturally the Syrian leaders
reacted. So, in 1836, at the synod marking the installation of a
new metropolitan, the official connection between the CMS
and the Syrian Church came to an end. The conservative
party within the Church had triumphed. But friendly relations

continued through the school and college at Cottayam, and reforms were set in train – but more slowly – within the ancient Church. Much good came in the end from the endeavour, but it did not result in the reformation of the Church for which many of those within the CMS had hoped and worked.

The West Indies 1827–1853

It was natural, considering the interest of its founders in the slave trade and the fate of the Africans so displaced, that the attention of the Society should be drawn to the West Indies. But for a number of reasons no direct mission work was embarked on for some time.

Baptist, London Missionary Society, Methodist and Moravian missions were working in the various islands, and so was the older Anglican society, the SPG, so the CMS presence seemed less necessary. But assistance was given to Christian laymen who acted as honorary catechists and started schools and churches. As the work of the Anti-Slavery Society (founded 1823) began to concentrate on changing the situation of those still enslaved (though the trade had been finished in 1807) and Thomas Fowell Buxton took up the torch from the failing Wilberforce, the CMS became more involved. From 1827 missionaries were sent to Jamaica and likewise to British Guiana, on the South American mainland. In 1833 the bill to free the slaves was passed in the British Parliament, and the day of emancipation was fixed for 1 August 1834. To the satisfaction of the Christians who had worked for it, that day passed peacefully with prayers and thanksgivings in the churches. Now the various missions attempted to increase their aid, especially in education and training schemes, for the slave owners had received compensation – but what had the slaves received? In 1836 CMS involvement in Trinidad commenced, and the number of men sent to Jamaica was increased.

But there was not to be a long future for the CMS here. Bishops had been consecrated for the dioceses of Jamaica and Barbados in 1824, and the colonial Church was increasingly able to take on responsibility. In 1842 the diocese of Barbados was divided into three, and from about this time the missionaries were phased out. A number of the ordained men (at least ten) stayed on as clergy in the local dioceses. One missionary, the Rev. Charles May, who went to Jamaica in 1835, died there in 1866, though his time with the CMS finished in 1836.

CMS involvement with British Guiana, although smaller, was to last longer. There it was not work among the ex-slaves, but with the Indian inhabitants. From 1829 a few men worked in Demerara and on the Essequibo River; the name of the Rev. J. H. Bernau is especially associated with this work, and he was there until 1853. The SPG took over responsibility in 1855.

With the emancipation of the West Indian slaves much of what had been hoped for at the time of the founding of the Sierra Leone colony had been achieved. William Wilberforce died in July 1833, knowing that the dream was now a reality. Zachary Macaulay, who had been responsible for much of the research which lay behind the campaigns for freedom, died in 1838. He had personally encountered slavery in Jamaica as a young man, and later had been the first governor of Sierra Leone. The heroic efforts of these two men, with many others including associates of the CMS, had met with success. This did not mean that the work of the Church was over, but now it could continue without the reproach of injustice which had held it back for so long.

3   A GREAT MISSIONARY
ADMINISTRATOR

Introduction

The 1820s and 1830s were years of uncertainty in Britain. The old and infirm king, George III, died in 1820 and was succeeded by his son, the prince regent, as George IV. His reign was marred from the beginning by his open quarrel with his wife, and his only daughter and heir, Princess Charlotte, had died in 1817. When he died in 1830 his brother came to the throne as William IV.

The instability of the monarchs was reflected in much conflict and instability in nation and Church. This was the period of great agitation over Catholic emancipation; it was a time of new views on prophecy which affected mission thinking; it was the time which saw the popularity of Edward Irving and the Irvingites, and of the rise of the Brethren under Darby and others, with defections from the Church of England. There were conflicts which divided the members of the CMS committee and secretariat, such as the case of the British and Foreign Bible Society and the inclusion of the Apocrypha in published Bibles. Some Bible Society supporters feared the rise of Socinian (Unitarian) views, and wished to make a doctrinal test necessary for membership. This move was defeated, but the supporters defected and formed the Trinitarian Bible Society. The other dispute had led to the formation of a separate Bible Society for Scotland. Then in the 1830s came the beginning of a new movement in the Church of England which was to become of great importance to the whole Church. In July 1833 John Keble preached his Oxford sermon on "National apostasy", and the Tractarian Movement was launched.

The Church of England had been comfortable and even the Evangelicals were beginning to settle down into positions where they were accepted and respected. They did not at first see where the views of the Tractarians might lead the whole Church. If they had, there might have been great apprehension, given the existing problems between the CMS and the bishops. But publicly at least the CMS did not take sides, and quietly pursued its aims of evangelism overseas and the awakening of the Church at home to pray and give for that end. Then in 1841 Henry Venn was appointed as a clerical secretary for the Society.

Henry Venn, clerical secretary of the Church Missionary Society 1841–1872

Unlike a number of missionary societies, the CMS has neither one supreme founding figure nor a single charismatic missionary figure who dominates its early years. Here there is no William Carey, no David Livingstone, no Hudson Taylor. Indeed, through its history, whether consciously or unconsciously, the Society has avoided the hagiography which sometimes occurs, and it has published comparatively few missionary biographies.

So the most outstanding personality associated with the CMS in its first hundred years is not a missionary pioneer and explorer, but an administrator. Henry Venn was never a missionary, he never travelled to visit any overseas mission field, he never saw at first hand the work he prayed for, agonised over, laboured for. His own work was primarily in an office – his own home became an extension of Salisbury Square. Although his duties were limited to the Society, and he never held high ecclesiastical office, he was, nevertheless, recognised as an ecclesiastical statesman whose influence extended far wider than his official role.

He was born in 1796, a few months before the death of his grandfather, Henry Venn the elder, while his father John Venn was Rector of Clapham and "chaplain" to the so-called "Clapham Sect". His mother died when he was only seven, and his father ten years later. Henry, the elder son, was left as guardian to his four sisters and one brother. At that age he completed the editing of two volumes of his father's sermons, foreshadowing his later editing and writing about and on behalf of mission.

Soon after his father's death he went up to Queens' College, Cambridge, and graduated in 1818. He was elected a fellow in 1819 and in the same year was ordained. More importantly, as it proved in his subsequent career, he attended for the first time a committee meeting of the CMS. (At that time any clergyman who was a subscriber was eligible to attend the committees.) He served a curacy in London, returned to Queens' as a tutor, and then in 1827 was presented to the living of St. John's, Drypool, Hull. Soon after moving to Drypool he married Martha Sykes of Hull – a very happy marriage terminated by her early death in 1840. He had in 1834 returned to London, as Vicar of St. John's, Upper Holloway, and resumed his earlier contact with the CMS. After Martha's death, which occurred when he himself had been seriously ill, he increasingly left his parish work to two curates and became more and more involved with the CMS. In October 1841 he was appointed "Honorary Clerical Secretary *pro tempore*", and that temporary appointment (officially made permanent in 1845) lasted for over thirty years, until just a few months before his death in January 1873.

He was the chief executive of the Society over an extremely important period in its development. The CMS's overseas work had started very slowly; though its foundation date was 1799 it was some years before it had any missionaries serving overseas, and well into its second decade before it expanded to more than one field. From the beginning the relationship with the official, established Church of England and its hierarchy presented problems, which increased with the need for the ordination of missionary candidates and the setting-up of churches in the mission areas. How does a state Church expand to colonies and realms outside the rule and law of its own nation? Venn consistently walked the tightrope suggested in his father's phrase at the founding of the CMS: "the Church-principle, but not the high-Church principle". He believed in, and fought for, the continuing existence of the CMS as a voluntary, independent society but always within the Church of England. He was in the truest sense a father of the world-wide Anglican communion.

He came into office at the time the Tractarian Movement was gaining ground and concepts of the office and role of a bishop were changing. It was likewise a time of the extension of British rule (however reluctantly) to the new colonies of white settlement (Canada: the Durham Report, 1839; New Zealand: the Treaty of Waitangi, 1840). The young Churches in these and other territories needed bishops – how were they to be provided? Likewise in India analagous problems presented themselves.

It was as a result of a conflict in India between the Bishop of Calcutta and the CMS over their respective spheres of authority that Venn was initiated into the controversy. Even before he became secretary he was entrusted with the writing of the "Appendix to the 39th Report", a policy statement which paved the way for a concordat with Bishop Wilson and also for new laws within the Society in Britain which, introduced in 1841, made it easier for the Archbishop of Canterbury, the Bishop of London (Blomfield) and other bishops to become members of the CMS.

Not that all problems were solved for good; over the next thirty years a number of issues arose where the CMS, represented by Venn, did not see eye-to-eye with a bishop. Venn was a man of strong personality and strong conviction, as were many of the bishops he dealt with. But he was personally courteous, by nature a peace-maker, and his opponents often became friends.

He feared not only some of the "Roman" doctrines being newly introduced by the Tractarians, but also the possible autocratic powers of a bishop, which within the Churches of England and Ireland were tempered by law and long-established custom. Venn, a low-Church Evangelical, was conservative in his attitude to Church and State, and he wanted to see the Anglican Churches overseas established under the legislatures of their territories or (as was the diocese of Calcutta) under British law. Here he and the CMS as a whole came into conflict with men like George Augustus Selwyn, the able first Bishop of New Zealand where, up to the bishop's arrival, all the Anglican clergymen had been CMS missionaries.

Selwyn's differences with the CMS over the ordination and licensing of clergy were lesser and negotiable problems compared with the differences over Church government. Venn wished to see a constitutional episcopacy established under law; Selwyn advocated a Church free of the State, but legally validated as "an autonomous society at law, capable of running [its] own affairs by internal legislation" [Yates, p. 122]. Church councils or synods would advise the bishop and prevent autocratic powers being wielded. It was Selwyn's view that prevailed in New Zealand, and was influential in other overseas areas, but in intent he and Venn were not far apart. Both wanted to see an episcopate pastorally based and responsive to the needs of Christians.

For almost all of his time in office, Venn differed in public and private with Samuel Wilberforce, Bishop of Oxford, over the place of episcopacy in the mission of the Church. Venn saw the bishop as "the crown of mission", necessary when a Church had been gathered; Wilberforce (and the Tractarians) saw the bishop as "the keystone of mission", necessary from the beginning. Wilberforce thus differed sharply from Venn, but without personal acrimony, as his tribute at Venn's death testifies. (He wrote to Venn's family, "I honour especially in him the dedication of a life to a noble cause with an uncompromising entireness of devotion which had in it all the elements of true Christian heroism.")

Important as Venn's views on the episcopacy and Church government are, he is remembered more especially for his teaching on the nature of native or indigenous Churches, and the relationship of Church and mission. Here he was truly a pioneer thinker, moving ahead of his fellows. He saw a difference between the missionary – the evangelist going out and preaching the Gospel and moving on – and the pastor, teaching and counselling in a settled situation. He strove to keep missionaries from becoming attached to stations – and for that reason had some difficulty with educational and medical missions, which tied the missionary down. He did not want to see "native Christians" plucked out of the local Church to become second-class missionaries, but he wanted to see them ordained as leaders in a local Church which would be "self-supporting, self-governing [and] self-expanding". When this happened, the scaffolding of mission structures could be removed. This would be the so-called *euthanasia* of mission. This teaching is now seen as almost an axiom of the missionary movement, but we do well to remember that this was not always the case, and how much we owe to Venn for his insight. He logically associated it with a high view of the ability of African, Indian and other new Christians to receive a theological education, to take responsibility, and to exercise leadership.

These areas by no means exhaust the spheres of Venn's contributions. In writing and editing, in deputations, as an unofficial adviser to the Colonial Office and to bishops, as an administrator and father in God to many missionaries, as an advocate of commercial development in the West African colonies – in all these and more he made important contributions. He was not always right, but his contribution to the Church Missionary Society and (what he would consider more important) to the mission of spreading the Gospel and building up the Church was, and still is, incalculable. As his successor, one hundred years later, wrote, "Venn was essentially an administrator of missions." But, if that should suggest something impersonal, Canon Warren added a definition of being an administrator: "to 'manage as a steward', 'to apply'." Venn, in very great humility, would have assented to the claim that it was his life's work to "apply the gospel". (Warren, *To apply the Gospel*, pp. 32–33)

Administration and extension under Venn

Venn became clerical secretary in 1841 at a time of severe financial embarrassment. In fact, the words used at the time were "a serious crisis". For many years income had remained in excess of expenditure, but now the expanding work rapidly reversed the position, and there were debts to tradesmen, loans from committee members, and little capital or property.

One resource the CMS has always had is well-qualified experts to call on. In this case four influential bankers formed a sub-committee to look at the whole financial position. They came up with some drastic proposals, and laid down important principles for future work.

Several missions were to be given up; no new missionaries were to be sent out except to fill vacancies; no new students were to be admitted at Islington except, also, to fill vacancies. A special fund was to be launched to pay off the debt, and a finance committee was to be appointed, to control all future expenditure. But the home organisation was to be extended, for with a little more spending there a much greater income might be produced.

The principles laid down were important for the future work of the Society. Self-support for overseas Churches and

the responsibility of a Christian government to provide for
Christian work and education in their territories were both
stressed. And also stressed was "the golden rule of restricting
expenditure within income". But this was not so easy to
apply. For recruits must be accepted and sent out without
complete knowledge of what the income will be, and unless
there is a policy of faith that if God sends suitable workers
he will also provide the means for supporting them, no
missionary society could operate. In their annual report,
written in fact by the new clerical secretary, the basic
principles of the Society were restated:

> Let it not be supposed that it is on gold, silver, or patronage
> that they found their hopes of success. God forbid! It is the
> faithful, plain, and full maintenance of those great prin-
> ciples of the truth as it is in Jesus, by all the agents and
> missionaries of this Society, without compromise and
> without reserve . . . It is the upholding of the Bible, and the
> Bible alone, as the foundation and rule of faith – upon
> which the blessing of God has rested, does rest, and ever
> will rest.

The general appeal was successful, and by May 1843 – the
time of the yearly annual meetings – all of the debt except
£1,000 had been paid off and a good beginning had been
made in the building up of a capital fund. By 1847 the
Capital Fund had reached £30,000; the new Special China
Fund had reached £15,000, and there was no deficit.

The number of missionaries sent out had been rising
steadily. A total of one hundred went overseas in the first
twenty-five years, up to 1824; in the next ten years, to 1834,
the same number sailed. From 1834 to 1840 another one
hundred went out; the peak year was 1837, when twenty-five
left. After the year of financial crisis the numbers dropped for
a while, but a total of four hundred was reached in the Jubilee
Year, 1849. Of course it is not just the total of those going out

which is important, but the number still serving. As the number of deaths dropped, the number of resignations rose. To take a sample, of the first 180 missionaries sent out, up to 1832, forty-two were still working in 1842, fifty-eight had died before that date, and eighty had resigned. These figures refer to men only; up to the jubilee year only forty-two women figure on the list of missionaries, and many of those were the sisters, daughters or widows of missionaries. Of those few single women who were sent out without being in relationship to a male missionary, few served for long periods. A German teacher, Sophia Hehlen, and an English teacher, Julia Sass, served in Sierra Leone for eighteen and twenty-one years respectively, and built up the Sierra Leone Girls' School into the Annie Walsh Memorial School, which has served the girls of Sierra Leone so well for so long.

The jubilee, 1849

So the Society came in 1849 to its jubilee, financially in good shape and with expanding frontiers. The jubilee was kept as a *year* from the May meetings of 1848. The jubilee statement records 350 missionaries sent out up to that point (with nearly forty more taken up on the field) and 127 of those still serving. The main celebrations were held in the middle of the jubilee year, around All Saints Day, 1 November 1848. Special services were held at St. Paul's and other London churches, and the jubilee meeting was in Exeter Hall on 2 November. There, one of the speakers was Bishop Samuel Wilberforce of Oxford, son of William Wilberforce. He was not, like his father, identified with the Evangelicals; indeed, he was sometimes a severe critic of the CMS, but he spoke as one who dearly loved the Society and its work.

Meetings were also held throughout the country and throughout the world, in the Churches established through CMS efforts and in the overseas Churches which supported it. At the jubilee, a specially-written hymn was sung, which has survived in our hymnbooks. Many who sang it rejoiced in the literal fulfilment of its words, "I hear ten thousand voices singing . . ." The author, Henry Watson Fox, had served in India for seven years, and he had just returned in ill-health and was appointed an assistant secretary in July 1848. But he died two weeks before the jubilee meetings at All Saints-tide. At the centenary in 1899 his son, Henry Elliott Fox, was clerical secretary of the Society.

The decade following the jubilee was full of controversies which cannot now hold us for very long, and which indeed we often find difficult to take seriously. The fear of "Papal aggression" was intensified by the Papal bull (October 1850) creating an archbishopric of Westminster and twelve dioceses. The Tractarians had increased in influence, and ritualists and bishops quarrelled openly in many dioceses. Archdeacon Manning, brother-in-law of Bishop Wilberforce, followed John Henry Newman to Rome, eventually becoming (like Newman) a cardinal. A number of other Anglican clergymen also converted to Rome, and well-known laymen and women. One defection from the Anglican Evangelical side was that of Baptist Noel, member of a well-known family and a strong supporter of the CMS. He became a Baptist, but no other Anglican Evangelical took a similar step.

This decade saw the jubilee of the "venerable Society" as the SPG was known, in 1851, and the first jubilee of the BFBS in 1854. In both CMS leaders participated publicly and generously. Of longer term importance to the CMS than some of the controversies which then loomed so large were the moves towards re-establishing convocation, and the Missionary Bishops Bill of 1853. In both these matters it must frankly be admitted that the CMS took stands which it later reversed. Stock (the first historian of the CMS), slow to criticise, speaks of "excessive caution" and "an undue backwardness to perceive the signs of the times, and to recognize the absolute necessity of Church developments which are now, and have been long since, recognized without reserve".

This period saw the increasing recognition of the CMS as a legitimate missionary arm of the Church of England, and also as a society representing the Evangelical wing of the Church. Its respectability had been aided by the accession of bishops as members, made possible by the change of rules in the early 1840s. Now, in the 1850s, the CMS saw several of its members becoming bishops. This was the period of the so-called "Palmerston Bishops", brought about by Lord Palmerston becoming Prime Minister in 1855 (the height of the Crimean War). Lady Palmerston was mother-in-law to Lord Shaftesbury, who was in any case a close personal friend of Lord Palmerston. The Prime Minister, scarcely a churchman, called on his kinsman for advice when vacancies occurred, and so a number of Evangelical parish clergy, already active members of the CMS were, through connection, raised to the episcopate. One was the Hon. and Rev. J. T. Pelham, brother of Lord Chichester, the CMS president, who in 1857 became Bishop of Norwich. Just as important, although he was not identified as an Evangelical, was the appointment of Archibald Campbell Tait as Bishop of London. This was the diocese whose bishop ordained for CMS, and an active bishop vitally interested in mission and missions was of great help and a stimulus to the Society.

For thirty years Henry Venn was the mainspring of CMS administration. He was never a "general secretary" but he was without doubt the leader of the team. His greatest gift was in committees, where he always sought to obtain decisions by consensus. He was especially gifted in the writing of drafts, minutes and despatches. The correspondence committee, the main organ of administration, met weekly, and attendances varied. There were eighteen elected lay members, many of whom through this whole period were connected with India – former Army officers or civilians in the Indian

Civil Service. Any subscribing clerical member was entitled to attend the committee, but the number who came regularly was limited. Venn tried to encourage potentially useful men to attend for long enough to understand what was happening, so that in the end they could profitably participate. There is no doubt that Venn's own ability and his dominance – though he was never a domineering figure – discouraged some from persisting in the attempt. They felt unnecessary while Venn was there.

Financial details were handled not by Venn but by others; the principle advocated by him, on which the CMS worked, was that God would provide what was necessary for his own work. This did not exclude prudent and sensible financial management. Increasingly money was raised through the associations which covered virtually the whole of England. Association secretaries – equivalent to the area secretaries of the present day – were appointed and paid from central funds to assist the associations, but not to control them. In some areas they were honorary; in others part-time, combining the CMS work with that of a small parish. The CMS sometimes found itself criticised for the expenses incurred by the association secretaries and the "deputations" who now were, increasingly, missionaries on leave.

But when economies were made in this area, giving fell, and the expenses for stipends and travelling expenses were justified by the results. It was, however, a continuing problem that the success of associations was largely judged by the amount of money raised for the CMS. This was in terms of the association's self-judgement. But their primary task was to educate, elicit prayer and to draw offers of service from suitable candidates. These aims were never lost sight of, but fund-raising was, as always, a more concrete activity. Children, young people, women, adults of varying educational and social class, were catered for in differing ways, and the numbers attending special services and meetings were impressive.

Most of this work went on without Venn's personal supervision, though his contact with missionaries, by letter and through personal interview when they were in London, occupied much of his time. But his major work continued to be in his own development as a missionary statesman and thinker. In particular, he was concentrating on the relationship between mission and Church, between evangelism and pastoral ministry, between missionary and pastor. He had come into office forty years after the foundation of the Society, and questions which had scarcely been asked at the beginning now urgently needed answers. Second- and even third-generation Christians were to be found in the CMS fields. So from 1851 to 1866 he wrote and issued three papers which together explain his thinking on *The Native Pastorate and Organization of Native Churches*.

In these papers he emphasised, first, the distinction between the work of the *missionary*, who preaches the Gospel to those outside, and that of the *pastor*, who teaches the young Christians. He realised early the danger of missionaries keeping control in their own hands and doing all the catechising and teaching, until they have no time left for evangelising. And he notes the fact that missionaries coming out of the English established Church are particularly liable to fall into the trap of doing all the organising for their converts, since they are used to a system where local Christians take little initiative in their parishes. He makes practical suggestions for avoiding this situation, the most important of which is the forming of converts into "Christian Companies" under an elder or "Christian headman". One thinks immediately of Wesley's class system, and of "small groups" in American (and other) Churches today. The "Companies" as they develop will become congregations, which in turn will form into conferences, until in the end there is the basis for a native episcopate, the training of local men as catechists, teachers and ministers, and the increasing support of such leaders by the local Christians. This would be the basis of the self-governing, self-supporting, self-extending Church for which Henry Venn became well known.

The work overseas

All this activity on the part of Venn and others, was directed towards continuing evangelism and the building-up of Churches overseas. During his period in office, some missions were discontinued, for financial reasons, or because mission became an impossibility or had no results, or, a happier reason, the locally organised Anglican Church was able to take over (as in the West Indies). The three earliest fields, West Africa, New Zealand, and India and Ceylon, continued to develop and expand, and some new missions were embarked on.

West Africa: the opening up of Nigeria

If any general theme can be drawn from the necessarily brief accounts of the founding of various missions world-wide, it should be that few missions have been established by outside agents alone. In instance after instance, we find that God has prepared an opening through local Christians, through expatriates already in contact with an area, through army officers, traders, and chaplains. Thus the contrast often made between the introduction of Islam, informally, by traders, merchants and travellers, and the "formal" introduction of Christianity by professional missionaries is by no means always true. Islam had its professional missionaries and the informal element is strong in the expansion of Christianity.

The establishment and growth of the CMS mission in Nigeria (as the region was finally to become) is a major example of this pattern. From Sierra Leone the Gospel went east and became established in the towns and cities of a vast area, and the CMS followed the Gospel. As always, it travelled in the persons of believers.

The special factor in the expansion of work in West Africa was the slave trade, which had removed hundreds and thousands of men, women and children from their homes, and taken them away on ships for transport to the West Indies and North America. When patrols of the British Navy began to intercept vessels carrying on the illegal trade, the recaptives were landed in Sierra Leone, where the colonial authorities with help from missionary societies tried to establish them in some kind of community. The adults were taught trades; the children were educated; many were baptised as Christians and were accepted into the already complex society of Nova Scotians, maroons from Jamaica, and freed slaves from England who formed the population of Freetown and its satellite townships. Many of the recaptives came from African societies with a strong and sophisticated tradition of trading through markets, and of commerce in general, and the acquisition of literacy increased their potential ability. European vessels had been trading along the coast of West Africa long before the advent of western missonaries; bright and adventurous young men of the coastal peoples sometimes found work on the ships. So as the Sierra Leone settlers became more prosperous, it is not surprising that their thoughts turned to the area from which some of them had so recently been torn away, and they started to look for ways of going back. As early as 1835 some of the liberated Africans were combining to buy condemned slave vessels, which they sailed back to Badagri and Lagos. Some made contact with their families, and the stories they brought back encouraged others. In 1839 twenty-three Yoruba merchants petitioned the governor of Sierra Leone to grant permission for them to go back to Badagri and form a permanent settlement there.

At the same time, CMS supporters in England were thinking of the relationship between Christianity and "civilisation" and how both could be extended. A leading figure was Thomas Fowell Buxton, whose book, *The African slave trade and its remedy*, was published in 1840. But he had been thinking on these lines for years already. The chief practical step he took was the sending out of the Niger expedition in 1841 – a joint Government-commercial-mission venture. The expedition was largely a failure; forty-five of the 150 European members died. But it gave wide publicity to the possibilities of commerce and trade on the inland stretches of the Niger, which was not missed by European merchants nor by the liberated Africans of Sierra Leone.

It also turned the eyes of missionary societies to the area, and because the expedition was reckoned a failure, the British Government stood back and it was left to the missions to take the initiatives. The CMS from Sierra Leone, Wesleyan Methodists from the Gold Coast, and Scottish Presbyterians from Jamaica, all planned new missions. All had the great advantage of black catechists and ministers, already trained, who would be more likely to survive in the difficult climate than white missionaries coming straight from Europe.

The Church in Sierra Leone was coming of age. In 1840 a Church Missionary Association was formed; in 1843 the first Sierra Leonean priest was ordained. This was Samuel Adjai (Ajayi) Crowther, of Yoruba origin, who had been freed from a slave ship and landed in Freetown in 1822. He visited England in the 1820s, and was the first student on the rolls of the Fourah Bay Institution. In 1842 he was sent by the CMS to the Islington College, after he had travelled with the Niger Expedition. His companions on that voyage were favourably impressed by Crowther, and afterwards, with Schön, the German missionary, he published *Journal of an expedition up the Niger* (London 1842).

The Niger Expedition and the rising interest in "re-immigration" to Nigeria came just at the time that Henry Venn was taking office in the CMS. West Africa had always come high in his interests since, as a boy, he had met at Clapham African boys sent to England for education. Now came a God-given opportunity to extend the mission in West Africa. Did he already foresee that here, perhaps, might be the test case for the "native Church"? It was already obvious that in New Zealand, Canada and the West Indies the "mission" would be absorbed into a colonial and largely white Church; the work in Australia, South Africa and the Mediterranean had been wound up, or soon would be. East Africa was an enterprise yet to be embarked on; in India and Ceylon were large and prospering missions which were complex in the relationships with bishops, the Company, other missions, and the ancient Churches. In West Africa there might be a clean slate, and a Church free of these complications.

Thomas Freeman, a Methodist missionary from the Gold Coast, acted before the CMS, and arrived in Badagri in September 1842. Soon he followed the immigrants to Abeokuta, where he made friendly contact with the local ruler, Sodeke. On his return to Badagri on Christmas Eve he met the first CMS missionary, Henry Townsend (working in Sierra Leone from 1836) who had just arrived. Townsend also visited Abeokuta, and met immigrants and Sodeke, who was keen to receive missionaries. But he was not then able to stay, and it was not until January 1845 that the first permanent CMS party arrived in Badagri. Townsend and Samuel Crowther were among the group, with Gollmer, a German missionary formerly in Sierra Leone, two Sierra Leonean schoolmasters, and several artisans, servants and a translator. So from the very beginning, German, English and Sierra Leonean missionaries were represented in the new work. They intended to proceed at once to Abeokuta, but the friendly ruler, Sodeke, had just died, and so the coastal city of Badagri became the first CMS base.

The CMS and the other incoming missions were to find from the beginning that plans and strategies were at the mercy of African rulers and of inter-group politics, and that no "sphere of influence" nor "consul" could make it easy for the strangers to live and work. The Yoruba-speaking peoples, among whom they first settled, were a vast nation divided into separate kingdoms, city-states and chiefdoms, and what the Yoruba did was to affect the whole course of the mission.

The Yoruba mission can be said to date effectively from 1846, when Townsend and Samuel Crowther entered Abeokuta. In Crowther the mission had an agent who was able to preach almost at once in his native tongue, and the first baptisms took place in 1848. In that year David Hinderer (another German) went to West Africa and despite warfare between Dahomey and Abeokuta he was able in 1851 to settle in Ibadan, with which his name was to be so closely linked.

Compared with the growth of the work in some other missions, affairs in Yoruba country matured fast. Most of the first missionaries came after experience in Sierra Leone, and they came accompanied by catechists and schoolmasters already acquainted with local vernaculars. Apart from Samuel Crowther, ordained in 1843, there were soon several other Sierra Leonean catechists ordained – Thomas King and T. B. Macaulay in 1854, and J. C. Taylor in 1856. Soon afterwards came the ordination of Nigerian-born men, though the first were the sons of Sierra Leone immigrants.

It was often through the demands of local people that advances were made; at least, what were afterwards seen to be advances, though the missionaries at first did not always see them as such. The climate of opinion was changing, and some of the former missionaries in Sierra Leone wanted to avoid what they saw as mistakes in the way the Church there had been directed and educated. This happened in the setting-up of Lagos CMS Grammar School, in 1859. The Rev. T. B. Macaulay, who had been working in Abeokuta, came into conflict with Townsend, and he was transferred to Lagos at Crowther's instigation. Here he set up the new school. It was welcomed by the local Christians but opposed by Townsend and some other missionaries. Later – but early considering the age of the mission – a Female Institution was opened in Lagos, in 1872. The first principal, jointly with his wife, was a German missionary, the Rev. A. Mann; another wife, Mrs. Lamb, also helped. But by 1885 single women were being appointed to the Female Institution. Most stayed only a short time, till removed by illness or marriage; the exception was an older English woman, Miss Marian Goodall, who had given up her own girls' school at Margate to go to Lagos. She served for over five years, much loved and appreciated; in 1895 she went at her own request to Abeokuta where, shortly afterwards, she died.

Another much loved woman was Anna, the English wife of the German missionary, David Hinderer. The Hinderers became identified with Ibadan, where they lived from 1853 to 1869, for part of that time isolated by the local wars. Anna Hinderer had no children – which probably accounted for her comparatively long life in the country. She took African children into her home, and became a mother to the Christians. The Hinderers' story became well-known in England through a memoir.

In addition to formal education, the CMS was especially diligent in Yoruba to provide industrial training. This fitted in with the "Christianity and civilisation" theme then prevalent. An industrial institute was set up at Abeokuta, and by encouraging apprenticeships under skilled immigrants, training was given in carpentry and other building skills, in architecture, in printing, and in medicine. Theological education was, surprisingly, much later in being established. As with the grammar school, some missionaries opposed the very idea of a theological education on theoretical lines. But another of the German missionaries, Bühler, conducted a training institution at Abeokuta until his death in 1865, and three of the first truly local pastors (that is, not the sons of immigrants) were trained by him. One of these was Charles Phillips, who was sent for education at Fourah Bay, and served as a catechist in Lagos until his ordination in 1876. In 1893 he was consecrated as one of the two assistant bishops in the Diocese of Western Equatorial Africa.

The Niger mission

The Rev. Samuel Crowther participated in all three Niger Expeditions – in 1841, 1854, and 1857. It was after the 1857 Expedition that the Niger mission began, but Crowther saw himself only as extending the Yoruba mission. Stations were established at Onitsha and Igbebe. But Henry Venn clearly and emphatically installed Crowther as the director of a new mission on the Niger.

If the CMS leaders at home had in the beginning seen the Yoruba mission as taking place in an area where it would be possible to start with "a clean slate", they soon became wiser. Warfare between the various Yoruba peoples (including those of Dahomey) was almost endemic. There was no central authority with which to negotiate, and little could be achieved by the various British consuls. The policy of the CMS of encouraging trade had succeeded almost too well. Traders were now a major force, and the mission often had to depend on them for mail, supplies and transport. Many of the Sierra Leone pastors and catechists (or their families) became involved in trading operations, and this resulted in connections between missionaries and traders where separation would have been more prudent.

Because the work commenced with the Niger Expedition, the first stations established were farthest inland, at Lokoja and Onitsha. From there the mission spread south, reaching Bonny and Brass in the Niger Delta, and finally Kalabari further east. The only staff Crowther had available were Sierra Leone catechists, some of whom were later ordained. There were able men, like William Romaine, who went to Onitsha in 1857, first as a scripture reader, then school-master and catechist. He was ordained in 1869, and worked on at Onitsha till his death in 1877, after twenty years there. The schools established and largely taught by these men were especially important, not only for what they taught, but also for the financial contribution they provided. The

CMS did not take full financial responsibility for the workers except at Onitsha.

In the years that this work was being established, warfare among the Yoruba groups was going on almost without a break. But the actual fighting was sporadic. The major conflict was between the Egba of Abeokuta and the people of Ibadan, both places where there was strong CMS work. The missionaries — Townsend at Abeokuta and Hinderer at Ibadan — tended to support the cause of "their" people, and the result was a general distrust of missionaries as allies of the threatening power, though evangelism resulting in many baptisms did not cease. Besieged by the Dahomeans, Abeokuta was especially prayed for by CMS supporters in England, and there was great rejoicing at its miraculous deliverance, in 1863. The Hinderers and Edward Roper were virtually prisoners in Ibadan for five years. So the British annexation of Lagos Island in 1861 only added fuel to the flame.

This general resistance to white missionaries was an additional reason for Henry Venn to press forward with his vision of seeing Samuel Crowther made bishop. The episcopal visits of the bishops of Sierra Leone were no longer sufficient for the large and growing work, if they ever had been. The first three bishops of Sierra Leone had all died after returning from visits to Lagos.

So Crowther must be bishop on the Niger — the crown of the native Church. But there was not yet a native Church on the Niger; inasmuch as a native Church existed, it was in Yoruba country. It is probably true that Venn would have wished to make Crowther a bishop with authority in Yoruba — his own land — but he was opposed in almost open rebellion by Henry Townsend, who in another time and place would undoubtedly have been a bishop himself, and who well knew his own abilities. (Townsend had been only twenty-one when he first went to Sierra Leone, and he was an extremely able and ambitious man.) The other missionaries, though not so bitterly opposed – none had any criticism of Crowther as a spiritual leader – were far from enthusiastic. The most general reservation was that "a black man" would not command the respect of the non-Christian Africans nor the white traders. Even Hinderer concurred in this view.

Townsend marshalled considerable support, and in fact Henry Venn's strategy was somewhat doubtful in this case, given that Crowther would be bishop in a missionary area, and one where he was not a native. But Venn was hoping and expecting to see, in the near future, Europeans serving under Crowther in an atmosphere of "collegiality and mutuality". Crowther himself, a naturally humble man, was well aware of Townsend's opposition. But Venn's pleas prevailed, and he was consecrated in Westminster Abbey on 19 June, 1864.

A number of factors prevented Crowther, in the years following his consecration, from getting the help and support he needed. Venn was getting old and nearing his retirement (he died in January 1873); continuing war and opposition to whites made it impossible to send missionaries inland; the CMS went through another financial crisis at the beginning of the 1870s, and offers of service dropped; of those sent out a number died. But more important, though harder to document, was a changing attitude to Africans, coupled with the view that the white man was a "natural" ruler; the partition of Africa and the high tide of imperialism were not far away. Whatever Crowther did or did not do, it is doubtful if he could have satisfied all groups at this stage of the mission's history.

He lived in Lagos, and could only visit the far-flung missions to supervise and advise once a year at the most. He was dependent on trading vessels to take him up the river, and he was generally five to six months on such a journey. In 1878 the CMS sent out the steamer *Henry Venn*, commemorating his beloved father-in-God, friend and patron. Potentially the vessel gave him independence, but the changing circumstances made it of less use than had been anticipated.

4   INDIA: BISHOP WILSON AND HIS SUCCESSORS, 1832–1876

India 1832–1876

By 1832 four bishops had been consecrated in England, successively, for the diocese of Calcutta. Each had made the long journey out, had been enthroned, and had entered on his duties. The first had survived eight years; the third less than eight months.

So there were no great expectations when the fifth bishop, Daniel Wilson, sailed. He was already in his mid-fifties. The situation was, as usual, complicated by the long interregnum caused by the distance. In the case of Bishop Wilson it was a year and four months.

But it was a matter for rejoicing that the new bishop was already a good friend of the CMS. He had been the Vicar of Islington, and the Church Missionary Institution was located near his church. Now he had offered himself for Calcutta, and his son, another Daniel Wilson, became Vicar of Islington.

One of his first tasks was to work for the establishment of new dioceses, for it was realised that this was necessary if the life of any bishop in Calcutta was to be prolonged enough for him to be useful. It happened to be coming up to the end of the twenty-year interval when the East India Company Charter had to be reviewed – an opportune time. Wilson had spoken with the Prime Minister and the Archbishop of Canterbury before leaving for India. Accordingly, provision was made in the East India Act of 1833 for "two separate and distinct Bishopricks [Madras and Bombay], the Bishops

59

thereof to be subordinate to the Bishop of Calcutta . . . as their Metropolitan".

So Daniel Corrie, one of the "pious chaplains" who had been Archdeacon of Calcutta and served during the inter-regnums, became Bishop of Madras in 1835. Sadly, he was to die there after only two years. Thomas Carr, archdeacon in Bombay, became its bishop in 1837. Ceylon was assigned to Madras diocese, and so remained till 1845, when it became a separate diocese.

Before the new bishops arrived, Wilson began his first visitation. Among his problems were the establishing of episcopal authority over missionaries of different backgrounds and societies, the relations with the corresponding committees, ministry to Christians of differing backgrounds, including soldiers, English civilians and Eurasians (Indian-Europeans), the training of local men, and the building of more and adequate churches. And always, the outreach to the Hindus, Muslims and others of the vast sub-continent.

Although Bishop Wilson was an Evangelical with close ties to the CMS, he was by no means "low Church" in his total view. He had good relations on the whole with the SPG, and when he came to deal with one of the most pressing problems, that of caste within the Church, he had need of all possible support. This problem was most acute in the Madras area, where the earlier German missionaries, working in the Danish mission with SPCK support, had not condemned caste-related behaviour on the part of Christians. After consulting with the SPG and CMS missionaries Wilson sent out a letter in Tamil on the subject of caste, to be read in all churches. There was resistance, but sufficient conformity to establish a new beginning in dealing with this very difficult and complex problem.

Early in Wilson's time in India the relationship between the CMS missionaries and the Syrian Church was coming to a point of change. In January 1836 the Metran, Mar Dionysius IV, drew up a document withdrawing the Church from the cooperative agreements previously entered into with the CMS. (See pp. 34–5) The continuing though changed relationship with the Christians of the ancient Church led to the theservice of many men who proved to be south India's greatest Christian leaders.

The CMS in India

By the time that Bishop Wilson came to India, the CMS work was organised into three area missions, each with its own corresponding committee to act as liaison between the missionaries on the spot and the parent committee in London. Originally all those serving on the corresponding committee were Christians from the white community: officials, army officers and the like. The missionaries met together annually in conference. The members of both groups often had years of experience in India. No wonder there were fairly frequent clashes with the bishops, who for some period of time were men with no previous experience in India. Wilson, although the friend of CMS, soon had his troubles. Corresponding committees which acted without reference to the bishop were just as likely to ignore the parent committee in Salisbury Square, London. One major problem was over the licensing and location of missionaries; another was the training and ordination of catechists and ordinands. The CMS soon found it advisable to appoint full-time mission secretaries, who acted as secretaries to the corresponding committees. After a few crises with consequent resignations from the committees it was possible to make new nominations and to establish committees which worked better with both bishop and sending body.

An inherited problem from the days when the missionaries were mostly German Lutherans was over the ordination of Indian workers. This, in Lutheran tradition, had been carried out by the missionaries themselves; now it was an episcopal prerogative. From the time of Bishop Heber the continental Lutheran missionaries received Anglican ordination, and in time that particular problem died out. But it persisted long enough to be one of the causes of the schism, in the mid-1830s, of C. T. E. Rhenius and his converts. Rhenius was one of the most able of the early German missionaries (Madras, 1814) and was leader of the flourishing work in Tinnevelly. After his death in 1838, and with the understanding help of missionaries like G. Pettitt, the schism was largely healed.

Modes of work

It has long since ceased to be the case (if it ever was) that missionary work consisted of preaching from the Bible under a palm tree. Education has from the beginning been an important adjunct to evangelism, though less so in India than in Africa. The circuits of simple village primary schools, using the vernacular and catering primarily for the children of village Christians, did come into being in parts of south India where there were fairly dense settlements of Christians, and in other areas where there were small-scale mass movements of lower caste and tribal peoples. But in India the higher-level English medium school was probably more important. The pioneer of the college of this type, catering for the young Brahmin and the socially élite of other communities, is generally accepted to be Alexander Duff, a Church of Scotland missionary who went to Calcutta in 1830. Alongside the regular formal classes, lectures, debates and discussions for a wider audience were often held, and these seem to have had a special attraction for Indian men.

Other missions followed Duff's lead, and the CMS was among them. Indeed, the CMS opened Bishop's College, Calcutta, which was a school as well as a theological college, in 1820, well before Duff arrived, but it did not so quickly find its place in the city. The hope and prayer for such institutions was that, through long and deep contact with the Scriptures and through the witness of Christian lives, students would be converted. This never happened in large numbers, but it did occur. One of the earliest and most noted of Duff's students to accept the faith was a Brahmin called Krishna Mohan Banerjea. Although baptised by Duff (in 1832) he became an Anglican while a teacher in a CMS school, and was ordained deacon in 1838, at the same time as another Brahmin convert, a long-serving catechist, Anand Masih.

Not all missionaries, over the years, were convinced that the perpetuation of residential schools which tied down missionaries in one place was the best use of personnel. "Itineration" was more in favour; it was seen as direct evangelistic work while the schools were, at best, only indirect. Certainly there were many problems such as obtaining suitable staff, and of giving Christian instruction to non-Christian pupils, not always legal, or permissible, or wise. There were few converts, but those few were important in that many became leaders in the Indian Church. Banerjea was one of the first; from the Robert Money School in Bombay came the Parsee, Sorabji Khurshedji, baptised in 1841; from the Noble School in Masulipatam came Ainala Bhushanam and Manchala Ratnam, both baptised in 1852. All these were later ordained. There were other high-caste Hindus, there were Muslims, Sikhs and at least one other Parsee who first heard the Gospel as students, were eventually baptised, and themselves contributed to "direct evangelism" as pastors of local churches.

One case where the educational work of the Church quickly affected the evangelistic work was in the North Tinnevelly Itinerant Mission. T. G. Ragland, a brilliant young scholar and fellow of Corpus Christi, went to Madras in 1845 as secretary of the corresponding committee. In his role of generally overseeing missionary work, he had a vision of an itinerating ministry which might do for the spiritually barren northern district of Tinnevelly what had already begun to happen in the south. He was himself willing to give up his secretaryship, but illness intervened, and he was able to make only one pioneering trip before he died in 1858, aged only forty-three. The two missionaries who really developed this work were David Fenn, a second generation missionary, and Robert Meadows, both Cambridge men. But from the beginning they were aided by Indian evangelists – Joseph Cornelius, of Syrian Christian background, and later by converts from Hinduism. One was Vedhanayam Viravagu, educated at the Palamcotta Seminary and at Bishop Corrie's High School, Madras. He worked as a catechist with the Itinerating Mission from 1855 to 1859, when he was ordained deacon, and from 1859 to his death in 1886 he served as a pastor to the church that was built up in North Tinnevelly. Another was William Thomas Satthianadhan, a convert who was trained at the Palamcotta Preparandi Institution, and was ordained deacon in 1859. In his own family Satthianadhan was an interesting example of the multiple strands going to make up the young Church. He was a convert from Hinduism, but he married a third-generation Anglican, the daughter of the Rev. John Devasagayam, who was ordained as early as 1830. The children of William Satthianadhan and his wife Anna, well-educated by any standards, became leaders in Church and in university circles.

Women and girls – missionary and Indian

Girls' education always lagged behind but it was not totally neglected. For a long time it had to depend on the rather haphazard help of the wives and daughters of missionaries. When the head of the family went on leave his womenfolk went too. These women usually became officially recognised missionaries in their own right only on the death of the father or husband. But in this period some gave quite exceptional service. One was Amelia Johnson, born Amelia Baker,

daughter of Henry Baker senior, the pioneer of Cottayam.
On her mother's side she was descended from the Kohlhoffs,
SPCK workers in India from the mid-18th century. Mrs.
Johnson, married and then widowed, ran the Normal Girls'
School at Cottayam with the help of her mother. That mother,
born Amelia Kohlhoff, was married in 1818, widowed in
1866, and remained at Cottayam till her death in 1888. The
widow of another pioneer had a similar record. Mary Davies
came to India in 1838 to be married to John Thomas of
Mengnanapuram. With her daughter Frances Thomas she
ran the Elliott Tuxford School in Mengnanapuram, and was
still serving in 1894, fifty-six years after first coming to India.

Another long-serving woman calls us to remember the
contribution made by Eurasian Christians, as they were then
called – the products of European-Indian marriages – and of
the "country-born" who served the Church. John Edmund
Sharkey was a Eurasian who was educated in CMS institutions. He served as a catechist in his home town of
Masulipatam, on the east coast north of Madras, and he
helped Robert Noble on the opening day of what became the
Noble School, in 1843. After ordination in 1847 he continued
work in the Masulipatam area for twenty years. In 1847 he
married a Eurasian woman, Ann Amelia Nailer, who made a
fine contribution on her own account, running a girls' school
at Masulipatam. In 1864 one of the periodic cyclones and
tidal waves which afflict the Bay of Bengal overwhelmed
Masulipatam. No missionaries died, but several of the Indian
clergy and their families were swept away and drowned. In
addition, half of the girls in the dormitory – thirty-three –
were drowned. Despite this terrible loss, Mrs. Sharkey carried
on after her husband's death in 1867 and till her own death
in 1878. The rebuilt girls' school was named the Sharkey
Memorial School.

Beginning in this comparatively informal way, girls' education nevertheless developed, and one advance was the
opening, in 1851, of the Calcutta Normal School, to train

women teachers for girls' schools. Various "Zenana"[1]
missions supplied missionary teachers – and, incidentally,
wives for many CMS missionaries. The Indian Female
Normal School and Instruction Society, which was the fore-
runner of the Zenana Bible and Medical Mission, was the
main contributor, and the CMS resisted several attempts to
take on specific "Zenana" work. It was not until 1880 that
the specifically Anglican CEZMS – Church of England
Zenana Missionary Society – was founded, but the IFNS
continued in close cooperation with the CMS.

The missionaries recruited

The Sharkeys were just two of a number of locally recruited
missionaries who strengthened the ranks in the mid-19th
century. In the case of the Eurasians they usually owed their
education to the English-medium schools the CMS had
established. Some were what were then termed "Anglo-
Indians" – of European ancestry but born and educated in
India. Others were British-born men – perhaps soldiers who
had taken their discharge and made their homes in India.
Some had little formal education, but they made up for it by
their natural abilities and their knowledge of the local society
and of Indian languages and dialects. One of the first was
William Bowley, ordained in 1825, who worked for the CMS
for twenty-five years. In the period we are considering at
least seventeen such men were "taken up" in India, and
enrolled on the list of missionaries. Some of the pioneering
work in new areas was done by these men. One was Thomas
Young Darling, who started as a lay agent, was ordained in
1851, and worked as a missionary for twenty-eight years. He
is noted in the *The Missionary Register* as "chief instrument in

---

[1]Zenana was the section of a prosperous Hindu home where the women were
enclosed.

the extensive work among the Malas of the Bezwada and Raghapur Districts". This was a small "mass movement" in a part of Telugu country. Darling was also involved in Telugu Bible translation. Another remarkable piece of service was that of William Cruickshank of Madras, blind from childhood. He taught at the Palamcotta High School from its inception in 1844 to 1870, and was an influence on several pupils who were later ordained. One of these was the Rev. W. T. Satthianadhan, who has been mentioned above.

Boarding schools were one type of residential care; another – though entered into reluctantly – was orphanages. The CMS has seldom emphasised the setting-up of orphanages, and has generally tried to avoid bringing up children in an isolated environment out of touch with the surrounding society. But on occasions this was the charitable and Christian thing to do. In India a series of famines in 1837–38 left a number of orphans for whom care was necessary. So an orphanage was established at Secundra (Sikandra) outside Agra, and another at Benares. A little earlier Mrs. Wilson (previously Miss Cooke), who had started the first school for girls in Calcutta, established a "female orphanage" at Agarpara. In several cases married couples (the Leupolts at Benares, the Hoernles at Secundra) supervised the orphanage, looking after both boys and girls. The children had not only to be cared for and educated, but prepared for life. An earlier historian writes about Secundra, "The orphans were carefully and lovingly brought up." They were taught Urdu, but were shielded from any knowledge of Hinduism and Islam, and thus grew up quite detached from the society round about them. As a result they also grew up without any remnant of caste prejudice. Employment had to be found for them, and one avenue was a trade which, because of its newness, had not become attached to a particular caste. This was printing. A printing press was established which became very successful – the Orphan Press. Other children educated at the orphanages became government clerks, railway employees, teachers and catechists. At least two were ordained and served the Church in northern India – Frederick Abel and David Jeremy. As time went on the orphanages emptied and in 1860 the one at Secundra was about to be closed when another famine struck and it was revived, with later famines maintaining the need.

We are accustomed to thinking of Christian missionaries as the pioneers of the Church – the advance guard who reconnoitre and stake out the claim. But in fact it was often the other way round in India. Others were the pioneers and the missionaries came in later as reinforcements, building up on foundations already laid. In the case of the CMS some of the Company chaplains and civilians serving with the Company first preached the Gospel in India, and by the time missionaries arrived there were a few Indian Christians ready to assist them. We have seen how Eurasian Christians and country-born Europeans backed up the overseas mission- aries, and how a chaplain like the Rev. James Hough, when appointed to Palamcotta, discovered the large number of Tamil-speaking Christians without schools, clergy or even Bibles, and did what he could to help them while calling in the help of missionaries.

There are many other examples of pioneering initiatives taken by those outside the professional ministry. The exten- sion of the Church in north India and in what is now Pakistan owed much to such initiatives. Sometimes they were civilians and sometimes army officers. It was civilians in Agra who founded a Church Missionary Association there in 1837 and asked for missionaries. It was not the absolute beginning of work in Agra, for two of the first Indian priests, Abdul Masih and Anand Masih, had been stationed there, but there had been a falling away of effort. A new appointment came just in time for help to be given at the time of the great famine in 1837–38, when the orphanage was set up. The work around Agra became extensive enough for Bishop Wilson to endeavour to have a new diocese of Agra created.

He failed in this, but Agra continued to develop as a Church centre.

As early as 1823 a CMS missionary went to Gorakhpur, on the Nepal border, at the request of a civilian, Robert Merttins Bird. Bird's sister assisted actively in the work until her death from cholera in 1834. Michael Wilkinson, the first missionary at Gorakhpur, later worked at Kotgur, near Simla, in what was called the Himalayan Mission. Kotgur is the Kotgarth of Kipling's *Kim*, where Lispeth, the Woman of Shamlagh, played the piano in the mission house (*Kim*, with its Muslim, Buddhist and Hindu characters; Eurasians, private soldiers and officers, army chaplains, Catholic and Anglican, provides a useful backdrop to the land we are discussing).

The Himalayan Mission never developed into a viable Church. More important in the long run was the work established in Peshawar, the Afghan capital. CMS missionaries had entered the Punjab in 1851, stationed at Amritsar, the Sikh capital. From before the turn of the century the Sikh state was growing in strength under the dynamic young Ranjit Singh, who eventually ruled the Punjab. After his death in 1839, without a strong successor, there was confusion, and war with the British forces became inevitable. In 1843 Sir Charles Napier took the province of Sind, south of the Punjab; in 1845 the Sikh army crossed the Sutlej River, the previous limit of their territory, and early in 1846 was defeated. After further battles, treaties, negotiations and risings, the Punjab was annexed by Lord Dalhousie in 1849. The two Irish-born Lawrence brothers, Henry (a soldier) and John (a civilian), had much to do with the Punjab in this period, and John Lawrence became the chief commissioner. He and his brother were two of the Evangelical Christians to whom the CMS in India owed so much. CMS missionaries continued in Karachi, Agra and Delhi, but officers in the occupying army wanted to see Christian work in the Punjab proper. This only became possible when another of the Christian officers was stationed in Peshawar as commissioner.

He was Major Herbert Edwardes, who accepted the request of some of the officers, and signed a memorandum to the CMS asking for missionaries. Those who signed (twenty-two military soldiers and eight civilians) also gave money for the project, as did private soldiers. In fact, sufficient was given for the CMS to have no initial costs except the allowances of the missionaries. The Rev. Robert Clark, already in the Punjab, went up to Peshawar and was joined by the veteran German missionary, the Rev. C. G. Gottlieb. One of the officers instrumental in getting up the petition retired from the army in 1855, and became a lay missionary. This was Colonel William Martin, who worked in the Punjab for five years and personally gave over £4,000 to the work of CMS and Moravian missions.

The work at Peshawar continued despite difficulties; it was a bad climate for Europeans and three men died and three more were invalided home after short terms of service. It was also considered dangerous, perhaps more especially for the Afghan and Indian converts. These were not numerous, but conversions there were, and from them came a number of future Church leaders. Daud Singh, the first Sikh convert, was ordained deacon in 1854; a Rajput man from Kotghur was baptised in 1853, and made a deacon in 1866. Perhaps the most famous was the former Muslim teacher, Imad-ud-din, who was baptised at Amritsar and made a deacon in 1872. He had been a learned Muslim and became a learned Christian, and his writings were widely used to help Muslim enquirers. Another Muslim of Amritsar, Imam Shah, became pastor of the local congregation of Peshawar. He married the daughter of the Rev. Daud Singh.

Other pioneering ventures in the north resulted from similar initiatives by army officers and civilians. One was the opening of the Kashmir Mission in 1864, the CMS's first genuinely medical mission, under William Elmslie, a Scottish Presbyterian doctor. Others followed after Elmslie's early death in 1872, and educational work in Srinagar followed.

Although it is difficult to pick out one missionary for a longer discussion, one missionary to India in the mid-19th century deserves to be remembered. He is James Long of Ireland, a clergyman and a gifted linguist, who served in and near Calcutta from 1840 to 1872. He took the part of the Bengali *ryots*, the serfs on the indigo plantations, as did other CMS missionaries at the time their conditions brought them near to insurrection (1858–60). The missionaries, naturally, were branded "political agitators", but were exonerated by a government commission and by the lieutenant governor of Bengal who "respectfully expressed his admiration of their conduct". But Long was to suffer more than criticism. He was asked by the Government to translate a Bengali play which dealt with the situation of the villagers and the plantations, and an association of European indigo planters brought an action for libel against him in the criminal courts. He was convicted after what was seen as an "outrageously partial" summing-up, and sentenced to a fine of 1,000 rupees and one month's imprisonment. A Bengali gentleman paid the fine; his month in prison earned him the respect and affection of thousands of Bengalis, and even some of the planters visited him in prison.

After his retirement in 1872 he remained active in travelling, writing and translating, and his last public action was a gift of £2,000 to set up the "Long Lectures" on oriental religion. During his life, and through the lectures after his death, he carried on the intent of communicating with and understanding those whom he sought to bring to the Christian faith.

The Indian Mutiny

There were developments and extensions in other parts of the sub-continent, as for example in the hills of Santal where a missionary was stationed from 1849. For Bishop Wilson of

Calcutta, now an old man, a climax came with the consecration of St. Paul's Cathedral, Calcutta, in 1847. In the
south work went forward steadily, and numerically it was
there that the strength of the Indian Church lay. Village
schools continued to teach the children of Christians; from
among those who attended the "higher" schools there was a
small but steady trickle of converts. In 1852 two Hindu
youths who had been pupils at Noble's school in Masulipatam
were baptised; in 1855 three more, one a Muslim. All five
were later ordained. There were likewise baptisms and
ordinations in the Bombay area around 1850, largely as a
result of the witness in the Robert Money School.

Then, on 10 May 1857, the "Indian Mutiny" burst onto
the relatively peaceful scene. On that day at Meerut, while
their officers were at church parade, the privates of the Sepoy
regiments rose and murdered them, fleeing afterwards to
Delhi and rousing the regiments there. From Delhi the revolt
spread to centre after centre – Aligarh, Agra, Cawnpore,
Lucknow, and many smaller stations. Europeans – men,
women and children – were murdered, and any Indians who
stood with them. The fort at Agra and the residency at
Lucknow were besieged for months.

So much has been written about the causes, course and
results of the Mutiny, and even on what to term it, that it is
impossible to discuss it adequately here. A few points need to
be made, however.

It was essentially a mutiny of the lower ranks of a mercenary
army. It was not a planned conspiracy, although once it
began there was undoubtedly collaboration. And it was
limited in the area it affected. The presidencies of Madras
and Bombay were totally free; it was in the Calcutta presidency alone that it was serious, and there only in the north-
west and central areas, not in lower Bengal. Surprisingly,
there was little trouble in the Punjab, and in areas where
there had been firm but compassionate administration there
was comparative peace. No Indian Christians were recruited

as soldiers in the Bengal presidency, and chaplains had been forbidden to evangelise among the Indian troops. So no Christians were directly involved in the rising.

The CMS suffered little in comparison with other missions, for no CMS missionary was killed, though a number lost all but their lives. At Delhi a considerable number of SPG missionaries, chaplains, Indian catechists, and their families, were killed; SPG and American Presbyterian missionaries died in other centres; likewise a number of chaplains. CMS missionaries went unarmed, and at Agra the calm and brave behaviour of French and his students at St. John's College was noted. Buildings and property belonging to the CMS were destroyed and looted to the tune of many thousands of pounds.

Though the worst was over when Lucknow was recovered in March 1858, peace was not officially declared until 8 July 1858. Thanks largely to the intervention of men like Sir John Lawrence (whose brother, Henry Lawrence, died at Lucknow) vengeance and punitive measures were restrained.

Meanwhile, Bishop Wilson in Calcutta endeavoured to call the administration together for a Day of Humiliation and Prayer in the cathedral; the governor-general did not then cooperate but later, in October 1857, declared a day of prayer. By that time Bishop Wilson, in his eightieth year, was too ill to be present; he died early in January 1858.

In Britain there was naturally great concern over all aspects of the conflict, and the reports coming in from missionaries were printed and widely circulated. In the manner of the time a public meeting was held at the Exeter Hall on 12 January 1858, chaired by the Archbishop of Canterbury as a vice-chairman of the CMS. There was no denunciation or bitterness at that or other meetings, and the speakers used their opportunity to call British Christians to renewed efforts for evangelisation in India. When men like Sir John Lawrence and Colonel Herbert Edwardes returned to Britain in 1859, they were received as heroes by the Church, and Edwardes preached at the CMS anniversary in 1860; a speech described as the greatest ever given on such an occasion.

To return to 1858, the greatest and direct result of the Mutiny was the complete transfer of all authority from the East India Company to the Crown. This transfer took place, officially, in November 1858.

After the Mutiny

After all the trauma and with the change of administration, the Church, like the country, slowly returned to a normality and a new balance. Lord Canning, who had been governor-general, was now named viceroy, and continued for four years. His qualities were more suited to the rebuilding of a nation than to giving a bold lead in time of war, and he took a stand against vengeance which was not appreciated at the time. For this he was given the nickname of "Clemency" Canning; what began as an insult became a title of honour.

As regards the change from Company rule to Crown rule, it was in administrative terms a relatively smooth matter, less disruptive than might have been expected. Changes were already in the air, and some were under way even during the period dominated by the Mutiny. A development in educational policy brought about the setting-up of the first universities in the presidency cities of Madras, Calcutta and Bombay in 1857. The universities were initially examining bodies only, and instruction was given in grant-aided colleges affiliated to each university. Here the existing Christian colleges had an important role to play, and bishops and some missionaries became fellows of the new universities and participated in their administration.

Other developments came in technical fields, and had important social results. The Indian Post Office was inaugurated in 1854, and by 1855 telegraphic messages between the main cities were possible. This had proved of the greatest importance during the disturbances of 1857. In social terms the railways were even more important; the first short line was opened in 1853 and by the mid-60s there was an extensive network. An incidental benefit for Eurasians and Indian Christians was employment possibilities in work where mobility and freedom from caste restrictions were an advantage. And now bishops might go on visitations with less stress and less expense. Irrigation works, canals and bridges were also improved and extended, and the better communications made the organisation of famine relief possible and were to save tens of thousands of lives.

Bishop Wilson's successor in Calcutta was a well-known English clerical headmaster, G. E. L. Cotton, and he proved to be the right man for the time. Interested in education, and able to maintain good relations with the CMS and the SPG, he was concerned for the pastoral care of Europeans and Eurasians as well as Indian Christians. In particular he took the situation of the poorer Eurasians seriously and did much to establish and maintain schools for them, and also for the children of the new type of expatriate – the engineers, mechanics and artisans who had come to India to work with the railways, the Post Office, and the canals.

Cotton's death was sudden: he was drowned in a river accident while out on a visitation. This was in 1866; his successor, Robert Milman, died in office in 1876. During his period as metropolitan the three bishops met for consultation (1873) – the beginning of what ultimately developed into the episcopal synod. Milman encouraged new developments on many fronts, and also regulated the development of the Church, becoming very necessary as it grew in size. Bishop Wilson had wanted to divide the diocese, which was larger than one bishop could care for even before the addition of work in Sind and the Punjab. Bishop Milman died in Rawalpindi in March 1876 during a visitation of the Punjab, and it was clear that the strains of travelling and overwork had contributed to his death. The case for division was revived.

In south India there had been a change of bishops in 1861, when Thomas Dealtry died. His successor was Frederick Gell, like Bishop Cotton connected with Rugby School, and also, through Archbishop Tait (to whom he had been chaplain) a friend of Henry Venn and the CMS. He served till his resignation in 1899, and died, still in India, a few years later. In south India the problem was one of success – there were twenty-seven Indian clergy, forty-four missionaries and forty chaplains. The number of Indian Christians considerably exceeded that of domiciled Europeans and Eurasians. But conditions varied greatly in different parts of the diocese, and the Church was at different stages of growth. The most pressing problem apart from the building-up of adequate local church councils was that of caste. It was accentuated when, as had happened in south India, large numbers of a particular caste had entered the Church during a population movement. In such cases the pre-existing social environment maintained its hold, for the need to interact with Christians coming out of other castes scarcely existed. Bishop Gell made extensive enquiries into caste attitudes, and it was clear that at least the minimal requirements laid down by Bishop Wilson were being adhered to. A highlight in the diocese during this period was a service at Palamcotta, in 1869, when twenty-two deacons and twelve priests were ordained. This was the crowning point in the service of the Rev. John Thomas, who had gone to Mengnanapuram in 1836, and served until his death in March 1870. His widow and daughter continued there for another half century.

It was obvious that this growing Church also needed more episcopal oversight than it could be given by one man living in Madras. Bishop Gell was anxious to appoint an Indian coadjutor bishop, which would be legally possible, while actual division of the diocese was impracticable. But on many grounds this was found to be a premature development, and a compromise was arrived at. Two experienced missionaries, one from the CMS and one from the SPG, were appointed. Each would have oversight of the area worked by his own mission.

The CMS bishop was Edward Sargent, son of an English soldier, who had been largely brought up in India. He was adopted by a missionary family and educated in CMS schools. He went to Tinnevelly in 1836 as a lay agent and later, after going to England and to Islington, came back as a missionary in 1842. Robert Caldwell of the SPG was a Scot who originally came to south India with LMS in 1838. A genius at languages, he spent a few years learning Tamil and went to Idaiangudi under the SPG in 1842. The two men were finally consecrated in Calcutta by Bishop Milman's successor, Bishop Johnson, in 1877. They were warm friends and an arrangement which might have been disastrous proved to be the right one for that time.

In Bombay the second bishop, the Rt. Rev. John Harding, served from 1851 to his resignation in 1868. He was succeeded by the Rt. Rev. H. A. Douglas, who served from 1869 to his resignation in 1876. He brought a group of Cowley Fathers (the Society of St. John the Evangelist), to work at Poona, and consolidated the SPG missionaries. Western India had never been one of the CMS's chief concerns; work there had started later and was less concentrated, and indeed the bishop felt that opportunities were missed for lack of staff, whether sent by the SPG or the CMS. Much work was carried on by several Indian clergymen, including the well-known Parsee convert, the Rev. Ruttonji Nowroji. Other clergy had been educated in CMS schools; one had been brought up in a Christian orphanage, and his son, later, was also ordained.

Missionaries

During the later years of this period, the type of missionary being sent to India was changing. Most of the men were ordained; many were university graduates, although this did not mean that they were more willing to teach in the higher level English schools and colleges. The number of German recruits was lower. After 1841 no more German missionaries were sent to south India, and very few to any part of India after 1860. When German names now occur, they are found to be of second or third generation missionaries born in India and educated in India and England. The last Germans were those who were accepted by the CMS within India after going to India with other missions, especially those who had worked in association with Pastor Gossner's mission (an independent German society). One of those, Paul Zenker, who went to India in 1866 and joined the CMS in 1869, survived to be interned by the government at the outbreak of the First World War.

For a long time leave or furlough to England was only allowed in cases of sickness; in the 1860s this policy was changed, and missionaries returned to their home Churches in good health and able to report personally on the work they were engaged in. Women were still not often recruited, and those whose names we find are still generally the daughters, sisters or widows of male missionaries. But often they accomplished remarkable work. One development was that of missionary conferences within India, both meetings of CMS missionaries in a restricted area, and a few large inter-denominational meetings. The first General Missionary Conference for all India was held at Allahabad in 1872. During the period of rebuilding after the Mutiny, a great debate on the position of the administration vis-à-vis Christian missions continued.

5   NEW WORK IN THE NEW WORLDS

New Zealand from 1842

In the twenty-eight years between 1814 and 1842 the situation in New Zealand had been changing rapidly. Where there had been a miscellaneous and usually transient group of whalers, sealers and runaway sailors, there were now a growing number of settlers who were committed to a long-term future in the islands. 1840 had been the crucial year.

Edward Gibbon Wakefield's settlement schemes had more or less forced the British Government into action, to give it some control over the activities of the New Zealand Company. Wakefield, a brilliant and eccentric upper-class Englishman, advocated a new type of colonisation which he promoted through the New Zealand Company. His first group of settlers landed at Petone Beach, near Wellington (at the extreme south of the North Island) in 1840. Knowledge of this prospect forced the British Government to act, and early in that year they promulgated the Treaty of Waitangi. It was signed before the settlers landed (with a good deal of help from CMS missionaries in getting consent from the Maori chiefs) but nevertheless the first years of settlement were bedevilled by conflict between Government, settlers, and the missionaries as advocates of Maori interests.

It was into this situation that the first Anglican bishop came, in 1842. George Augustus Selwyn, scholar of Eton and St. John's, gentleman, was influenced by the Tractarians but was not at all an extreme Ritualist. New Zealand's isolation required a bishop, and the influx of settlers increased the need. Selwyn's first relations with the missionaries were warm and friendly, and they on their side were delighted with this capable, athletic man who walked, rode and rowed the length and breadth of his diocese, and was preaching in Maori a short time after landing. In 1843 he held his first confirmation, and in the same year he appointed the Williams brothers archdeacons. Soon he moved his headquarters from the CMS station at Waimate, in the far north, to Tamaki, in Auckland, a growing centre of population.

But it was not to be expected that a strong, self-reliant and superficially autocratic man like Selwyn could avoid the differences with the CMS which the roles of bishop and missionary society seemed to make inevitable. Selwyn was not in fact an autocrat; he was to encourage and promote the synodical forms of Church government, but he also held a high view of his office. In ordaining CMS catechists to the diaconate he required a pledge from them that they would go wherever he, as bishop, should require; he saw this as especially necessary in the unsettled conditions of New Zealand. This requirement was made without prior consultation with the CMS and, though they admitted the special circumstances, the parent committee was not willing to allow such a pledge as a general rule. The result was that the CMS suspended for some time the presentation of lay agents for ordination.

The difficult conditions in New Zealand had not yet interfered with the increasingly strong work. In several areas Churches were growing, and Maori Christians were reading the New Testament (published in 1836) avidly. Boarding schools provided higher education for some, and Bishop Selwyn founded St. John's College to train young Maoris (and, in the original plan, Pacific Islanders) for ministry to their own people. There was much material advance, and the stories of Maori converts thrilled English readers of mission periodicals.

But the ordination pledge was not the only difficulty which arose. The CMS missionaries (and their Maori converts) also stumbled at a churchmanship more "advanced" than that to which they were accustomed. More serious was Bishop Selwyn's reluctance to ordain men as priests unless they met, in general, English educational requirements for ordination, such as knowledge of Greek. This affected English lay agents, who had been busy acquiring Maori, as much as the Maori deacons. As a result no Maori was ordained deacon until 1852, or priest till 1860. However, from that date the numbers increased steadily, but largely, it must be added, through ordinations by the new (CMS) bishops. In general the Maori clergy fulfilled all the trust placed in them. The question of educational standards was always debatable. Bishop Tucker in Uganda took the other line; probably Bishop Selwyn's policy was defendable in a colony where English educational standards would increasingly be applied.

In New Zealand, after the early (and largely abortive) start with artisan missionaries, most of those sent were pastoral workers, catechists, and ordained men. An industrial school and a training college were carried on, but most training was incidental and "in service", performed by the missionary on the spot. There was virtually no organised medical work and remarkably few women workers. In fact, the very few listed are all missionaries' daughters. But work among women and girls went on, directed by the wives and daughters, unrecognised and unlisted, to whom the Church owes so much. In later years the daughters of Bishop William Williams conducted a boarding school for girls in Napier. Boarding schools for boys – St. Stephen's, in Auckland, and Te Aute College in Hawkes Bay – were founded by CMS missionaries but were never CMS institutions as such. The way in which New Zealand was evolving as a colony made it less necessary for missionaries to be involved in systematic educational, social and medical work, and freed them for evangelism and pastoral care.

So we find from an early period a particular missionary associated with a particular area where he had lived for many years, knowing the language and people intimately, and in many cases becoming archdeacon or bishop officially after having served *de facto* as such. In a remarkable number of cases an ordained son followed his father in the same area. So it was with William Williams in Hawkes Bay; he was the first Bishop of Waiapu and his son, Leonard, its third. Similarly with Richard Taylor in Wanganui and the American-born Seymour Mills in the Rotorua area. New Zealand missionaries were also remarkable for their long periods of service, often without any return to England. Octavius Hadfield, the greatly-loved apostle of Otaki and the Waikanae coast and the second Bishop of Wellington, was fifty-five years a missionary and bishop. His wife was a daughter of Archdeacon Henry Williams. Even today one may visit the Maori church at Otaki built and dedicated in 1849. Hadfield was ill during the building and much of the supervision was done by his young future brother-in-law, Samuel Williams, the founder of Te Aute College. Otaki was in the sphere of the great and formidable Maori chief, Te Rauparaha, whose son and nephew had become Christians and turned the old man away from violence at the end of his life; he is buried in its churchyard. The church is decorated with Maori motifs and around the communion table are the words *Tapu-tapu-tapu* – "Holy, holy, holy."

Meanwhile, despite progress in many areas, relations between Maoris and white settlers degenerated. At the root of it all was land, and it is hard even now to see how the bloodshed and tragedy could have been avoided, given that the country was to be a colony. In the 1840s there was fighting in Wellington, Nelson, and in Henry Williams' "sphere of influence" in the far north; in the 1850s the "King" movement affected the centre of the North Island, and in the 1860s the severest fighting of all came in the Taranaki wars. Also, in 1865, occurred the violent murder at Opotiki of Carl Volkner, a German missionary, in an incident related to an anti-white religious cult known as Hau Hau. Another missionary, Thomas Grace, narrowly escaped. But in this land of dreaded cannibal warriors, Volkner's was the only violent missionary death. The firm and sympathetic handling of the situation by Sir George Grey, New Zealand's greatest colonial governor, kept matters from getting worse. However, in 1853 the settlers were granted internal self-government and it became harder for any governor to do justice to the Maori position.

Land was also at the root of a personal tragedy for Henry Williams, the real pioneer of the New Zealand CMS mission, and here we see a rare example of misjudgement and resulting injustice on the part of Henry Venn. Given the distances and difficulties of communication it is surprising that such incidents happened so seldom.

The two Williamses had large families who were educated in New Zealand. How were they to be provided for? Some became missionaries themselves (two sons and three grandsons were ordained, and three daughters married CMS missionaries); but for others the missionary bought land as was then legally allowed and settled it on sons to enable them to farm. During the early settlement period when the illegal purchase of land was becoming an issue, Governor Grey accused the missionaries of obtaining land unfairly. The governor persuaded Bishop Selwyn, and the CMS listened to them, but did not give a fair hearing to Archdeacon Henry Williams. He, since he believed himself to have acted rightly and legally, refused to admit guilt by giving way. Finally, and cruelly, the CMS committee disconnected him, in 1849. Only two years later they saw their mistake and exonerated the missionaries, but Henry Williams was not fully restored and vindicated till 1854. He worked on faithfully till his death in 1867, having never returned to England since his departure in 1823.

The longest survivor from the early missionary group was Jane Williams, the wife of Bishop William Williams. She arrived in 1826, saw her husband and her son become bishops of Waiapu, and died in 1896, after seventy years in New Zealand.

Selwyn's work as a missionary bishop was remarkable, but in the end he may be remembered best for his work in establishing synodical Church government in New Zealand, and for the clarity with which he saw the place of a non-established Anglican Church in the colony. Henry Venn had pressed for a continuing relationship with the Crown, and for a Church in some way established. Selwyn saw that in a new land a new way was called for. The Church deriving from the English established Church should in New Zealand be a self-directing body. Venn's apparent clinging to an out-dated establishment stemmed largely from his fear that an independent Church might move, doctrinally, away from reformation principles, and that the bishop of such a Church, unrestrained by English law and custom, might prove an autocratic dictator. Selwyn took care of those justifiable hesitancies in the constitution he worked out for the Church of the Province of New Zealand, a constitution afterwards used as a model in other developing Churches. When in 1867 Selwyn came back for the last time after a visit to England during which he had been persuaded to accept the see of Lichfield, it was to set things in order for his departure, and to preside over the fourth meeting of the general synod. There were now six bishops in the country, and two were CMS missionaries; there were also about twenty Maori clergymen, and a number of ordinands in training.

Lands of the Utmost West: missions in North America

Of all the areas where CMS missionaries worked during the 19th century, the North-West America Mission and the slightly later North Pacific Mission seem to have left least trace in the memory of the society. In New Zealand the early role of the CMS is still recognised, but few Anglicans in Winnipeg, Manitoba, know of the important part played by the CMS in the growth of their Church, the diocese, and also of the University of Manitoba.

The name of the earlier mission was later changed to North-West Canada Mission, and that gives a much more accurate idea of its scope. The first clergyman who was associated with the CMS in this area was the Rev. John West, who went to Rupert's Land in 1820 as a chaplain to the Hudson's Bay Company, the *de facto* rulers of the Rupert's Land and North-Western Territory areas. He was taken up by the CMS in 1822, and from York Factory, where he landed, he took two "Red Indian" boys down to Red River (Fort Garry), the site of Winnipeg-to-be, for education. One of those boys was to become the first ordained Anglican clergyman of Indian origin (the Rev. Henry Budd, Sr., ordained in 1850).

West served one year under CMS auspices, and in the next twenty-six years only a few men were sent to Rupert's Land. Three of them worked in the Red River area. One man, James Hunter, who arrived at the Red River in 1844, went up later to the Mackenzie River and pioneered work there. He was responsible for much translation into Cree.

All this was before the Dominion of Canada existed, and Fort Garry (later Winnipeg) on the Red River was just a cluster of wooden buildings with a scanty and mixed population of adventurers and traders. The hardships of the intensely cold and long winters without adequate supply routes to bring in necessities were very great indeed. But by 1837 there were at the various mission settlements around Red River a community of six hundred baptised Indian Christians. When the Bishop of Montreal was able to make a visitation, in 1844 (2,000 miles, by birchbark canoe and on foot) he confirmed 846 candidates. But such a journey could not often be made. So in 1849 a bishop was consecrated for a new diocese called Rupert's Land – David Anderson. From that date the CMS gave greater and more consistent help, though in 1842 North-West America had been one of the missions marked for abandonment during the time of financial crisis.

Bishop Anderson served until 1864, and in that period seventeen men were sent out or "taken up" as CMS missionaries. He ordained several Indians and others who were variously described as "country-born" or *métis* – men of mixed origin, often Scottish-Indian.

The work expanded geographically as well as in numbers, and expanded also to other Indian groups beside the Cree – the Blackfoot, Swampy Cree, Plains Cree, Sioux, and also to the Eskimo of the far north. The expansion of stations and the need for supervision naturally resulted in a division of episcopal duties. John Horden, who pioneered work in Hudson's Bay, became in 1872 the first Bishop of Moosonee, which included the Hudson's Bay area. And all this was happening at the time of westward expansion, the planning of the Canadian Pacific railroad, and the emergence of the Dominion of Canada. As white settlers came in, there was a need for ministry for them, and inevitably the nature of the work in the southern parts of British North America (1867 – Canada) changed. Manitoba became a province in 1870.

Bishop Anderson's successor was Robert Machray, an Oxford-educated Scot from Aberdeen, who set about the division of his unwieldy diocese with energy, and began to organise for self-support. The taking of weekly collections in churches was instituted, and a dangerous innovation it appeared to some. But Bishop Machray found it "impossible to call forth self-support without also calling forth self-government", and he instituted a conference of clergy and lay delegates which to us seems quite unexceptional, but was then to some an even more dangerous innovation. Still, that was the way the tide was flowing, and it was obvious that an Anglican Church in Canada must emerge. The CMS kept up a steady stream of clergy, some men still sent from England but increasingly men "taken up" in Canada though still supported from England. One or two a year, they were often ordained after arriving in their place of work, and they enabled the bishops – by the mid-1880s there were seven dioceses in the area once covered by the one diocese of Rupert's Land – to continue outreach to the scattered communities of Indian and Eskimo peoples. Meantime other parishes had transferred to a "settled ecclesiastical system of self-support", with some assistance still from the SPG, C&CCS,[1] and also where appropriate the SPCK.

The CMS, as well as continuing to support missionaries, made another significant contribution. It gave an annual grant to St. John's College, the theological training institution developed by Bishop Machray. The grant was mainly used for scholarships, and the £600 a year, which was a considerable sum at that time, was in the long run received again with a hundred-fold increase. As the years go on and more and more of the men on the CMS list are "of North-West Canada" and "in local connexion", it is apparent that for most of such men the phrase is added, "St. John's Coll., Winnipeg." St. John's eventually became a constituent college of the University of Manitoba, and in time one notes that many of the men "in local connexion" are graduates of that university. By 1895 there is a Canadian CMS which is itself sending out men – to China and then to Japan. With ten dioceses stretching from the forty-eighth parallel to the far north, and with continuing work among Indians, Eskimo and white settlers and miners, this Church has come of age. We may trace its

---

[1]C&CCS – Originally the *Colonial and Continental Church Society*, it was founded as the *Colonial Church Society* in 1838, with the aim of supplying pastoral care for British settlers overseas. It later became the *Commonwealth and Continental Church Society*, continuing the same role, recruiting chaplains for overseas positions mainly concerned with ministry to expatriate British men and women. It is now called *Inter-Continental Church Society*.

growth in the career of one clergyman, Robert McDonald of
Manitoba, probably a *métis*. Educated at St. John's, he was
ordained deacon and priest in 1852 and 1853, by the first
bishop of Rupert's Land. He served first at Islington mission
(named at the request of an English donor) and then pioneered in Alaska at Fort Youcon (Yukon) and Peel River, and
in 1875 was made archdeacon of Mackenzie River. In 1884
he received an Hon.D.D. from his Alma Mater, St. John's.
He translated Scriptures and other materials into three Indian
languages, and died as late as 1913, after serving the cause of
the Gospel for sixty-one years.

North Pacific Mission –
Duncan and Metlakhatla

In many parts of its various fields throughout the world, the
CMS was invited or urged into work through the vision of an
English Christian who saw a need. This was very much the
case in India, where Christian army officers and civilians
pioneered before the mission. On the coast of British
Columbia it was a naval officer, Captain James Prevost,
who asked the CMS to send a mission to work among the
Tsimshian Indians on the northern coast. He did more than
ask; he offered a free passage in his vessel for a missionary.
There was not much time to be lost, and the CMS quickly
selected a young man who had already been in their Highbury
training college for over two years.

The young man was William Duncan, and his story was to
be largely the story of the North Pacific Mission. It was later
to be generally known as the Metlakhatla Mission from the
Christian settlement founded by Duncan. For many years
one of the CMS's greatest success stories, it later became in
many ways one of its most embarrassing failures.

· Duncan was born and brought up in Beverley, the town in
Yorkshire which is the site of the great minster. He was

educated in the local national school, and at fourteen went to work in a firm which owned a tannery and were dealers in hides and skins. He became a travelling salesman, and was helped and influenced by the Christian head of the firm. He was also active in the life of a local Anglican church, and in fact became a model of the young English working man intent on improving himself by discipline, self-education, and Christian training. He was intelligent, pious, genuinely religious and well-intentioned, but, it would seem, rather humourless and self-important also. His links with his family seem weak, and he never married.

When he left with Captain Prevost (in 1856) he was twenty-four years old; not ordained, he had been trained as a schoolmaster. He was first landed on Vancouver Island, and had to stay for several months at Victoria, waiting to go north to Fort Simpson, a centre for the Tsimshian. He started to learn the language and made useful contacts while lodging with the Hudson's Bay Company's chaplain, the only Protestant minister in Victoria. Finally he was able to go to Fort Simpson.

It is impossible now to find out if Duncan was very different from the other young working-class men who through their religious connections rose educationally and socially and, in many cases, were in the end ordained and passed into another social class. He appears to be a classic case, and his situation prevented some of the restrictions which probably held others back. He went out as a missionary pioneer and was never under a senior clerical colleague; indeed he usually had no colleague at all. He himself was a schoolmaster and not a clergyman; his work had early success and he came to trust his own judgement. In very many respects he was an ideal missionary, following faithfully the insights of Henry Venn as he started to build up a Christian community. He learned the vernacular and refrained from preaching until he could do so without an interpreter. He spent time carefully observing the local culture, and did not try to make abrupt

changes, even of customs which distressed him. He visited
the sick and gave practical help. He was above all careful
not to move too far ahead of the people he was seeking to
influence.

What he did not realise about the Tsimshian was that,
though he was the first missionary to work among them, they
had been in close contact with traders and such settlers as
there were for two generations, and were unusually ready to
make cultural adaptations where it seemed to their advantage
to do so. They were beginning to realise the danger of losing
their rights over land and water to the incomers, and their
chiefs saw that a man like Duncan could be an ally and an
intermediary with the alien government (which in fact at
that time was the Hudson's Bay Company). And more
changes were now rapidly taking place. In 1858 the Gold
Rush came to the Fraser River. In the same year the mainland
became a Crown Colony, and the man who as chief factor of
the Company served as governor now was confirmed as
governor of Vancouver Island and British Columbia.

Duncan was alarmed at the social disintegration induced
among the Indians by these changes. The fur trade was
collapsing, and thus poverty was increasing; as was the drink
traffic. There was opportunity for the men to make money by
prostituting their women. Instead of small numbers of the
Fort Simpson Indians going to Victoria to earn money,
whole boatloads were leaving.

Thus Duncan turned to consider a solution not new but
not in general a part of CMS policy. It was to establish a
model village where Indians willing to abide by Christian
rules laid down by the missionary could live separated from
the increasingly evil and disruptive influences of the trading
ports and trading forts. Typically Duncan took time to put
forward his plan and make the move, and the location was
suggested by the Tsimshian themselves. It was the site of
a former settlement, about fifteen miles from Fort Simpson.
He began to talk about the possibility in the summer of 1859,

but they did not leave till May 1862. He put no pressure on individuals to go with him, and initially only fifty moved. They understood clearly what would be asked of them in the new settlement. Duncan was not choosing between Christianity and civilisation for his protégés, but hoped and believed that they would receive both together. Temperance, hard work, Sabbath observance, education; all this would lead to increased material prosperity and religious benefits which would build a utopia in the wilderness. Henry Venn had always encouraged missionaries to look for ways to increase the productivity and wealth of native Christians, and Duncan was in many respects only following his mentors. He received a larger and more rapid access of population than he had expected, for in 1862 smallpox spread rapidly from Victoria, and it was estimated that in two years almost one third of the native people died. A number of small tribes with little previous contact were led by their chiefs to Metlakhatla, and Duncan accepted them and began to forge them into the community. One of his first steps was to open a store which kept prices low, sold only "acceptable" goods (no paint for the traditional face-painting) and made the settlement less dependent on the Hudson's Bay Company. It also provided Duncan with cash for development. A schooner for trading trips to Victoria gave similar independence. A sawmill provided work and timber to build houses and public buildings. Eventually there was a large church as well as the school, guest-house, court-house and jail. There was a fire-brigade, local police-force, and a brass band. Metlakhatla became a well-known name in CMS circles; Duncan's reports were often published in the *Church Missionary Intelligencer*. Outside visitors, including officials of the Canadian Government, sent back glowing reports of the settlement and its Indian Christian community. Nevertheless, the CMS had some cause for concern. Although Duncan had kept in close touch over many aspects of his work, on the one subject of a "native Church" he was not prepared to take advice.

Baptisms had taken place from 1860, but Duncan had resisted all efforts to bring "his" people to confirmation and to allow the Holy Communion to be celebrated. In fact, he did not want an *Anglican* Church, and was not prepared to compromise. Although he spoke Tsimshian fluently, he did not translate much into the language, and emphasised English in the school. So the older people were dependent on oral translation from the English Bible for their knowledge of the Scriptures. In general, as time went on, there was more emphasis on material progress than on the life of the spirit, and it was becoming obvious that Metlakhatla was an autocracy under the control of one man. Ordained colleagues sent to work with Duncan did not survive long; either they left completely or were moved to outlying centres. Duncan himself was offered ordination and refused it. He was unmarried, so he had no close companion with whom to share the strains of his leadership.

During most of the twenty years during which Metlakhatla grew and flourished, there was no close episcopal supervision. Bishop Hills of Columbia diocese was responsible, but in 1879 it was decided to divide the diocese, and this brought the settlement under more direct observation. The northern section where the CMS worked was to be in the diocese of Caledonia, and a former CMS missionary in India was consecrated as its first bishop. William Ridley proceeded to visit Metlakhatla and the other stations, and experienced the same ambivalence of feeling in the contrast between the secular and religious progress. There was continuing concern about Duncan's absolute refusal to allow any Indian Christians to experience the Lord's Supper. He continued to assert that they could not be trusted with the Sacrament, and would turn it into a fetish.

In addition to the internal problems, there were now external tensions. Duncan's old friend the chaplain at Victoria had clashed with Bishop Hills over matters of ritual, and had aligned himself with a breakaway, "reformed" episcopalian

Church in the United States. This did not help to affirm Duncan's faith in the Church of England.

Finally Bishop Ridley was forced to assert his leadership, with the support of the CMS. Duncan was given an ultimatum. He was asked either to come to England for conference with the CMS, or to follow the bishop's plans for religious instruction, or to hand over the mission and leave the settlement. When he failed to follow any of these courses he was disconnected, by letter.

Duncan, as might have been expected, stayed on at a divided Metlakhatla, now separated from the CMS, for five more years. Bishop Ridley, on the Metlakhatla site, continued under great difficulties, aided by new missionaries and with less than one hundred of the old population adhering to his work. It became apparent that complicated questions of land rights and of leadership roles were involved, in addition to Duncan's dominating position.

In 1886 the CMS sent out two men on a commission of inquiry, but it was now far too late to heal the deep divisions. The dilemma for the CMS and Bishop Ridley was in practical terms solved when in 1887 Duncan and about six hundred of his loyal followers moved north to a site in southern Alaska which had been granted to them by the Government of the USA. Here, at New Metlakhatla, on Annette Island, another prosperous community evolved. Duncan lived there until his death in 1918.

His separation from CMS was probably inevitable, but it was not well handled, considering his twenty-five years of faithful service. The story illustrates vividly many of the strains liable to arise in the work of CMS missionaries, whose theological loyalties were stronger to an evangelical and anti-ritualist position than to the Church to which they were linked. The strain of advocating a policy of material development, and the difficulties of moving from a mission community to a native Church are also clear. The CMS may also have learned something about the danger of giving too much publicity to a seemingly successful enterprise, without looking carefully into its whole background. Duncan's problems were from the beginning intensified by his isolation from other missionaries and by the lack of clerical supervision. In fact, his early success made him confident and unwilling to take counsel, and the ability he had in the vernacular gave him a great advantage – which ultimately became a disadvantage – over other workers. For all his knowledge of Tsimshian culture he failed to understand their emphasis on leadership. He was right to insist on the ultimate choice which should be made by native Christians on the organisation of their Church, but he was insisting on that choice at a period when no native elder had been affirmed in a role of spiritual leadership, and this was the weak point in his case. If he had been willing to share leadership with "his" Indians, there might still have been a division from the CMS, but it would have been of a different kind. The wonder is not that the conflict with Duncan occurred, but that it was almost unique in the history of the CMS.

The East Africa Mission 1844–1875[1]

What began as the Abyssinia Mission became, almost imperceptibly, the East Africa Mission. As the Society's work extends, it will be impossible to mention even briefly all the new fields. But the step into East Africa soon became, and has remained, important. From it opened up the Kenya mission, the Tanzania (German East Africa), Uganda and finally Ruanda missions where strong and large Churches have grown up.

Abyssinia had had a unique attraction for explorers, including missionaries, for a long time, as the land of Prester John. This mountainous region of a Christian king and

---

[1]Originally called the Eastern Equatorial Africa Mission.

people, historically and in legend (if one could ever disentangle the two) connected with the ancient Jewish kingdom and with the Apostolic Church, has caught the imagination of many. Then south of the Christian Amharic peoples were the Muslim and pagan tribes such as the almost unknown Galla. Missionary after missionary had as his object the reaching of the Galla.

Johannes Ludwig Krapf, like many of the most outstanding German missionaries to serve with the CMS, was from Würtemberg. He was at the Basel Seminary in 1837, and went straight out to Abyssinia under the CMS without visiting England. He remained in Abyssinia for almost seven years, latterly making an effort to reach the southern Galla around Shoa. But ultimately he was expelled and (with his young wife) took a ship from Aden to go south. It had occurred to him that there was more than one route to the Galla. After a shipwreck they found a second vessel, which was on a trading journey, and they called in at ports as they went south. So they put briefly into Mombasa harbour, and got a glimpse of their future base. Going on to Zanzibar, the great island metropolis which was to be so important in the missionary history of East Africa, they were offered spheres of work nearer at hand. But Krapf's vision was unwavering, and by May 1844 he was back on Mombasa Island, and immediately plunged into the translational and linguistic work which was to be his most important contribution. In July his wife gave birth to a second daughter, and was dead within a few days. She was buried, at her own request, on the mainland opposite Mombasa Island. The motherless baby was soon buried with her, and in his loneliness Krapf was given the vision of a chain of mission stations linking across Africa from east to west.

But for the time being he stayed on alone, working at languages and making tentative exploratory journeys in the immediate hinterland. In June 1846 he was joined by Johannes Rebmann, a fellow-countryman who had also been a student at Basel. Together they moved to live on the mainland, building a house, and eventually they set off on the expeditions through which their names became well-known.

They made several exploratory journeys inland, and their reporting of the snow-topped mountains Kilimanjaro and Kenya were geographically of the greatest importance. But unlike their fellow missionary explorer, David Livingstone, one does not get the impression that "the excitement of the chase" has taken over. First and foremost they were, and remained, missionaries. But in their own lifetimes of service they saw few results. They were the forerunners who take out the stones and prepare for planting – they scarcely even planted seed. A poor cripple, Mringe, was Krapf's first-fruit. Krapf returned to Europe in 1856, though he made later visits to the East African coast. Rebmann laboured on, often alone and latterly quite blind, until 1875. He held the fort and in 1875 the CMS at last revived the East Africa Mission. In the next year the Uganda pioneers arrived in Zanzibar. Krapf and Rebmann and their few colleagues, in addition to their contributions in translation and in exploration, laid the foundations of a home-base from which the evangelisation of all East Africa could expand.

6   THE FIRST CENTURY

The home committees, etc, from the death of Henry Venn

When Henry Venn came into office in 1841, the Society was going through a period of financial difficulty, from which it made a good recovery. The number of recruits sent out continued to rise; between 1849 and 1855 another hundred sailed, and the financial support kept pace.

But in Henry Venn's last years there was again difficulty. There was a deficit in 1870, and men were kept back. In 1872 the position was even more serious: "Failing treasury and scanty supply of candidates." There were no offers from university men and Islington College was only half full. The reasons were complex, and Henry Venn was not at fault – but as far back as 1862 he had felt he was not able to work adequately, and was trying to resign. Inevitably aspects of the work suffered. CMS missions were now in their third generation; many senior missionaries had resigned or died, and replacements were not forthcoming. (There were actually by this time a number of second-generation missionaries, and the granddaughter of Nyländer, Annie Catherine Schon, who in 1858 married Edward Higgens, missionary in Ceylon, represented a third generation.)

No early replacement was found for Henry Venn, and he struggled on till 1872, seeing further retrenchments and no rapid financial recovery. There was little money to send men out – but there were also few candidates to send. Finally the committee accepted the inevitable, and the Rev. Henry

Wright was installed as Honorary Clerical Secretary. He was from a wealthy family, and had shown his ability as a pastor and administrator in several charges, notably in Nottingham. One of his first innovations was a Day of Intercession. The first was held on 20 December, 1872. Three weeks later, in January 1873, Henry Venn died. He had been in harness, though often unwell, up to less than a year before his death.

Wright's period as clerical secretary was marked by real advances in organisation, especially in publications, and by 1874 the income was again rising. In that year seventeen men and one woman were sent out.

A few years before Henry Venn's retirement, in 1867, a lay secretary was appointed whose tenure reminds one of the formidable Dandeson Coates, lay secretary in the 1830s. Edward Hutchinson's special brief was the financial, legal and business affairs of the Society, but he saw the CMS as a lay society and he himself therefore as its principal representative. He achieved much for the CMS but, as Stock remarks, he "claimed for the Society a freedom from the control of bishops beyond what a clergyman like Henry Wright thought reasonable", and this was not helpful in the Ceylon controversy, which troubled the Society from 1876 to 1880. It does, however, serve to show that the rather heavy-handed way in which Bishop Crowther was treated by Hutchinson was not purely the result of racial prejudice; Hutchinson was heavy-handed also with Bishop Copleston.

Wright's period as secretary came to a premature and tragic end in August 1880. He was on holiday with his family in the Lake District, and drowned while bathing in Coniston Lake. The cause was possibly a heart attack. He had gone on vacation with a number of concerns on his mind; 1879 had again seen financial difficulties and a number of men ready to be sent out had been kept back.

Another cause for great concern had been the Niger Mission, and the relations between Bishop Crowther and the new missionaries. It was Hutchinson rather than Wright who communicated with Bishop Crowther, since he had, under the devolved responsibility taken by different secretaries for different missions, the responsibility for African fields. Thus it was Hutchinson who went with others to Madeira in early 1881 to meet with missionaries and clergy from Nigeria and discuss the affairs of the mission. Of course, by that time Henry Wright was dead, but perhaps his earlier involvement might have changed the situation. The plans decided on in Madeira did not in the long run solve the difficulties. Shortly after coming back to England Edward Hutchinson tendered his resignation. He subsequently went to Canada and was ordained there, and after a period in Scotland returned to Canada where he died in 1897.

Meanwhile the committee had quickly fixed on a successor to Henry Wright. It was in fact Wright's brother-in-law, a Southampton clergyman, the Rev. Frederic Wigram. Appointed in October 1880, he took up his duties in January 1881. But thanks to Hutchinson's organisational skills, his duties were somewhat different from the ways of the previous régime. Hutchinson devised the group system which was to prevail in Church Missionary House for many years to come. The overseas fields were divided into groups, and one of the secretaries took responsibility for each group, with précis of all foreign correspondence prepared separately for each group.

Frederic Wigram continued as clerical secretary up to 1895. This was a period of remarkable progress in the Society, in respect to the income received, the numbers sent out, the advances in organisation, the reputation of the Society within the Church of England, and in the developing relations with the "new dominions", where colonial associations were formed. Wigram and his son Edmund (later a missionary in the Punjab) made a round-the-world journey in 1886–87, visiting mission fields as well as Australia and New Zealand. This was the first time that a mission secretary had made such a journey, though by now of course some of the secretaries were former missionaries.

Before we close this discussion of Wright and Wigram as secretaries, their family contribution deserves to be mentioned. Of their children, who were first cousins, no less than ten became missionaries.

Moody and Sankey, Keswick, and university men

During the last quarter of the 19th century several new influences were operating which were to be important to the CMS both in the short and long term. This was the period of the great evangelistic missions led by the Americans Moody and Sankey, which made a notable impact on the Churches of Britain. It was also a period of smaller quieter movements which had a deep effect on evangelical Christianity. Again the transatlantic element was important, especially in the Holiness Movement with Hannah and Robert Pearsall Smith, that was influential in establishing the annual Keswick convention.

For over half a century, as we have seen, evangelical influences had been strong at Cambridge, first through the ministry of Charles Simeon at King's College. His friendship with the Venn family, and his great interest in India, maintained a connection with the CMS. A Church Missionary Union was founded at Cambridge in 1858, and in 1862 a daily prayer meeting was commenced. At the same time in the USA a revival was touching the Churches, and the movement reached Britain. There was also on both sides of the Atlantic a desire among Christians to know more deeply the work of the Holy Spirit, and to live a life of "Holiness" – or the "Higher Life". Those who distrusted this movement feared the heresy of "perfectionism". In the 1870s these various influences converged.

Dwight Moody, the American evangelist, was already well known by reputation in Britain when he came over by invitation in 1874. After taking meetings in Scotland, Ireland and Liverpool he came to London in 1875 with his singer colleague Ira Sankey. Among those converted at his meetings was a wealthy businessman, Edward Studd, once a planter in India. Studd had three sons at Eton and he made it his business to influence them for Christ. One by one they went on to Cambridge where they became known as cricketers and also as Christians. Charles, or C. T., was the most outstanding player, though not at first as active a Christian as his older brother Kynaston. It was Kynaston (later Lord Mayor of London) who was the instigator of the invitation which in 1882 brought Moody and Sankey back to England for a mission to Cambridge. But the mission could never have taken place without the prayers and organisation of the CICCU – the Cambridge Inter-Collegiate Christian Union – which in March 1877 had been formally constituted to bring together Christian men in all the colleges. The CICCU owed much to the pre-existing Christian Missionary Union, and the CMS was in its turn to owe much to the CICCU.

The desire for holiness – a closer walk with God and complete victory over sin – was present among many Christians including those recently touched by the 1875 mission. In 1873 an American Quaker couple, Robert and Hannah Pearsall Smith, had come from Philadelphia with a message that the Christian life need not be only a constant and hard struggle; that it could be a joyful resting in the presence of God through the Holy Spirit. They met prominent English Christians and in July 1874 were the guests of honour at a conference/houseparty at Broadlands, the home of William Cowper-Temple.

Cowper-Temple, a Member of Parliament, stepson of Lord Palmerston and brother-in-law of Lord Shaftesbury, was an active Christian with very wide contacts in the Church and in politics. At the houseparty the Pearsall Smiths met a cross-section of British Christians of all ages and all wings of the Church, from George Macdonald to Mrs. Sumner of the Mothers' Union. Cambridge students were included among those invited to Broadlands, and these influences also contributed to the founding of the CICCU in 1877 and the Moody Mission in 1882.

But perhaps the most important ongoing result of the Broadlands conference came when in September 1875 a similar conference for the north was arranged at Keswick in the Lake District. The man responsible was the vicar of Keswick, Canon Harford Battersby, already a strong supporter of the CMS. It was not an easy thing for him to do. He was much opposed and even abused by former friends who saw the movement as perfectionism heresy. But the annual conference persisted and grew into the great Keswick Convention "for the deepening of the spiritual life", with its lasting and important influence on the Church and on missions in general.

Here we cannot go into detail about the effects of the mission of 1882 on Cambridge and the CICCU. But after a difficult start the prayers of the CICCU members and of many others were more than answered. Meetings were crowded and young men in large numbers made public commitment to Christ. And many soon proved their sincerity by offering for overseas service as missionaries.

In 1884 and 1885 the cause of missions received great publicity through the offering for service, and subsequent departure for China, of the group who became known as the Cambridge Seven. They went out, not with one of the old, now respectable missions like the LMS or CMS, but with the almost unknown China Inland Mission, a faith mission founded and led by the young James Hudson Taylor. Not all of the seven were actually Cambridge graduates, but all were young men with Cambridge connections, from families of social and financial standing. Britain was not used to thinking of such men as potential missionaries. One was Studd's son, the MCC cricketer C. T. Studd; another, Stanley Smith, was stroke oar of the Cambridge boat. Studd and Stanley Smith spoke at several universities, not so much about the CIM and China but more as witnesses to the Lord they served. Finally there were farewell meetings for all the Seven at Oxford, Cambridge and London. The final meeting at Exeter Hall in February 1885 was packed – a new kind of missionary meeting which the young men used to preach the claims of Christ.

The CMS soon benefited also from this new wave of enthusiasm for missions. But it was not just shallow enthusiasm; it was soundly and deeply based. All the Cambridge Seven gave long and faithful service in China; one, the Rev. William Cassels, finally came on to the CMS roll of missionaries in 1895, when he was consecrated Bishop of West China.

In the year that the Cambridge Seven went out, five Cambridge graduates were sent overseas by the CMS. In 1887 it was ten. In 1886 thirty-one Cambridge men signed a letter to the CMS stating their hope and intention to offer themselves as missionaries. Of that group twelve were in fact accepted and sent out. In this period a trend already observed increased. From the beginnings of the Society to 1880 the number of university graduates sent out had been 156 (over half of these coming from Cambridge). But in the next fourteen years, to 1894, there were to be 170 graduates, of whom one hundred came from Cambridge.

Medical Missions: the beginnings

The CMS was in no way ahead of its time in establishing medical missions, and in fact medical work has never been as prominent as with some other missions. Both the sending nation and the receiving nation influence the missionary society, and it may be suggested that the growth of medical education in Scotland and the importance of Scottish medical schools caused the various Presbyterian missions to stress medical work to an unusual degree in almost any area where they worked. There was not the same emphasis in the CMS.

The CMS was initially very reluctant to send out doctors, except to give help to the missionaries and their families. Medical work and any but the most elementary educational work were seen as distractions from the main task of evangelism. The first missionary listed as a "medical missionary" was Henry Graham, who went to Sierra Leone in 1829. He withdrew after only two years, and it does not seem to have ever been intended that he would commence any formal medical practice.

The extreme difficulty of establishing even a toe-hold in Muslim areas, and of obtaining a hearing for the Gospel, was what seems to have forced the possibility of medical missions on the CMS. The first real medical mission – and missionary – was in Kashmir. But, as in so many areas, a national Christian was in some senses the pioneer. Abdul Masih, baptised in 1811, from a Muslim background, who became an evangelist in Agra, used his limited medical knowledge to treat patients and was known as the "Christian doctor".

Kashmir, where the first modern hospital dispensary was established, was a protected Native State, and missionaries and other Europeans went there on holiday, but the Maharajah allowed no one foreign to stay over the winter. The Rev. Robert Clark, one of the pioneers of the Punjab mission, went to Srinagar in 1864 with his wife, who started a dispensary. Soon it was attracting a hundred patients a day, and an Indian catechist brought in by the Clarks was preaching to them. The success was almost too much too soon, and when a man was converted and baptised there was an officially-arranged disturbance. The Clarks had in any case to leave before the winter. But English Christians in the army and in civilian service in the Punjab pleaded with the CMS to establish the dispensary. They found a doctor and offered help with the costs. The doctor, William Elmslie, was a Scot and a Presbyterian, but the CMS accepted him, and he opened his dispensary in Srinagar in 1865. This grew into a hospital, and when he went on leave medical replacements were found. Elmslie came back in 1872 with an able and devoted wife, but that summer a cholera epidemic struck. In October the tired and overworked doctor had to trek out over the high passes, for the Maharajah would not even in these circumstances allow Europeans to stay over winter. The journey took more than three weeks, and although Margaret Elmslie walked so that her husband could be carried in her litter, they reached the Punjab only for William Elmslie to die. He was just forty.

At that point the British authorities put pressure on the Maharajah to allow expatriates to stay year-round in Kashmir. The medical work was the reason for this change of policy being requested, and replacement doctors were found. Two stayed only for short periods, and then came the Neve brothers, Arthur and Ernest, whose names became associated with Kashmir.

Medical work was started early in China, where Duncan Main (another Scot) started an opium refuge in Hangchow in 1881. In the north-west frontier of India, another "hard field", a chain of hospitals was established – at Dera Ghazi Khan (1878), Amritsar (1881), Quetta (1885), and Bannu (1892.) The pioneer at Amritsar was an Afghan, the adopted son of the Rev. Robert Clark, who had received his medical education in Edinburgh. Henry Martyn Clark's work became a centre of evangelism, and he himself was active as a writer both on Islam and on medical topics.

Persia, Egypt and Palestine were three further areas where medical work was especially important, and where local women trained as nurses and midwives played a leading role. As early as 1895 a woman doctor, Henrietta Cornford, was sent to Egypt. She had qualified at Brussels and Edinburgh, but left on her marriage after only a year in Egypt. The next woman doctor, Mary Harmar (also qualified at Brussels and Edinburgh) went to China, and soon afterwards married a fellow CMS missionary, an ordained doctor from Ireland, Samuel Synge.

The Society had, up to the 1880s, no special committee for dealing with medical missions. It was the special need of the Punjab which drew attention to the subject, and in 1884 a sub-committee was appointed to consider the matter. In July 1885, following their report, certain resolutions were adopted. They endorsed the desirability of medical missions under certain circumstances, but added that "The medical work should always be subordinate to the spiritual."

There had been a suggestion that a new society should be formed to supply medical needs, as it was recognised that extra expenses were involved in such missions. The alternative recommended was a Medical Mission Auxiliary Fund, administered by an auxiliary committee, and this was formed. But little further action was taken until in 1891 a Medical Department was set up. Dr. Herbert Lankester was then appointed Honorary Secretary, but a more important step was taken in 1894 when Dr. Lankester retired from his private medical practice and was appointed Physician to the Society and Secretary to the Medical Board. The first function related mainly to the examining of missionary personnel; the second related to his work as secretary to the Medical Mission Committee, where he was to oversee the work of medical missions and also to support the raising of the auxiliary fund through meetings, exhibitions and literature. From this time the work of medical missions continued as a regular and organised part of CMS work.

Medical work did not have quite as crucial a role to play in Africa (outside of Egypt), for in most of Africa schools rather than dispensaries were the key to contacting large numbers of people. And in the British colonies medical services were early established by the Government. But there were still needs not met, and some hospitals were set up which in time became an integral part of the work and witness of the Church. Often the vision of a particular doctor was influential.

In Uganda it was the Cook brothers, Dr. Albert Cook and Dr. John Cook, who pioneered. Albert Cook went to Kampala in 1896 and his younger brother followed in 1899. They built up the hospital on Mengo Hill, next to the cathedral. In 1899 Albert Cook was married to Kate Timpson, a nurse trained at Guy's Hospital who had been among the group of women who walked up from Mombasa in 1896. Together the Cooks made a formidable medical team. Mrs. Cook's special contribution was in the training of African nurses, both male and female.

In Egypt where the CMS had to re-establish its work after the early and on the whole abortive entry through Malta, medical work played an important part. In 1899 an Irish missionary doctor, who in 1885 had gone to Aden, was sent to Cairo to establish medical work there. He was Dr. F. J. Harpur, whose name was to become so closely associated with the work at Old Cairo that the rebuilt and extended hospital was finally named after him. It was not until 1893 that his move to Cairo became permanent, but he was to stay there for over twenty years.

The early use of women in the Church Missionary Society

After the CMS was founded in 1799, it was several years before women were free to attend its public meetings, let alone serve in any public capacity. So it is not surprising that female missionaries were not even to be thought of. In fact, it is more surprising that as early as 1820 the names of two women were entered on a second list in the *Register of Missionaries*. This List II was of "Female Missionaries". Both were sent to Sierra Leone. Mary Bouffler, a schoolmistress from London, lived for five months. The second, Hannah Johnson, was sister to the German missionary, William Johnson. She served for two years before marrying a widowed colleague.

These two pioneers are in a pattern which continues. Single women who went abroad, especially to Sierra Leone, did not often survive long. But those who did were likely to marry either a bachelor missionary or a man whose wife had died, often in childbirth. Very many of the women in the early lists went out with, or to join, an unmarried brother. What happened when the brother married? Others went to join the family of a sister. Quite soon we find the daughters of a missionary, or a widow, being taken on to the list, which means receiving an allowance. While the father or husband lived this was not necessary, and so years of faithful service go unrecorded.

The rapid turnover through marriage of women missionaries was so great that some Church leaders believed it was a waste of money to send women out. Bishop Daniel Wilson of Calcutta formed strong opinions on the subject. In 1842 he wrote to an English clergyman who had suggested a lady for service in India:

> No: this lady will not do. I object from the experience of my Indian life, and indeed upon principle, to single ladies coming out unprotected to so distant a place, with a climate so unfriendly, and with the almost certainty of marrying within a month or two of their arrival . . . Ladies don't know their own minds, and no one can, or ought, in our Protestant church, to deprive them of a natural right. I give them all credit for sincerity of intention; but no single lady remains such in India, from the rarity of such persons, and the opulence of our services.

In fact, the bishop exaggerated. A few women married within months, but many served for two or three years, and doubtless did much good in contacting women and girls even in a short period.

It was India which opened as the first real arena for women's work. It was soon obvious that only women could contact women in all but the poorest Muslim and Hindu families. Since the missionary societies as constituted were not prepared to act, special organisations were set up. Within India a Ladies' Female Education Society was set up in Calcutta in 1824, and in 1834 the Society for Promoting Female Education in the East was founded. One of the first women to work overseas for any length of time (she is number four on List II) was Miss Cooke, who went to India in 1820 with the British and Foreign Schools Society. In 1822 she was taken into CMS connection, and shortly afterwards married a CMS missionary. But after his death she continued work for women and girls for several years.

This is the first example of another repeating pattern. Widows were the first long-serving female missionaries. Of course wives, no matter how much they did alongside their husbands, were not counted as missionaries, but if they survived their husbands and continued, their earlier time of service is sometimes actually mentioned. Thus Mrs. Mary Beale, who in 1840 went to Sierra Leone to be married. Her husband died in Africa in 1856, and she stayed on in Sierra Leone as a teacher till her own death in 1866. She had been in Africa for twenty-seven years, at that time a remarkable length of time. Her son followed her to Sierra Leone, though he was invalided home after only two years.

Other widows also served for considerable periods. Jane Hooper went to Benares, India, with her brother in 1861. In 1864 she married, but after her husband's death she stayed on teaching in the Female Normal School for four years. After her return to England she offered as an "honorary missionary" and went to Palestine accompanied by her daughter, Charlotte Low. Margaret Duncan married a missionary doctor working in the Punjab, William Elmslie, the pioneer of Kashmir, but he died after only a few months of marriage. She continued in the Punjab for five years before she returned to England. Three years later she married a widowed missionary colleague and returned to the Punjab, but this time it was she who was to die after less than a year of marriage.

The CMS has always been a family-based mission, and after sisters, wives and widows came daughters. At a time when, in England, it was customary for daughters to stay on with their parents and find their occupation in the affairs of the parish and village, it was not surprising that missionary daughters did the same. It is hard to know when their service began, for often they were only taken into CMS connection on the death or retirement of the father, so that a separate allowance could be paid. Often widows and their daughters worked on together. Two famous examples were the widows of the pioneers of Tinnevelly and Travancore in south India, John Thomas and Henry Baker. Mary Thomas came to India on marriage in 1838. Her husband died in 1870, and she remained actively working till her own death in 1899, after sixty-one years in India. Amelia Baker was born in India, of a German missionary family. She married in 1818 and after her husband's death in 1866 continued missionary work till her own death in 1888. In both cases daughters, sons and grandchildren were serving as missionaries at the same time as their mothers.

The first missionary daughters to be listed as missionaries in their own right were the children of Gustavus Nyländer, one of the Berlin Seminary missionaries, who stands third in the list of those sent out. His first wife died, and his second wife was a Nova Scotian, one of the former slaves resettled in Sierra Leone. She also died, leaving two little daughters, and when their father, the veteran of the Sierra Leone missionaries, died in 1825 the CMS took the two girls to England to complete their education. In 1831 they returned and served as school teachers. Both eventually married fellow missionaries but the familiarity with the climate which took them through the danger of fever could not protect them in childbirth, and both died within a few years of marriage. Anne Elizabeth died in 1837; Hannah in 1839. Anne Elizabeth's baby daughter Annie Catherine grew up and married a CMS missionary (Higgens) serving in Ceylon. She also had a daughter who worked with her father in Ceylon and who in 1893 was taken into CMS connection, though she had been an honorary missionary from 1886. Three generations of women thus served the CMS.

To summarise: up to the year 1886 103 women had been enrolled as missionaries; in the same period there were 1,041 men. Of these women forty-eight – close to half – were the sisters, daughters or wives of male missionaries. In addition to the widows and sisters "taken up" on the field, a number of others were taken into connection after working in a mission-related post. It is obvious that, whatever the theories were, there was work for women and somehow women were found.

But from 1887 the pattern changed. In that year seven women were sent out, and in the eight years following there were 207. What caused this rather abrupt change in policy?

Very certainly there were changes in social and educational patterns for women within England. Conditions overseas were rather more acceptable, and travel rather less hazardous. The use of women missionaries made by the China Inland Mission indicates a change in attitude and an example which might be followed, although the CIM policy was greatly criticised at the time it was inaugurated. The role of women in the home organisation was also changing. In 1885 a Ladies' Church Missionary Union for London had been formed. The Indian Female Normal School and Instruction Society was sending women to work in India, and the Zenana Bible and Medical Mission and the Church of England Zenana Missionary Society had been organised for the same purpose, and were sending out an increasing number of women. About this time the CEZMS even had talks with the CMS regarding a possible union. Although this did not happen (till after another half century) they remained in close and friendly cooperation. Another society formed to send women overseas, the Female Education Society, was dissolved in 1899 and some twenty-three women, working in India, China and Palestine, were transferred to the CMS lists.

No formal change of policy was announced by the CMS, but early in 1887 the committee responded to an appeal from Bishop Parker of Mombasa by passing a resolution that they were ready to send out a small party of "suitable ladies" in the event of such ladies offering "and the necessary funds being provided" (Stock, vol. III, 368). An appeal also came for ten ladies for Palestine. A number of suitable women did offer, and before the end of 1887 one had sailed for Mombasa and one for Jaffa. In 1888 thirteen women went overseas, and it is interesting to note that from this time onwards fewer rather than more married in the field. One of the women who went out in 1888 was the first of a new breed – a university graduate with a degree in mathematics. Katherine Tristram became principal of the Bishop Poole Memorial Girls' School in Japan. In 1889 the number of women recruits was eighteen.

In addition to the general changes in society and the appeals from church leaders, there was within the CMS another factor directed towards a new policy. This was the attitude and vision of Eugene Stock, the influential editorial secretary. His biographer wrote of him:

Long before others realized it, he saw that if women converts were to have full place in the life of the church of their own country, women missionaries must lead the way. This was impossible while they lacked due recognition in the administrative work of the mission. He expedited as much as he could their slow admission first to consultative bodies, and finally to full executive work . . . On the home side his policy was the same. His was the first C.M.S. department to offer central work to a woman. In days when it was not unknown for a clerical member of the C.M.S. staff to leave the room if a woman rose to speak, even in a semi-public meeting, he put forward women speakers both in London and the provinces. He took a leading part in the formation of the C.M.S. women's department in 1895, which had a share in both home and foreign work. (Gollock, 1929, pp. 171–172)

At the end of the Jubilee year, 1899, 550 women stood on the CMS List II. The number of men who had been sent overseas at that time was 1,556. The difference is great, but the development is seen when we compare the figures for 1885. Then it was ninety-nine women and 1,018 men. Over 400 women had proceeded overseas, or been taken up, in less than fifteen years. This indeed set the scene for the new century, when women were to be of increasing importance in their number and in their work.

7 NEW FIELDS, NEW DEVELOPMENTS

Nigeria: the new missionaries

In the late 1870s, when major internal changes were in any case taking place in the Yoruba and Niger missions, and in the affairs of the large trading companies on the Niger, the last and most extensive Yoruba war broke out. The European powers saw their chance to intervene, and France (in Dahomey) and Germany (in the Cameroons) joined Britain in taking control over inland as well as coastal territories. Mission work was extending, with a number of new missions (including Roman Catholic) coming in, and with some of the earlier societies (like American Baptists) regrouping after the American Civil War. Where did the African congregations and the African missionaries fit, in this changing situation? As an African historian has written, "from suppliants seeking protection in the country, the European missionaries became protectors, and their attitude towards Africans changed accordingly. From fellow-men and brothers, though not without rivalry, they were becoming part of a ruling caste." And at the same time that ideas of national and ethnic superiority were spreading, a new and subtle form of spiritual superiority was affecting many of the younger missionaries.

The post-Civil War period in America was a time of spiritual revival, and from the USA these revival movements came to Britain. Notable was the evangelist D. L. Moody and his musician colleague I. D. Sankey, whose 1875 London campaign profoundly affected both East End and West End.

In 1882 the two men led a mission to Cambridge, and this was to be a breakthrough in the recruiting of university men for overseas mission.

But ultimately more influential in the Nigerian situation was the visit to England in 1874 of the American Quaker couple, Robert and Hannah Pearsall Smith. Their teaching on the "higher life" led eventually to the setting-up of the Keswick Convention, and to a new emphasis on holiness. Some who became involved crossed the line into a dangerous "sinless perfectionism"; even for those who stopped short there were still dangers. When men holding such views came into contact with Christians living in another culture, their views, though not in themselves racist, appeared very much like racisim. It was out of this situation that the new breed of CMS missionaries came.

After a long period when no white missionaries could go inland, and when African clergy had been totally in charge of their churches, the CMS began at the end of the 1870s to reassert its position. From 1867 to 1880 African clergy had been running the work at Abeokuta, and the pastor from 1877 was the Rev. James Johnson. He received a favourable report when the Bishop of Sierra Leone was able to make a visit in 1879, but in 1880 he was withdrawn and replaced by a white missionary.

This happened where there was no criticism of his work; but reports were going to the CMS, often from white traders, of misconduct on the part of CMS agents. When the mission steamer *Henry Venn* was sent out, the CMS appointed a lay agent as "accountant of the missions". The Rev. Henry Venn's successor as regional secretary for Africa, E. J. Hutchinson, no longer had complete confidence in Bishop Crowther. This was in 1878, and in the same year two African clergymen were appointed as archdeacons, to share Crowther's burden. But because of the "unfavourable reports" received about the agents in the up-river stations, a committee was formed in Lagos to go into the affairs of the Niger mission. The bishop and the two archdeacons were members, and three ordained missionaries, the lay accountant, and another more senior missionary, the Rev. J. B. Wood, who was secretary. He had served in the Yoruba mission since 1857. As a result of the investigations of this committee several of the African clergy were, in 1883, given notices of disconnection. A meeting was held in Madeira to which the English parent committee sent representatives, but neither party – for by this time the white and black missionaries were clearly two parties – was satisfied. It was now clear that Europeans intended to take over the running of the Niger mission.

But Crowther was still the bishop. No accusation of dishonesty or misconduct ever touched him; at worst he was guilty of weakness or lack of decision in dealing with his staff. From 1887 the new missionaries descended on him – "Able, young, zealous, impetuous, uncharitable and opinionated." Some arrived with, and some later joined, Graham Wilmot Brooke, a young pioneer who had earlier travelled alone through West Africa and the Sudan, and convinced the CMS to let him in 1890 take men out for the "Soudan and Niger Mission." In effect, the Niger mission was to be divided. From Lokoja north was to be the Soudan and Niger mission. Three or four African agents were removed to allow the "Soudan Band" to establish themselves. To the south the new mission was to be the Lower Niger and Delta, and here also English missionaries were to be in charge. The management committee which was taking control out of the hands of Bishop Crowther met in Onitsha in August 1890. As even the official history of CMS admits:

That meeting issued in a lamentable crisis. The two nationalities entirely failed to agree as to either the policy or the *personnel* of the Mission, and although the brethren on the side of greater strictness succeeded in carrying the disconnexion of certain agents, they did not consider this enough, and the Secretary, acting for the C.M.S., gave separate notice, in its name, of the suspension of some others from its employment.

Lest it seem that the African staff were wholly without defence, it should be added that Ashcroft, the lay accountant, was dismissed in 1882 for rudeness to Bishop Crowther, and that the lay secretary of the parent committee, Edward Hutchinson, was obliged to resign in May 1881, after questions concerning his handling of the Niger mission affairs.

At the August 1890 meeting, when the secretary overruled in favour of the missionaries, and men ordained by Bishop Crowther were suspended without his consent, the bishop rose and announced his resignation from the committee. This was in fact the desired result on the part of the missionary members, who now appointed some of their own number to be responsible for the local superintendence of the work.

Archdeacon Dandeson Crowther, the bishop's son, who was one of the clergy censured at the meeting, reacted by taking the Delta Churches out of CMS superintendence without (as might have happened) declaring them an independent Church. By June 1891 J. A. Robinson, who had been a leader in the mission and the "Soudan Band", had died; at the end of the year Bishop Crowther died. In March 1892 Graham Wilmot Brooke died. With other deaths and resignations the whole enterprise had collapsed.

But how was Crowther to be replaced? There was no question of another African bishop at this point. The Rev. Joseph Hill, who had served in West Africa and then in New Zealand before resigning, re-offered and was acceptable to the Archbishop of Canterbury. Two "Native Assistant Bishops", Charles Phillips and Isaac Oluwole, were consecrated with him in June 1893.

The CMS and the Anglican Church in Nigeria survived this difficult period with less defections than might have been expected, and the Church continued to grow.

New Zealand

As the Anglican Church in New Zealand developed, the relationship with the CMS obviously had to change. And so, as the early historian of the Society records:

> In 1883, the Society put the New Zealand Mission on a new footing. The Committee felt strongly that the C.M.S. funds ought not to be drawn upon permanently for ministrations to a few thousand Maoris now living in the midst of a large and flourishing British Colony. . . . There could never be a really independent Native Church for a small minority of the population. [A scheme was drawn up] under which the Maori Mission was assigned to a local Board.

So from one point of view the CMS in New Zealand had accepted the euthanasia which should be the aim of mission as a Church grows. But from another point of view the CMS in New Zealand was just about to begin. In 1892 the New Zealand Church Missionary Association was founded (and, at the same period, CMAs in Victoria and New South Wales, Australia). As early as 1893 two women went out as missionaries to Japan – accepted and financed from New Zealand but located under the English parent committee. The first to go from Australia were the Saunders sisters from Melbourne who went to Ku-Cheng, China, in 1893.

Up to the CMS centenary in 1899 nearly twenty men and women from New Zealand and Australia had gone to Africa, Persia, China, and India, as well as Japan. One last name deserves mention. In 1899 Frederick Augustus Bennett was recorded as a missionary of the Society "in local connexion in New Zealand Mission". He was transferred to the New Zealand Maori Mission Board at the end of 1902. This Maori clergyman was to become the greatly-loved first Bishop of Aotearoa, and the true successor of bishops like Williams and Hadfield. Since the Maori members of the Church were comparatively few and scattered, the Church of the Province of New Zealand finally gave one suffragan bishop in the diocese of Waiapu responsibility for Maori Anglicans all over New Zealand. He was given as his title the Maori name for New Zealand, Aotearoa. Bishop Bennett served his people and the country long and well and (like Bishop Williams) a son was later to follow him in the same office. He is buried near St. Faith's Church on the shore of Lake Rotorua, and in that church is an etched window of Christ as a Maori *rangitira* (chief), walking on the waters of the lake. The later history of the Maori Church in New Zealand has not always been happy, partly because of the situation of a minority people among a dominant immigrant population. But we can assert that without the work of the Church it might have been much worse, and that within the Church the Maori and his culture have been recognised. Bishop Bennett and others like him have ministered to their *pakeha* brothers and sisters, as well as to their own people.

Eastern Equatorial Africa from 1875

Rebmann, the German missionary who had played a large part in the discoveries and mapping of the East African interior, lived on at Rabai, near Mombasa, till 1875. His wife died in 1866, and much of the time he was alone as far as missionary companions were concerned. He was becoming blind; there were just a few converts around him, but he continued his translation work. From many points of view he was a pathetic figure, but he maintained a Christian presence on the mainland which was soon to become a bridgehead for dramatic expansion.

It was the slave trade in the Indian Ocean which revived the flagging CMS interest in the East African coast. Naval vessels were intercepting Arab *dhows* carrying slaves, as they had earlier done around the West African coasts, and the rescued slaves had to be settled somewhere. The CMS committee in London took up this new Abolitionist cause, and there was much discussion about a suitable site for a freed slave settlement. The Seychelles, Zanzibar and Mombasa were all mentioned; in the meantime, from about 1850, slaves were landed at Bombay, India, and dispersed locally. Some came into the care of a CMS missionary, and finally an institution known as the African Asylum was set up at a Christian village near Nasik, inland from Bombay. There men and women were educated and trained in useful skills and many became Christians and were baptised. Eventually it occurred to missionaries that there might be a place for these folk in the continent whence they had come. In 1864 two young men, who both originated from the southern Tanzanian coast, went to Rabai with their wives, and two women from the same area were sent as wives for two of Rebmann's converts. The men were Ishmael Semler and William Jones, and they were later joined by George David. They made occasional visits back to India and visited Zanzibar, but they were more permanent and useful colleagues for Rebmann than the CMS missionaries who were from time to time sent out.

Meanwhile discussion about a site for a settlement continued, and at the same time the interest of European powers in the East African coast and its hinterland was rising. The CMS decided to revive the dormant East African mission, and in November 1874 sent out the Rev. W. Salter Price, a long-serving CMS missionary in India, who had been the main inspirer of the African Asylum. He was asked to find a site for a village near Mombasa, and to reorganise the mission. Price persuaded Rebmann to retire, and the veteran left for Europe in March 1875. In May a plot of land was bought on the mainland, opposite Mombasa Island, and named Frere Town, after Sir Bartle Frere, who had been much involved in the slave trade issue. The site was obtained just in time, for in

September 302 rescued slaves were landed and handed over to the care of the CMS. Price had come out with several new missionaries, but none had survived very long at Frere Town; however, he had the help of the Nasik men, who were able to communicate with the recaptives. Once again the Western missionaries were helped and strengthened by indigenous Christians, who in this case had passed through capture and recapture, and years in a foreign land, which could now be seen as a preparation for a new work of God.

So after a long period of stagnation matters began to move again in the East Africa mission, and a number of recruits were sent out to Rabai and Frere Town. But the CMS could not possibly have anticipated the next development, which was to open up one of the most exciting and dynamic mission ventures in the whole history of the CMS.

The link was David Livingstone, who died in the southern interior of East Africa in 1873. His companions on his last journey, and the faithful servants who at great personal risk preserved his body and carried it to the coast, were "Nasik boys" whom he had personally engaged in India. One of that group, Matthew Wellington, went to Frere Town in 1874 and proved of great service to Salter Price.

Livingstone's "discoverer" of 1870, H. M. Stanley, had through his contact with Livingstone acquired a respect for missionary work, as well as a continuing interest in Africa. So when in April 1874 Stanley arrived in Buganda in the course of his trans-African journey, and met the young Ganda ruler or *kabaka*, his first instinctive reaction was to write to England and ask for British missionaries to come over. So the famous letter to the *Daily Telegraph* was published in November 1875, having been almost miraculously preserved through the intervention of General Gordon after the murder of its Belgian courier.

Within two days of the publication of Stanley's appeal, the CMS received an offer of £5,000 towards a mission "to the Victoria Nyanza", from a friend who signed himself "An

Unprofitable Servant." The CMS Committee met immediately to consider whether this call was indeed from God. There were not lacking on the committee men of affairs – like Lord Lawrence of India – to point out the great obstacles. But the memory of Krapf's vision of a chain of mission stations stretching from east coast to west coast was before them, and this carried the day. The gift was accepted, and more contributions and offers of service came in. Despite all difficulties a party was got together and eight men sailed as early as April 1876. The Uganda enterprise started on a high note, and it was to continue to challenge and excite British Christians for many years to come.

The party was made up first of several young and well-educated men – the naval officer Shergold Smith, the doctor John Smith, an ordained man, C. T. Wilson, and the Scots engineer Alexander Mackay. Then there were three older men, one, O'Neill, an Irish architect, and two artisans, and a younger artisan builder. Of the whole group, four were Scottish or Irish, and several were not Anglicans. At the farewell meeting, Mackay reminded the committee that "within six months they will probably hear that one of us is dead." His prophecy was soon fulfilled, for the Scottish builder, James Robertson, died at Zanzibar within three months, and in December 1877 Shergold Smith and O'Neill were murdered on Ukerewe Island, Lake Victoria. Dr. John Smith died near the Lake in May 1877. Two others had returned ill, and in fact, only Mackay and the Rev. C. T. Wilson lived to work in Buganda itself.

Mackay proved in many respects to be the model of a pioneer missionary. He was obliged to return to the coast, ill, on the first journey inland, but aided the party by organising supplies and finally reached Rubaga (the capital of Buganda) in November 1878, having been reunited south of the lake with C. T. Wilson, who had been alone for five months. The King of Buganda, Mutesa, was not as receptive to the missionaries as Stanley's letter had led the CMS to hope. Mackay

and Wilson were restricted in where they could go and the
contacts they were allowed to make, and it was clear that
Mutesa was hoping for arms and ammunition from the
strangers. Mackay countered these demands to some extent
by his practical work as a smith and engineer. They were
able to make friends with the boys and young men who
thronged their dwelling out of curiosity, and they held services
in Swahili, while they themselves began to learn Luganda.
There were a few local men available as translators who had
been in Stanley's caravan, and who could use some Swahili
and English.

Meanwhile, in England, when news was received of
the deaths and illnesses, a "Nile Party" of four men was
assembled to travel out via Egypt and Khartoum as reinforcements. They were promised and received help on their way
from General Gordon. One man had to return ill but three,
including Felkin, a doctor, reached Rubaga in February
1879. In April two others, Stokes and Copplestone, came
from the south. Stokes had been at Mpwapwa, the mission-
cum-staging post 200 miles from the coast. So for a brief
period there were seven CMS missionaries within reach of
the Kabaka and his court.

But the situation soon changed. The missionaries were
facing internal problems of leadership, and factors that were
to continue to plague the work in Uganda were already
present. The Protestant missionaries had to contend with
Islam, personified in the Arab traders who made (sometimes
false) allegations to Mutesa; with Roman Catholic missionaries, French by nationality, who arrived in March 1879;
and with Mutesa's suspicions of British and French designs
on his territories, highlighted for him by Gordon and the
Turks in Khartoum. The instructions issued to the missionaries had warned them not to interfere in local politics —
but there was no escaping the effects both of local and of
international pressures. At one point the group decided
to withdraw completely, but in the end this was not done.

Stokes and Copplestone left for the south in June; Wilson and Felkin took the northern route to England in May 1879, accompanied by three envoys whom Mutesa was sending to the British Government. Mackay still had two missionary companions, and he worked at his practical pursuits and at language learning. Through these contacts they were able to get to know and to teach young Ganda men. In April 1881, when both the other missionaries had gone, an older clergyman, Philip O'Flaherty, arrived. He made good progress with language learning and translation, and a year later conducted the first baptism, of five young men.

The original Eastern Equatorial Africa mission was now sub-dividing and becoming a cluster of missions. In 1878 the Usagara mission was separately identified with the setting-up of Mpwapwa and later, in its vicinity, Kisokwe and Mamboia stations. Here Charles Stokes, Henry Cole and Joseph Last worked; here their wives, the first white women to live away from the coast, worked with them and all three died within a few years. Charles Stokes, the Irish "adventurer" as many called him, showed himself to be a gifted caravan leader who was of great service to the mission before and after he retired from the CMS (in 1885), getting parties through to Uganda. His first wife, who had been a UMCA missionary, died at Mpwapwa after only a year of marriage. He later married a Ganda wife, and their son, Charles Kasaja, never knew his father. Stokes was executed in the Congo Free State in 1895, accused of gun-running. The little Charlie Stokes was entrusted to the Church of Scotland Mission for education, and he became a trusted hospital assistant at Kikuyu (near Nairobi) and a boyhood friend of a young Kikuyu called Jomo Kenyatta, also a protégé of the Presbyterian missionaries.

A little later (1885) the Taita and Chaga missions were begun in the hills east of Kilimanjaro. Taita was to come within British East Africa and so continued a CMS mission; Chaga came into German East Africa and the work there passed to Lutheran missionaries. Even in Taita, the missionaries benefited from Krapf's linguistic labours, for he had made vocabularies of the language.

In Uganda, affairs moved with an incredible rapidity. In 1882 the first baptisms took place; in 1883 the first Holy Communion was celebrated with African Christians. They were not officially confirmed; there was no bishop to confirm them. During 1882 a new party came from England via Zanzibar and Mpwapwa; the leader of the six new missionaries was a young English clergyman, James Hannington. Recurrent illness allowed him no nearer than Uyui, on the south of the lake, and he was obliged to return to the coast and England. There, when doctors passed him as fit again, he was chosen and consecrated as first Bishop of Eastern Equatorial Africa, and he sailed again in November 1884.

He spent some months setting matters in order at Frere Town, and visited the Taita mission. He went to Zanzibar and established a warm relationship with Bishop Smythies of the UMCA. Perhaps most important of all, he ordained as deacons the two "Nasik men" who had carried on the work of the ministry long and faithfully, William Jones and Ishmael Semler. Several of the white missionaries were admitted to priests' orders. But he had now to consider his duty to proceed to Uganda and give similar help to the Church there.

Mutesa, the Kabaka of Buganda, had died in October 1884. His successor, Mwanga, was a young man of eighteen without his father's experience and wisdom. The rumours of white nations in the Sudan to the north, and the activities of white explorers nearer at hand, combined to unsettle him, and the Arab traders did their part to make him distrust all white men. More than that, there was a legend in Buganda that conquerors would come from the east. Mwanga exhibited his power and his cruelty when in January 1885 he had three young readers cruelly put to death. But this did not make the

Ganda turn away from the missionaries. In July 173 attended a church service and thirty-five communicants were recorded. At almost the same time Bishop Hannington left Frere Town on his journey to Buganda. He made the decision to go by the north-eastern route, through Maasai country, and not by starting from Zanzibar and approaching from the south of Lake Victoria.

He was accompanied by the Rev. William Jones and by about 220 porters. This route was shorter, and the bishop had twice been as far as Kilimanjaro. In terms of food supplies and health it was a better route, and the Maasai gave them no real trouble. By early October they were almost within sight of the lake. At a place called Kwa Sundu the bishop divided the caravan. He left William Jones with most of the men, proceeding with fifty, and promised to send messengers back when he arrived at Rubaga. Jones heard nothing good or bad until 8 November, when two men came to his camp with a story that the bishop had been captured and killed. It was some time before he could believe the truth of the report. But a few of the bishop's African companions escaped, and brought convincing testimony. Jones waited for almost a month before taking the remaining men of the caravan on the sad journey back. He used some of the trade goods to make a flag of blue cloth on which was sewn in white letters ICHABOD – "The glory has departed." The women at Frere Town heard by way of Zanzibar that the bishop had died, and believed that all their menfolk had died with him. Sadly, some had. But on 4 February 1886 (after a journey of less than two months) they were firing signal guns as they approached Rabai, and the women rushed out to see the caravan approaching. Jones led them back, but the much-loved bishop was not with them. To many, the glory had indeed departed.

It was not understood for some time that the death of the bishop and his companions was by order of Mwanga. Many thought that he had become involved in a local quarrel.

But within a short time the great persecution in Buganda showed where matters stood. In the first part of 1886 some two hundred young Ganda Christians, both Catholic and Protestant, were put to death in the cruellest ways, and truly died as martyrs and witnesses for the faith they had professed for so short a time. In no other Anglican mission has there ever been such a testing and such a response. It was only five years from the first baptisms. Mwanga's reasons for fearing the missionaries and the Christians were complex; the reasons for the acceptance of the faith by these young men were also complex. But they died for the faith of Jesus as they knew it, and we are told that the earlier martyrs went to their death singing a hymn, "Daily, daily, sing to Jesus." Just before the bishop was speared to death, he is reported to have said, "Tell Mwanga I die for Buganda, and that I have purchased the road to Buganda with my life." So James Hannington became East Africa's first martyr bishop, and he was joined by the scores of young men "who loved not their lives unto the death".

Another bishop, Henry Parker, formerly a missionary in India, was quickly consecrated and sent out to take Hannington's place. He also spent six months at Frere Town, and then set off for Uganda, but this time by the southern route. Again, the bishop did not arrive in Buganda. It was fever, and not the Kabaka, that kept him back. He died at Usambiro, south of the lake in 1888. In the same place were buried four other missionaries. One was Alexander Mackay, who left the capital for Usambiro in October 1888. There he continued with his work and witness, and no appeals to "Come home!" could move him. He had now been over ten years without a break in the vicinity of the lake. No missionary had yet died of illness in the northern area, but many had died in the south. Now illness struck Mackay, tired out with heavy manual as well as spiritual labours. He died in February 1890, and his body was later taken to Kampala and reburied outside the cathedral on Mengo Hill. He was

supremely the practical and pious missionary for whom
Stanley had appealed, and the title of his biography still
remains his tribute – "Mackay of Uganda."

This Uganda was no longer an isolated spot on a few
missionary maps; it had become a focus of interest for
European powers in reality, and not just in the imagination
of Mwanga. In 1888 the Imperial British East African
Company (IBEAC) received a charter, in the British tradition
of chartered trading companies. It was at the very time that
the enmities between Arab Muslims, French Roman Catholic
missionaries, British Protestant missionaries, and their
groups of followers were at their height. To the north Egyptian
and Sudanese interests complicated the issue. Mwanga
became a prisoner of the Arab/Muslim faction, and managed
to escape to the south of the lake. All the missionaries,
Catholic and Protestant, had now left Buganda. In June
1889 they returned, and a Christian army was organised
which defeated the Muslim faction and re-installed Mwanga.
Meanwhile, officers of the IBEAC and a German explorer,
Carl Peters, were approaching (separately) from the east.
After a period of confusion Captain Frederick Lugard, for the
Company, acquired Mwanga's signature on a treaty, giving
the Company the right to intervene and maintain order in
the kingdom. This was at the end of 1890.

Intergroup fighting continued sporadically for several
years. The aligning of the Anglican converts with one nation
(they were known as the *Bangereza*, the English) and the
Roman Catholics (*Bafransa*, French) with another was an
unfortunate trend which was to bring trouble in time to
come. Mwanga distributed the offices in his administration
between the two groups. The Company now embarked on
the building of a railroad to link the coast to the interior and
to make trade and administration possible. But it could not
for long meet the heavy costs involved, and decided to withdraw completely. The CMS was alarmed, for they feared
internal warfare and also the possibility of another European

power or Egypt entering in. This would damage the young Church even further.

By this time a third bishop, Alfred Tucker, had been consecrated for Eastern Equatorial Africa. He at last journeyed up by the southern route and arrived in Buganda at the end of 1890.

Despite the unsettled conditions – he himself wrote that it was like "a volcano on the verge of an eruption" – the state of the mission was encouraging. Thousands came to worship at the church on Namirembe; thousands more were crying out for books and teaching. Before Mackay's death he had completed the translation of Matthew into Luganda, and now a gifted new missionary, George Pilkington, was publicly set aside to continue Mackay's work.

The fascinating story of Uganda's coming under British control cannot be told here in full. When the IBEAC felt obliged to withdraw the CMS intervened – not as a body for that was not possible – but by mustering financial help and the political influence of individual members. They made it possible for the Company to stay on in Buganda until the British Government declared a Protectorate, in August 1894. There were still many ups and downs, including a mutiny of Sudanese mercenary troops in 1897. During an assault on Luba Fort, near Jinja, the translator, George Pilkington, was killed, shot by a Sudanese soldier at close range. He had responded to an appeal from British officers, and he wanted to share the hardships of his Ganda friends. It was a great loss for the young Church, but by the time of his death the manuscript of the whole New Testament was ready, translated largely by him with much help from Ganda Christians. Parts of the Old Testament, the Prayer Book and catechisms, hymns and reading sheets had also been prepared.

With regard to the native ministry, Bishop Tucker took the opposite line from Bishop Selwyn of New Zealand. At his first visit in 1890–91 six Christians were publicly set aside for work as lay readers. On Trinity Sunday 1893 three of those men, and three others, were ordained deacons. "Unlearned and ignorant" men, as the bishop observed, but they had been "tested and tried in the fires of persecution, and had laboured for years in the service of their Lord, without pay or earthly reward".

From a very early stage the Gospel was being taken out to other parts of Buganda and the whole protectorate, now called Uganda, by the Ganda Christians. In the beginning Swahili was used by the missionaries as they taught the men and boys of the court who understood the *lingua franca* of East Africa, but now it was to be Luganda which was the medium, though translations into many vernaculars were to follow.

Bishop Tucker from the beginning set an example in itinerating; he was always travelling and was a constant help and example to the overseas and the local missionaries. From 1890 to 1900 he made four return journeys from the coast to the lake on foot, though on the last of these, in 1898, he was able to travel the first hundred miles by train. Later journeys were by rail and then lake steamer. After his first journey, by the southern route, he always went to Uganda by the northern route and returned by the route through German East Africa, visiting missions on the way. As well as these major journeys, he walked hundreds of miles on visitations – from Frere Town to Taita, Taveta and Jilore; from Mengo to Toro, Ankole, Mboga, beyond the Mountains of the Moon; to Busoga and Nkole. He often suffered from fever and had to be carried; there were enormous swamps, rivers and lakes with crocodiles and hippo, crossed in leaky dug-out canoes; there were thunderstorms and there was blazing sun. Tucker was a talented artist, and made sketches when forced to wait for the caravan to catch up. Despite the weariness, he loved the journeys and the services he took in the little thatched churches. There were many confirmations; in Kampala in the great thatched cathedral there were commissionings and ordinations; sometimes sadder ceremonies like the funeral of

the six British officers killed in the Sudanese mutiny. He
entered into the joys and sorrows of them all.

In several areas Bishop Tucker set in motion modes of
work which were of great importance for the future. He
quickly realised the need for women missionaries if the
Church was not to grow lopsided. Having made a successful
and comparatively easy journey to Uganda by the northern
route in 1892, he gained permission to take a party including
women by that route. But it was 800 miles, and only ten years
since Bishop Hannington's death. No wonder there were
criticisms! But he made very careful preparations and in
1895 he went up with a party of twelve missionaries, five
being women. They made the trip safely in twelve weeks, and
received a tremendous welcome when they came into the
city.

Their arrival was important not only for the care and
teaching of girls and women (three were nurses) but also as
the pioneers of more formal education for both boys and
girls, including mixed schools. But something more was
needed, and a missionary who arrived in 1897, Charles
Hattersley, became the pioneer organiser of village primary
schools, which were in the end to cover the whole country. By
the end of 1898 there were already nearly 700. John Purvis
who came in 1895 and Kristen Borup, a Dane who came via
Canada in 1897, re-started on a more systematic basis the
industrial education pioneered by Mackay. Borup later
transferred to the Uganda Company, which took over from
the CMS much of the responsibility for commercial and
agricultural developments.

Wherever Bishop Tucker travelled, he found men and
women eager to learn to read, and to be taught the basics of
the faith. Teachers were called for, and hundreds of faithful
Ganda went far and wide to teach and preach. In those early
days patterns were being established which would come to
be seen as normative in all the East African territories where
the CMS came to work. A central church/school would be set

up, with a licensed lay reader or even an ordained clergyman in charge, and then a circle of little "outschools" or
"synagogues" where teaching went on during the week and
where services were held on Sundays. About once a month
all would gather at the central church for preaching and
communion.

The Ganda went to the pygmies beyond the Mountains of
the Moon; to Mount Elgon among the Bagishu; to the other
kingdoms; in each place baptisms took place and a Church
began to arise. In 1890 ninety-three were baptised; in 1894
it was 1,724, and the numbers continued to rise. It was by
any standard a successful mission, but there were dangers
inherent in the success. By the end of the century plans were
being made for teacher-training and for theological education,
for certainly much depended on the standards of the clergy
and the teachers. Boarding schools, specifically for the sons
of chiefs, had been established; Mengo High School and
Kings' College Budo. There was soon a similar school for
girls as well.

Medical work was also introduced as another means of
contact, and of service, for there was absolutely no treatment
available, and much need. In Uganda it was the brothers
Cook – Dr. Albert who arrived in 1896 and his brother Dr.
John, 1899, who pioneered. Albert Cook in 1900 married a
missionary nurse, Kathleen Timpson, trained at Guy's, who
had walked up from the coast in 1896, and she was responsible
for setting up nursing training in the hospital on Mengo Hill
which her husband founded. The little dispensaries on the
mission stations were for a long time as important to the
people as the larger houses of healing.

Bishop Tucker's final contribution may be seen to be his
emphasis on the relationship of the missionaries to the African
Church in the constitution that he introduced. Even before
he arrived in 1890, a Church council had been formed in
Mengo, and from his return in 1892 Tucker was building up
the council into a synod. He drew up a constitution in which

white missionaries would come under the same rules and regulations as the Ugandan clergy and lay workers. This was resisted by many of the missionaries. Before he finally left Uganda (1909) Bishop Tucker was induced to make compromises which allowed the constitution to be adopted. The missionary standing committee retained certain powers relating to the missionaries, but in comparison to most mission fields "Uganda was blessed with an enlightened policy directed towards the early autonomy of the African Church." (J. V. Taylor, *Growth of the Church in Buganda*, p. 8.)

As early as 1904 Bishop Tucker travelled into what was then called Kavirondo, and which was still a part of the Uganda Protectorate, and, with a missionary called John Willis, selected a site for a mission station. Willis became the pioneer of the work in this area, and later was to succeed Bishop Tucker as the second Bishop of Uganda. For by this time the huge diocese of Eastern Equatorial Africa had been divided. The two dioceses which resulted were Uganda and Mombasa, and another former missionary in India, William Peel, became the first Bishop of Mombasa.

The mission work in Uganda had preceded the arrival of the colonial government, but expansion in British East Africa (which became Kenya) followed the flag. Missions, Catholic and Protestant, went inland with the railroad, and the CMS was among them. The first inland station, Kabete, was near the new town of Nairobi, and the earliest CMS missionary came from Taveta. Gradually stations went further out, and the CMS became established in Kikuyu and Embu territory to the west and north of Nairobi. The work in Kavirondo originated in Uganda, and so three spheres of Anglican influence were established in Kenya – the coast, the highlands, and Kavirondo. One of the pioneers of the highlands was Douglas Hooper, a veteran of the journeys to Uganda, who later worked at the coast and buried his first wife at Jilore, north of Mombasa. He went with his second wife, a doctor, to Kahuhia, after medical advice prevented him from returning to the coast. With him went a coast Christian, Harun, as his cook – and also as his translator. Other Christians from the coast and from Taita-Taveta went inland with the missionaries. They were able to preach immediately in Swahili and were soon using the local vernaculars.

So again native Christians were pioneers alongside the missionaries and even on a local scale a missionary moving on to found a new station was likely to take with him a few converts from his earlier station. They often did not go far in miles from their place of origin, but they were true pioneers, carrying the Gospel to new frontiers.

One unusual feature of the mission in Uganda was not repeated in British East Africa (Kenya) or in German East Africa (Tanganyika). In Uganda there were for many years no other Protestant missions of any kind. Only the CMS and Roman Catholic missions were found there. This was not the case in the other territories. In Kenya especially, mission comity agreements were very necessary. In the very large territory of Tanganyika, there was little overlapping. The CMS had given up the work around Kilimanjaro, but continued to work in Usagara, a difficult area where there were many discouraging features. There were thoughts of withdrawing and handing over to a German mission, but this was not done. In due course missionaries from Australia and Canada were located there, and geographical extension took place into Gogo country, further inland around the administrative centre of Dodoma.

So from the situation as it was in 1875, with only a tiny handful of Christians around Rabai, near Mombasa, Christian schools and churches connected to the CMS were by 1914 to be found in very many – if not all – parts of East Africa. Two bishops headed two large and populous dioceses, with ordained African clergy, lay readers, teachers, catechists, and many missionaries from Australia and Canada as well as the British Isles. The Universities Mission to Central Africa was established along the coast of Tanganyika and in the south. But even so it would have taken a brave prophet to predict that in these three (now independent) nations there would be by 1980 three provinces of the Anglican Church, with over thirty dioceses, all but one headed by an African bishop.

The Jerusalem bishopric, and missions to Muslims

When the CMS turned again to the countries of the eastern Mediterranean in the last quarter of the 19th century, it saw the mission as a new start. In fact there was never a complete break, but the later work certainly had a new emphasis. Earlier, though the call to evangelise Muslims was never disregarded, there persisted the belief – somewhat naive – that preaching and teaching the Scriptures would swiftly bring about a reformation in the Orthodox Churches, and that Muslims could then be evangelised through and by the Orthodox believers.

This was in the end seen to be a false hope. In the later work the emphasis was laid on the winning of Muslims, and missionaries were wary of appearing to proselytise the Orthodox. The Mission Press in Malta had long since been closed down, but the distribution of scriptures continued, mainly through colporteurs employed by the Bible Society. At Syra, Smyrna and Constantinople missionaries had stayed on in retirement after the official CMS withdrawal. Translation was continued, but there was little else they could do except through personal contact, and that mainly when visitors came to them. One feature of the Mediterranean/ Muslim missions was the long service of the missionary personnel. Thirty-five, forty, fifty years' service is recorded.

A strange and unique feature of this work was the affair of the Jerusalem bishopric. Naturally there was no Anglican – indeed no non-Orthodox, non-Roman – bishop in the holy city. The advent of one was brought about by the unlikely alliance of Lord Shaftesbury (then Lord Ashley), a warm supporter of the London Jews Society, and King Frederick William IV of Prussia. The bishop was to be appointed alternately by the British Crown and the Prussian Crown, and he was to minister to Anglicans and Lutherans in the holy land. A Jewish convert, the Rev. Michael Solomon Alexander, was consecrated in 1841, after appropriate legislation had been passed in the British parliament. The CMS was not at all involved at that stage. But Bishop Alexander lived for only four years after his consecration, and the CMS became more involved with the choice of Samuel Gobat. A Swiss by nationality and a former CMS missionary in Lutheran orders, he was at the time he was chosen teaching in Malta. He had to be ordained priest before he could be consecrated bishop, and there was a good deal of opposition (mainly from English Tractarians) but in 1846 he was consecrated – "The first Bishop from CMS ranks." He naturally turned to the CMS for help in carrying out his mission. In 1851 two missionaries were sent to Jerusalem; one of these, the Rev. Frederick Klein, was to work in Palestine and then Egypt for fifty-two years, until his retirement in 1903.

But it was not until the mid-1870s that the deeper involvement of the CMS in mission to Muslims really began. Bishop Gobat by that time had weathered some storms, especially over accusations of proselytising. His position was very difficult, for almost any action would be criticised either in England or in Prussia. Work was started in Nazareth, Jaffa, Haifa and Nablus, mainly with German missionaries. Gobat earned much gratitude for starting a network of elementary day schools in Christian areas, to which Muslim boys also came for lack of any alternative, and a boarding school in Jerusalem was also set up. As Gobat grew older he wished to hand over projects he had started to the CMS to ensure their continuity, and this had begun when he died in May 1879. His successor was consecrated in the same year but lived only until 1881. The Jerusalem bishopric then lapsed for several years, and was not revived until 1887.

Meantime, the CMS was entering into other areas. One wholly new field was Persia, a country long high in the interest of a number of English CMS supporters. This came about partly because of Henry Martyn's translation of the New Testament into Persian, and his death after passing through Persia on his way home. Robert Bruce, an Irish missionary working in the Punjab, obtained permission to visit Persia in 1869 to study Persian; during his visit a serious famine occurred and he was able to bring some relief. He wished to stay on, and finally in 1875 the CMS committee formally adopted the Persia mission. Although he had at first little help, his own translation work and medical work by his colleague (an ordained doctor) went on, and services were conducted in Persian. There was also an Armenian school. In 1883 the former Bishop of Lahore, Bishop French, visited and performed episcopal functions; he confirmed sixty-seven and ordained an Armenian pastor. This was the beginning of the little Episcopal Church in Persia. The distribution of Persian and Armenian scriptures went on. Later, in 1893, Persia received its second "retired" bishop in the person of Edward Craig Stuart, who after twenty-seven years in India and seventeen in New Zealand (where he was Bishop of Waiapu) was to spend another seventeen years in Persia. He came with a daughter and was later joined by two nieces, one of whom was a doctor. They may mark for us the importance of medical work, and work by women, in Persia. Bishop Stuart, described as "a missionary in episcopal orders", continued in Persia till his death in 1911. In 1883 work had been opened in Baghdad as a branch of the Persia mission, and again medicine and women workers were important.

In Palestine quiet work continued at a number of stations and out-stations. The long-serving German missionaries provided continuity, and now in the 1880s the CMS was able to send reinforcements. From 1881 to 1887, when there was no bishop in Jerusalem, visiting bishops were entrusted with episcopal functions. Finally, "in the teeth of vehement opposition from the High Church party", as the early CMS history has it, a new bishop, G. P. Blyth, was consecrated and arrived in May 1887. He was warmly welcomed by the CMS missionaries and was himself warm in the praise of the CMS at first, but ultimately the strain of working with those of differing theologial views within the Anglican Church, the criticisms of the High Church party in England, and the very real difficulties of maintaining good relationships with several ancient Orthodox Churches brought on a dispute. Bishop Blyth made public very serious charges against the CMS and its mission in Palestine. This was in 1890, and it was a *cause célèbre* in English church circles (and indeed in national newspapers) throughout 1891. The principal charge and the underlying cause of the problem was still the accusation of "proselytism". But what was a missionary to do when a Greek or a Syrian Christian came to him begging to be admitted into a "Scriptural" Church? The Archbishop of Canterbury called in "five prelates" to arbitrate on the case rather as had happened in the Ceylon controversy eleven years earlier. The *Advice* finally issued by the bishops vindicated the CMS, but made little difference to the practicalities of the situation. Nor did it prevent Bishop Blyth from continuing to make criticisms.

In 1882, after a period of twenty years without a missionary, work was re-opened in Egypt. Earlier the aim had been to influence the Coptic Christians; now it was to be a mission to Muslims. In 1882 Britain had occupied the Nile valley, so from some points of view it was an opportune time to re-enter Egypt. The missionary chosen to go to Cairo was the Rev. F. A. Klein, veteran missionary in Palestine and of course fluent in Arabic. Work went ahead slowly at first, with few missionaries appointed, and the real step forward in Cairo came, as in many other Muslim centres, with medical work. Dr. F. J. Harpur, who had been briefly in Aden, went to

Cairo in 1889, and among the women sent to Cairo from 1890 onwards were several trained nurses. In 1896-97 buildings were erected for the hospital in Old Cairo, which was to become and remain a well-known place in the story of the CMS in Egypt. In 1898 and 1899 two outstanding missionaries were sent successively to Cairo – Douglas Thornton and Temple Gairdner. They added a ministry to university students to the existing work, for both had been largely involved in student work before joining the CMS. Since they discouraged the reception of Coptic Christians into the Anglican Church, numbers remained small, but there were some conversions from Islam and a much wider general influence.

It was very clear by the end of the century, when the second phase of work in Muslim countries had been under way long enough to form some conclusions, that no quick or easy way of evangelisation among Muslims had been found. Many CMS missionaries had for even longer been in contact with Muslim societies in northern India, where the situation was little different. Medical work, which was appreciated, and which gave contacts with men and women, was one method. Schools were also appreciated. The use of women in these missions was much more extensive than might have been expected, given the restrictions on women within these cultures. In the seven years from 1888 to 1894, thirty ladies went to Palestine, and in the same period six went to Egypt, five to Persia and four to Baghdad. These included more than one woman doctor, several trained nurses, and experienced teachers. Other features of the work in these missions was the continuing use of German missionaries, valued especially for their linguistic gifts, and the use of older missionaries who transferred there after long service in other areas.

8   ORIENTAL UPS AND DOWNS

China (to 1895)

In their first annual report the committee of the CMS mentioned China. They had chosen for their name, after all, the society for Missions to Africa and the East, and China was, to many, *the* East.

The discussion in that first annual report was over the possible publication of portions of the New Testament which had been translated into Chinese. The CMS decided that it should be done by the specialist society, the SPCK, but ultimately they were produced by a society which did not exist at the time of the report – the British and Foreign Bible Society. And little more was heard of China for some time, as the work started in West Africa and New Zealand, and as the committee fought to gain the right to evangelise openly in India.

But China was not forgotten. Henry Venn, who was later to write on Xavier and his missions to the East, must have helped to maintain an interest. Catholic involvement had continued after the death of Francis Xavier, but in the 18th century Christianity had been prohibited in China by imperial decrees, and the Roman Catholic presence was officially confined to Macao, the Portuguese enclave on the coast.

China in its immensity calls out for comparison with India. Although a larger area with a somewhat larger population (which can only be estimated), China was in many respects a more unified country than India ever became before the

British imposition of unity. From the 17th century China was
ruled by the Manchus, a dynasty of foreign origin who were
assimilated to the traditions of Chinese culture, and maintained control with the aid of an administrative bureaucracy
which long antedated their rule. China maintained a very
strong cultural identity and a contempt for all things foreign;
it was united not only by its imperial rulers and the administration, but also by a common written language and a philo-
sophical system, Confucianism, which provided a firm religious foundation for the literate classes. Folk beliefs persisted
around Confucianism as the prevailing religion of the peasants and urban poor. No caste system existed to perpetuate
legally the subservience of a section of the population,
although slavery, mainly of the domestic variety, was widespread. In theory the administrative posts were open to any
who passed the requisite examinations, and in practice some
at least did enter the bureaucracy from the poorest sections.

Desiring no contact with the West, foreigners were confined to a few coastal cities, and there were no chaplains or
resident expatriates to pave the way for missions, as in India.
There was no ancient Christian Church, and only a very
small number of Russian Orthodox Christians in the cities
of the interior and Roman Catholics at Macao and in the
coastal cities.

How China was finally opened up for the entrance of
missionaries in the 1830s and 1840s is one of the most shame-
ful episodes of Western economic imperialism. To their credit,
missionaries and the Church in England worked and spoke
against it, but the fact remains that China was opened up for
trade in opium, and that without the Opium Wars (1839–
1842 and 1856–1860) there would have been no treaties and
no access for foreigners – at least for a very long time.
Missionaries were included as foreigners, and so came in
because of the provisions of the treaty which ended the first
Opium War. It is no wonder, then, that the history of the
Church in China should include episodes of violence against

Westerners unparalleled in any other sphere of work in the 19th century.

The first Protestant missionary, however, preceded the first Opium War by some thirty years. He was Robert Morrison of the London Missionary Society, who was unable to go inland, and devoted himself to language study. He was able to support himself as a translator for the East India Company, and, with Robert Milne, he had by 1818 translated the whole Bible into Chinese. He also founded a college at Malacca. In 1829 the American Board sent two missionaries to China, and in 1835 and 1837 the American Episcopalians (PECUSA) began their involvement with China. Already we see the beginning of a trend, for USA involvement with China was to continue to be deep and significant whether in love or in hate, and the British involvement – certainly with CMS – was never so great. There are many ways in which China was the India of the USA.

Despite these new initiatives, relations with China were no more open, and the new missionaries could not leave Singapore or the coast. In fact, a new edict against Christianity was proclaimed in 1835. Just at that time, the CMS contacted an unusual semi-independent missionary named Charles Gutzlaff, a Prussian who had been an agent of the Netherlands Missionary Society, and who was using Chinese agents to distribute literature in the interior. It was at least in part a response to his activities that the new edict was promulgated.

The CMS contacted Gutzlaff for information and in 1836 sent out Commander Edward B. Squire on a journey of enquiry. But he never got past Macao, for by the time he arrived the troubles preceding the Opium War were building up, and the actual war was declared in 1839. In 1840 he returned to England to report, but the time to enter China did not seem opportune.

The Opium War was caused by the East India Company aggressively seeking markets for the opium raised in India, and the Chinese Government doing its best to prevent its import. In military terms the British were easily able to overcome the Chinese forces, and when the Chinese sued for peace the Treaty of Nanking ceded Hong Kong to Britain, and opened five "treaty ports" for foreign trade and residence – Canton, Amoy, Fuh-chow, Ningpo and Shanghai. Lord Shaftesbury, to his credit, wrote at the time, "We have triumphed in one of the most lawless, unnecessary and unfair struggles in the records of History." What was the reason? £1,200,000 a year in the Indian revenue.

Nevertheless, this treaty opened the door for missionary work in China. A number of Protestant missionaries were soon in the treaty ports and Hong Kong. In 1843 an anonymous donor gave £6,000 to the CMS as the nucleus of a China fund. In June 1844 two missionaries sailed for China. They were commissioned to visit all the treaty ports and Hong Kong and report on the most suitable place to settle. Eventually one, the Rev. Thomas McClatchie, settled in Shanghai; the other, the Rev. George Smith, returned to England in poor health in 1846.

Here the beginning of another continuing trend may be seen: both men were ordained, and both were university graduates. All the first men sent out were graduates, a large proportion being from Ireland and graduates of Trinity College, Dublin. Although China never took the first place in the affections of the home constituencies, and was never numerically favoured, there was a definite bias in the sending of those recruits reckoned to be the most promising and able. Doubtless this was in part because of the known difficulty of learning Chinese.

In 1849 an important step forward was made. The Rev. George Smith who had returned in 1846 in poor health, and had subsequently become well known through his writings and speaking engagements, was consecrated to the new diocese of Victoria, Hong Kong. Another special gift provided the nucleus of an endowment. Bishop Smith set out with a party of university men – some to accompany him to Hong Kong, others to go to Ningpo (where two men were already in residence) and others to start a new work at Fuh-chow. The recruits included one qualified and experienced medical doctor, who was to be the founder of the work at Fuh-chow, William Welton. Medical work was to be, relatively, of great importance in China. Another of the new recruits, Frederick Gough, who went to Ningpo, opened the first opium refuge, a form of work unique to China and similarly of importance in the special circumstances. Gough served for thirty-four years at Ningpo and retired only in 1881, to die in 1889.

With the arrival of Bishop Smith and his party (he was just in time to preach in Hong Kong on Easter Day, 1850) the work of the CMS was considerably augmented. Welton and a second man went to commence work at Fuh-chow; Gough joined two already at Ningpo; Hobson joined McClatchie at Shanghai where he had been since 1845; and Moncrieff stayed at Hong Kong, where a school (St. Paul's) was commenced. In 1851 the first baptisms took place: two men were baptised at Ningpo and three at Shanghai. The work at Ningpo flourished to the extent that by 1885 there were sixty converts there. Ten Protestant missionary societies were now working in the five treaty ports and Hong Kong; half of these and more than half of the missionaries were from the USA.

But at the same time that the new missionaries were establishing themselves, a new cloud was looming over China. A movement known as T'aip'ing ("Great Peace") was gaining power and influence. China, it must be remembered, was ruled by a foreign dynasty, and not every Chinese citizen was happy with the régime and his position under it. In the 1830s a young scholar called Hung Hsiu-ch'uan, discontented with his failure in the civil service examinations, formed a society centred around a new religion which has been described as "a monotheism tinged with fundamental Protestant Christianity". Hung had read Christian publications and personally met missionaries at Canton. His followers came from the unemployed of the cities, poor peasants and others, and their numbers were augmented by the sufferings caused through various natural disasters. In 1851 a new state was declared, and the rebels made their base at Yungan. Besieged there by the Imperial Army, they broke out and surged on to capture Nanking in March 1853. They were to hold this city till July 1864.

Missionaries and the consuls of foreign powers found it hard to explain or classify the T'aip'ing. Were they Christian or not? They sought peace for the Chinese, but death for the Manchus; they were totally against idol-worship and thousands of idols were pulled down and destroyed. They were also totally against the use of opium. They circulated Christian publications and announced their intention of supporting Christian teaching in their new state.

So a civil war, varying in intensity at different times and in different geographical areas, continued, and the work of missionaries continued despite it. Bishop Smith appealed for new missionaries to take advantage of the anti-idolatry feelings, but between 1854 and 1861 only seven recruits were sent to China and with retirements and deaths there was no overall increase in staff. While the civil war continued the British and French became involved in another dispute (the "Arrow" incident) which escalated into a second Opium War.

Whatever the occasion of the dispute, it was the dissatisfaction of the Chinese and the European trading nations over the import of opium which lay behind it. This led to a British expedition under Lord Elgin which finally took Peking and destroyed the great Summer Palace. Humiliating terms were included in the Treaty of Tien-tsin between Britain and China, including a clause allowing unrestricted entrance of opium into China, and the free entrance and protection of Christian missionaries. As the Ningpo missionary Russell clearly saw at the time, this left the missionaries in a serious dilemma, for previously they had at least been able to deny their complicity in the opium trade, but this could not now be done. "The inconsistency is but too transparent; the thought of it is most awful. Where shall we find relief, except in Him who is wont to educe the greatest good out of the direst evil?"

There were further problems even after the Elgin expedition and the first treaty, and T'aip'ing was not finally extinguished until July 1864, when an army of irregulars led by the Englishman who became famous as "Chinese Gordon", together with Imperial troops, retook Nanking. Terrible massacres were perpetrated by both sides. In the whole episode, from beginning to end, it has been estimated that from twenty to thirty million Chinese, probably more, died.

Now with some kind of peace, there was the possibility of easier entrance for missionaries, and the possibility also of beginning work in the interior. The CMS continued to be handicapped by lack of suitable workers, although there was progress, including the ordination of two Chinese deacons (in 1863) and the opening of new schools, including one for girls, with the help of the Female Education Society. Up to this time the only women working with the CMS were missionary wives.

In 1864 Bishop Smith retired, and it was desired to divide the diocese and appoint a bishop for north China, and Russell, the pioneer of Ningpo, seemed ideal for this post. But the man designated for Victoria, Hong Kong, the Rev. C. R. Alford, objected to having his diocese confined to the very small island of Hong Kong, and Russell returned from leave in England unconsecrated. Bishop Alford reached Hong Kong in October 1867. He travelled extensively and energetically, while Russell was made mission secretary for China (a new post) and was given *quasi*-episcopal powers of superintendence. Bishop Alford resented the lack of support from the Church as a whole, considering himself too dependent on the CMS who were unable to provide him with the staff he wanted. By the late 1860s the policy of retrenchment with falling giving and falling offers of service was in sight. The matter of the new diocese was settled by compromise in 1872, when Bishop Russell was finally consecrated. Both dioceses, North China and Victoria, were to include parts of mainland China, and the chaplaincies in North China would come under the Bishop of North China. Bishop Alford was still not satisfied and resigned. His successor was John Burdon, CMS pioneer in Peking from 1862, who had gone to China in 1853. He was consecrated third Bishop of Victoria in March 1874.

Meanwhile, a new missionary society had been founded, and commenced work in China, which was to prove important for the Christian Gospel in China, both for its own work and for the influence it was to exert on other societies. This was the China Inland Mission, founded and directed by James Hudson Taylor, who had initially worked, from 1853 to 1860, with the China Evangelisation Society, connected with Gutzlaff. In 1866 he sailed back to China from Britain with a party of fifteen. Thirty years later the CIM had 641 missionaries in China. In three particular ways the CIM impressed other societies, even when they were critical: the vision of the needs of the interior; the use of Chinese clothing and identification as far as possible with the Chinese people; and the use of single women in evangelisation.

The first single woman sent to China by the CMS was Miss Matilda Laurence, who joined the Russells in Ningpo. Mrs. Russell herself was accepted as a missionary in full connection after her husband's death in 1879, but no other women were sent out until 1887. From 1889, however, a large number were located to China – five in 1889, nine in 1891. Before they arrived the CMS utilised the services of the Female Education Society, for there was much to do on behalf of Chinese women, and although they were not in purdah as in parts of India, only other women were effective contacts. Chinese women were trained and used in evangelisation.

The peace which now existed was an uneasy one, and all

foreigners were seen as threats. But the Christian converts suffered more than missionaries. The Roman Catholic missionaries came under the protection of the French consular staff, and the Protestant missionaries felt themselves and their converts under the shadow of persecution because of Roman Catholic policies. The work of that Church in orphanages had from the beginning led to misunderstandings, for the babies taken in were inevitably frail, and many died. This gave rise to accusations of murder and worse against the foreigners and this was, incidentally, an accusation which persisted down to the 1950s and the time of the Communist takeover. In 1868 there were riots at Yang-chow which involved the CIM, and in 1870 a serious massacre at Tientsin, which was anti-French and anti-Catholic. Several RC missionaries, including nine Sisters of Mercy, were killed, and some fifty RC converts; the French consulate, the RC cathedral, the sisters' house, and several Protestant preaching chapels, were destroyed. The murder of the sisters was in part at least related to the children they purchased and baptised. Protestant Christians were arrested and threatened, but released by the magistrates, showing that a distinction was made. The French government demanded reparation, but an agreement was postponed because a worse conflict had broken out in Europe – the Franco-Prussian war.

In these incidents the CMS was not involved, but later one of its missions was also to become the victim of violence. Robert Stewart, an able Irish missionary, went to Fuh-chow in 1876, and had commenced a school and theological college, for which buildings were being erected. The site and the buildings had been approved by the local mandarins, but in August 1878 a mob attacked and burned the buildings, and the mandarins, who had actually been viewing the work in progress when this happened, made no attempt to control the mob. Other incidents occurred and the Church authorities could obtain no satisfaction.

Still, the Church was expanding, and when Bishop Russell

died in 1879, after thirty-two years in China, the opportunity was taken to rearrange the episcopal spheres. The SPG was now working in the Chefoo area, and the North China diocese was divided to allow for a new diocese. The northern section kept the name of North China, and an SPG missionary was appointed as bishop; the remaining area was designated the diocese of Mid China and, as its bishop, was consecrated, in 1880, the older of the two Moule brothers, George Evans Moule, who had served in Ningpo from 1858. He and his brother Arthur, (Archdeacon Moule) not only gave long years to China themselves, but also a total of six children who returned to China as missionaries. (A fourth son of Archdeacon Moule became a CMS missionary in Japan.)

Further important work developing in this period, beside the schools and the circuits of small churches, was medical work, and notably the hospital in Hang-chow which grew out of an earlier opium refuge, run by Dr. Duncan Main, trained at Edinburgh University. The work of a good hospital helped to mitigate the continuing and cruel persecution of converts.

The FES continued to help with the CMS girls' school at Fuh-chow, and the newly-formed Church of England Zenana Missionary Society took up some women who offered to the CMS and sent them out; one of the first, Miss Gough, was the daughter of a CMS missionary. Other CEZMS ladies followed, and Robert Stewart and his wife recruited a number in Ireland. Later, following a visit of theirs to Australia, two sisters from Melbourne, Harriette and Elizabeth Saunders, were located to the South China mission, sent out by the Victoria (Australia) Church Missionary Association in 1893.

In July 1895 the Stewarts and a number of these newly-recruited women had a meeting together, at the time of the English Keswick Convention, while they stayed in holiday cottages owned by the CMS just outside Ku-cheng. There was a good deal of general unrest, and some scurrilous pamphlets and posters abusing missionaries and the

Christian religion were circulating. Some missionaries in widely separated places were attacked, and in a few cases killed; others were wonderfully preserved. CMS missionaries had up to this time suffered no physical harm in China.

But early in 1895 news had come of an anti-authoritarian society called "Vegetarians", and for a while the women and children were evacuated from Ku-cheng to Fuh-chow. By the hot holiday month the danger appeared to be over, and most had come back and gone out to the more isolated cottages twelve miles from Ku-cheng.

Early in the morning of 1 August, a band of "Vegetarians" attacked the two cottages where the missionaries were staying. Very quickly Mr. and Mrs. Stewart, the two Australian sisters, and four CEZMS missionaries, were killed. The Stewarts' five youngest children were there, with their nurse, who was also killed. The children escaped from the burning house, but two were injured and later died. One CEZMS lady, also terribly injured, escaped; eleven were dead.

CMS missionaries had been killed "on active service" before, but never so many, together, and including women and children. There was terrible shock among the expatriate community in Hong Kong, who held a protest meeting and demanded vengeance. But the missions involved, and other missionary societies in England, when they were able to arrange a meeting in London (on 13 August – the cable system had enabled such news now to be communicated rapidly) used it for praise and prayer, and no word of vengeance was uttered. They declined the offer of the British Government to press for compensation from the Chinese authorities. So some good came out of the tragedy, and the number of those enquiring about Christianity in the area increased in the months after the massacre. Violence was far from over in China, but as it happened the CMS was not to suffer so much in the greater violence of the Boxer Rising which was shortly to come.

Japan to 1897

After China, Japan. After the opening of the great eastern giant, the opening of the mysterious and almost unknown islands connected to China in so many ways.

Like China, Japan had first been entered by Roman Catholic missionaries in 1549. For a period the Jesuit missionaries came in numbers and reaped a great harvest, but by 1587 there was reaction, expulsions, and a terrible period of persecution. By 1637 it seemed that no Christians remained. Earlier, in 1624, almost all foreign nations were banned from Japan, and no Japanese were allowed to leave the country; in effect, Japan was sealed off from the rest of the world. So it remained for 230 years.

The reopening of Japan came about largely through initiatives of the United States of America, and it was likewise American missions who first entered. American Episcopalians came in 1859. For a number of years they were totally circumscribed in what they could do – they could not preach, or teach religion openly; they could and did teach English in Japanese schools, they learned Japanese themselves and distributed Chinese scriptures discreetly. These were understood by educated people.

The breakthrough came after the great revolution of 1868, when the social and bureaucratic structure of Japan was turned around – by the free choice of its "barons", the Daimios. The emperor, the Mikado, was confirmed in his authority and his capital was moved to what became Tokyo. The treaties made with the USA and with Britain in 1858 could now be fully implemented, and the people and leaders of Japan were open and willing for change which would enable Japan to benefit from the technical advances of the West. In 1872 the public notices which forbade the practice of Christianity were removed, and although the law was not changed, it was not enforced.

During this time – in January 1869 – the first CMS missionary landed at Nagasaki – the Rev. George Ensor. In 1870 he was joined by the Rev. H. Burnside. They were both sent out supported by a specially designated gift, and by 1873 public Christian services were being held.

As with China, Japan never became a "leading" CMS field, and American missionary societies were always more prominent. The SPG and the CMS were the only English societies to enter in the early period. Small-scale work – daily preaching and teaching – began to be effective, and in 1876 six people were baptised and confirmed (by the Bishop of Victoria, Hong Kong) at Osaka. By the end of 1882 there were about 600 baptised Japanese in association with the CMS and the other two Episcopal missions (SPG and American).

Up to that time the episcopal functions were carried out through visits from the Bishop of Victoria. There was also a bishop for the American Episcopal work. Now it was arranged that the Archbishop of Canterbury would nominate an English bishop, hopefully acceptable to both the CMS and the SPG. He nominated and consecrated a CMS missionary in India, the Rev. Arthur Poole, who sadly lived only till 1885. His successor was the Rev. Edward Bickersteth, also a missionary in India with the Cambridge Brotherhood in Delhi. His family background (as a grandson of the early CMS secretary) assisted his acceptance by the CMS, and he was a much loved bishop up to his death in 1897.

The work in Japan went on in several centres, Osaka being the chief, with regular preaching, and with teaching in schools and in smaller groups. Church schools were also founded – the Bishop Poole Memorial Girls' School and Momoyama School in Osaka. Whatever arguments there were elsewhere about the merits of evangelistic as against educational work, it was clear that in Japan education and especially the teaching of English would continue to be the main route to contact with the Japanese people.

In 1884 a theological school was set up in Osaka. It was called in English "Holy Trinity Divinity College", and the Japanese name was, literally, "The One-God-in-Three Teaching House". Bishop Bickersteth saw the need for the proudly nationalistic Japanese people to have their own Church, and as early as 1887 – only eleven years after the first baptisms – the Japanese Church (Nippon Sei-Kokwai) was organised from the three Episcopal missions. At that time there were only three Japanese deacons, but fifty Japanese lay representatives were present at the organising meeting. Although, as in other areas, many Christians came out of the poorer classes, there were already in the Japanese Church well-educated professional people, and for this reason and others it was right for its time. By 1900 at least seventeen Japanese men had been ordained, and one missionary had been sent to work in Formosa.

In Japan, unlike many other fields, the missionaries had virtually no internal help from Christian groups within the country but outside the mission. There was no ancient Church to be revived, no Company chaplains, no already converted nationals who had travelled abroad. But they did receive some voluntary help from expatriate Christians who were teachers in government schools, and a few contacted in this way later came back as missionaries. The use of women missionaries in Japan was extensive and demonstrated their value as evangelists among young men, not just as workers among women and girls. The opening of Japan came just as the CMS was ready to send out women, and by 1894 over thirty had gone to Japan. One was Katherine Tristram, a university lecturer in mathematics, who seems to have been the first woman graduate sent out, in 1888. She became principal of the Bishop Poole Memorial Girls' School. Many of the men who went to Japan were graduates; like China, Japan was perceived as needing the best candidates. The women were also generally of the higher social and educational background, demonstrated by the large proportion who were honorary missionaries, and who were connected with CMS dignitaries.

The early historian of the CMS mentions in particular the influence of women missionaries in teaching classes of young men. "In most mission-fields any such influence is neither possible nor desirable; but Japan is exceptional, as it is in so many other respects." Classes among police officers, schoolboys, soldiers and doctors, were all held. English was usually the first attraction. But the Bible was also studied in Japanese and a number of baptisms were reported. Women missionaries also conducted a training school for Bible women, and taught girls, but mainly in day schools; there was little hospital work (a leper hospital had been opened in 1895), few boarding schools, and no orphanages.

Another interesting and responsive field was opened among the Ainu, the indigenous Caucasoid people of the northern island, Hokkaido. The Rev. John Batchelor went to Hokkaido in 1883, and reduced the Ainu language to writing. By 1885 the first baptisms had taken place, and in the 1890s a considerable number were baptised.

With the growth of the Church, and the inevitable difficulties of travelling in an island nation, it seemed advisable to divide the diocese, and in the mid-1890s the two dioceses became four. Two were reserved for the "American mission"; two others for the "English" (CMS or SPG) work.

In the early days of missions in Japan, there was great optimism about the possibility of Japan becoming a Christian nation. There were conversions among the socially and politically prominent, including members of the legislature. The traditional beliefs seemed weak and moribund (compared to Islam and Hinduism) and there was such a strong desire to absorb the best of Western thought and skills. There was no caste system, and in many ways Japanese culture seemed compatible with Western culture and so (it was hoped) with the religion of the West.

But by the end of the century such hopes had dulled. The Churches were growing – slowly – and there were able and faithful Japanese clergy. But "there had been a kind of half-patriotic reaction against Western influence, and Christianity was looked upon as a disloyal religion." Buddhism and Shinto, the nationalistic cult, re-established themselves as a result. In Japan the missions had never played much part in organised educational, social or medical work, for the excellence of local institutions made this unnecessary. So there was no large bureaucracy for supervising primary schools, or dispensaries and hospitals, which in some missions had given an illusion of importance and influence. English classes and a few good secondary schools were important in making contacts, but in Japan actual preaching and teaching of various groups – young, old, professional, occupational – had been the main outlet of the missionaries. Progress was thus slower, but when it came it was real.

Ceylon (Sri Lanka) to 1886

Ceylon, the beautiful island at India's southern tip, has been in many ways a microcosm of the missionary problems of larger countries. In Ceylon, beside the indigenous Singhalese people, there was a considerable community of Tamil-speaking people who had been settled for centuries in the northern peninsula known as Jaffna. They differed in language, appearance and religion from the Singhalese. Later large numbers of Tamils came to the coffee plantations in the central hill country as migrant labourers. There was a considerable Burgher community – analogous to the Eurasian community in India – of mixed Dutch or Portuguese and local ancestry, and usually at least nominally Christian. In the cities and on the coffee estates there were many British men and women who needed the ministration of chaplains. A number were Scottish and so not of Anglican background.

The CMS had sent its first missionaries to Ceylon in 1817–1818, and chaplains continued in a few places, but for a considerable period no bishop was appointed, though the Bishop of Calcutta and then of Madras came on visitations from time to time. The SPG gave some support to three local clergy, but sent no missionaries until after the appointment of the first bishop in 1845. But in the confined island situation the missionaries of very different traditions did not always cooperate well, and the first-comers, the CMS, having been left so long almost alone, tended to act independently of the bishop and the rest of the diocese.

The CMS had sent twenty-two missionaries to Ceylon from the beginning to 1848 when ten of these were still working there. They found their work discouraging and their reports expressed this. By 1849 there were some 3,000 adherents, but only 300 communicant members, which showed the continuing effects of the Dutch policy of forced conversions, by which men who wished to progress in government service had had to become Christians. The schools with nearly 3,000 pupils were more encouraging. But in 1850 the missionary community suffered a double blow when two missionaries, still young and vigorous, died. One had been head of the Cotta Institution, and after his death the CMS took the chance of changing its nature from that of a training institution for catechists and (hopefully) local clergy, to that of a general fee-paying school, accepting Christians and non-Christians and giving a good general education. With a new and able missionary head (C. C. Fenn, later a CMS secretary) it prospered in this new role.

Two other new ventures were the Singhalese Itinerant Mission (sometimes called the Kandyan Itinerary) which sought to reach non-Christian villagers in the hills around Kandy (from 1853); and, from 1854, the Tamil Coolie Mission, reaching out to the Tamil migrant workers, some of whom were already Christians. For this work Tamil-speaking catechists from Tinnevelly and Mengnanapuram (in India) were also used. Some of the planters, not necessarily Anglicans, helped in this work with money and their interest, and served on a committee to administer it, but the work was distinctly Anglican and under the CMS missionaries. The work among the permanent Tamil community in Jaffna also continued.

So some progress was being made, and with the support of the SPG the bishop was able to allocate staff to better advantage. But the administration of the CMS and its relationship to and with the bishop continued to cause problems, which finally led to what became known as the "Ceylon Controversy".

Before that period, however, there was, from 1862–1864, something of a Buddhist revival, with aggressive efforts by Buddhist priests to bring people back to the traditional faith. It was successful in turning thousands of nominal hereditary Christians back to Buddhism, but it also had an opposite and beneficial result in making other nominal Christians realise that the two faiths were incompatible, and in their consciously choosing the Christian faith. So by the time that the Ceylon mission celebrated its jubilee in 1868, there was a more hopeful spirit.

In 1850 the CMS had sent George Pettitt, an experienced Tamil-speaking missionary from south India, to be secretary of the mission, and to build up in Colombo a Corresponding Committee. But the attempt was a failure, and in 1854 the administrative responsibility reverted to where it had previously been, to the missionaries in conference. Pettitt was, however, effective in building up the Church in Colombo. He himself conducted services in English, Singhalese and Tamil at the new and afterwards well-known church erected at Galle Face. He returned to England in 1855 and the services continued under his successor, the Rev. Henry Whitley, who, sadly, died in an accident in 1860.

Three bishops served Ceylon from 1845 to 1874; the third, Bishop Jermyn, became ill and retired after only three years.

His successor was Reginald Stephen Copleston, "a brilliant young Oxford don of decidedly high-Church views." As well as being devout and missionary-minded he was tall and handsome, and a brilliant linguist, and he was so young that his consecration had to be postponed until he reached his thirtieth birthday. Afterwards his opponents were to call him the "boy bishop". Unfortunately, when he arrived in Ceylon in February 1876, there was no experienced archdeacon who might have advised him, and the dominating personality among the CMS missionaries was William Oakley, a strong figure who by 1876 had already served in Ceylon for forty-one years, without leave in England. He had been the secretary and treasurer of the Ceylon mission for many years, and was not accustomed to compromise or consultation with high-Church views.

Bishop Copleston was genuinely concerned for an extension of mission, and he wished the chaplains located in different centres to participate in mission as well. He therefore asked the missionaries, who were often working in the same geographic area as chaplains, but among a different population, to inform the chaplains of what they were doing, and cooperate with them. Unfortunately many of the chaplains were men who had arrived recently and knew no language but English, and senior and experienced missionaries saw themselves being treated as curates to their juniors. Still more difficult, the chaplains were in many cases "advanced churchmen", and the missionaries strongly disagreed with the services they led and the furnishings of their churches. The bishop also demanded that all layworkers – which here meant the Tamil catechists participating in the Tamil Coolie Mission – should come directly under the bishop's jurisdiction. But the missionaries, who had recruited them and who paid them from CMS funds, regarded them as directly under their own authority, and this claim was one that persisted. The Tamil Coolie Mission was financially supported by many planters, a proportion of whom were non-Anglican,

and although the teaching given and the church groups
organised were strictly Anglican, any "high-Church
ritualism" introduced would destroy the working relationship
which allowed the Tamil Coolie Mission to function under
CMS direction. In 1876 matters came to a head in a deep
disagreement between the Rev. W. Clark, senior CMS missionary connected with the Coolie Mission, and the bishop.
There were misunderstandings and misjudgements on both
sides, and the bishop's youth and inexperience was clearly a
factor, but behind such misunderstandings lay the distrust of
the Evangelical churchmen for the new ways – pictures and
altar crosses and innovations in celebrating Communion.
The bishop finally withdrew his licence from the twelve
ordained missionaries. The bishops of the province intervened
and interceded, and within a month the bishop had returned
the licences of all, except that of the Rev. W. Clark.

Naturally news of the affair arrived in England, and not
only to the committees of the CMS. The religious press,
already divided over ritualism, found all their prejudices
confirmed either by the reports of "low-Church missionaries"
in league with "dissenting planters", or of the "ritualistic
boy-bishop". The CMS General Committee discussed the
issue in October 1876, passing a series of resolutions "by
which they claimed that they were entitled to expect that a
bishop would not withdraw a missionary licence once granted
without duly assigned legal cause". In addition, they
would not admit that the bishop had the right "to assume to
himself the management of a mission of theirs or of any
part of it"!

The Bishops of India and Ceylon, meeting in March 1877
for the consecration of the two suffragan bishops for Madras
diocese, took advantage of the occasion to confer together.
An important principle was at stake, and it was expressed in
a part of the resolution they passed on the relations of missionary societies and diocesan organisations: ". . . That the
Bishop of every Diocese is in the last resort responsible for all

teaching given and all work done in the name of and under the authority of the Church."

The CMS received the resolution and later in 1877 adopted a memorandum concerning it. Four points were made which had an importance that reached far beyond the island of Ceylon. They maintained: (1) that individual churchmen had a right to carry on missionary work and "to control, within proper limits, the organisation created by them"; (2) that the work carried on with a society's funds cannot be controlled by a diocesan organisation; (3) that a bishop appointed by Letters Patent, with legally-defined powers, is in a different position from a missionary bishop with undefined authority.

The fourth point was that the "ecclesiastical arrangements for Native Christians in countries like India and China, where they will be the majority, must differ from the arrangements in colonies like Canada and New Zealand, where the Natives, being a small minority, are naturally absorbed into the Colonial Church".

Thus the "ultimate rights" of a bishop depended on whether he was a bishop appointed by Letters Patent (i.e. within a British territory) or whether he was a missionary bishop. And it must be added that the fear which underlay this conclusion was that a missionary bishop of the "wrong views" – not a low-churchman or an Evangelical – could, when without the constraints which existed in a Church established under law, destroy all that the CMS agents had built up. Copleston was undoubtedly seen by most of the CMS missionaries in Ceylon as such a bishop, and they were determined to oppose him.

Although the new metropolitan, Bishop Johnson of Calcutta, and Bishop Gell of Madras thought that their resolutions had settled matters, actions by the missionaries in Ceylon during 1877 soon worsened the situation. But the local events were only a part of a drama of much more extensive importance. Who controls clerical and lay workers in a mission field? The appointed bishop or the workers themselves, responsible only to a lay body in a distant country?

In 1878 the affair was discussed at the second Lambeth conference, from which, at that time, the CMS stood aloof, and the misunderstandings and confusion deepened. Later in 1878 the CMS missionaries refused to participate in a Communion service led by the bishop, in the cathedral in Colombo, because they objected to the ritual followed. Bishop Copleston behaved with generosity and restraint, and in May 1879 a service was held at which one of the missionaries presided and the bishop and all clergy participated. But the difficulties were not settled, and there was a real danger of schism, with a separate "native Church" being set up.

In the end the Archbishop of Canterbury was asked to arbitrate, and he did so, calling on the Archbishop of York and the Bishops of London, Durham and Winchester. The Church in Ceylon was still — at that time — an established Church and so "the tribunals of the Church of England might be presumed to have 'legal cognizance' of what went on there." Furthermore, even an informed "opinion" coming from five such leaders would have great weight with both the Society and the bishop.

The actual negotiations were long and difficult, but Archbishop Tait persisted, and the "Opinion or Advice" was delivered to the Society on 1 March 1880. The matter of licences for clergy and the situation of lay agents was clearly and definitely laid down, but in many other areas the "Opinion" left the situation open and did not pass judgements on the past.

Henry Wright, acting for the CMS, and Bishop Copleston now had to work out the details and, with goodwill and give and take on both sides, this was achieved. Henry Wright had also to take into account the views of more conservative English Evangelicals. If he gave away too much, the whole situation might again become inflamed, and this time, perhaps, schism would not be avoided.

But the concordat did work, despite the difficulties. And in 1881 the Government of Ceylon announced their decision that the Anglican Church in Ceylon should be disestablished. Financial support would be phased out over five years. The Church was now forced to consider its future constitution and an assembly was summoned. In the discussions which took place during the interim period the experience of the CMS in other colonies was important, and the constitution finally adopted, in 1886, was based on that worked out for New Zealand by Bishop Selwyn and his clergy, who included CMS missionaries.

At the time of the Ceylon jubilee, in 1868, the growth of the Church in Ceylon was felt to have been slow and disappointing; in 1888, as the new independent Church got under way, the outlook was brighter. There were 6,500 adherents, and 2,000 of these were communicants; there were now thirteen local clergy and the number of children attending the church schools had also increased. Progress continued, and Trinity College, Kandy, was seeing non-Christian pupils coming into faith frequently. One other milestone should be mentioned. In 1886 William Oakley died. He was seventy-eight, and had been in Ceylon for fifty-one years, without ever returning to England. His death and the new constitution marked the end of one era and the beginning of another.

9   TAKING STOCK: CMS AT THE CENTENARY AND AFTER

Introductory survey

In 1899 the CMS celebrated its centenary, not only in England, but all around the world. The Editorial Secretary, Eugene Stock, had completed for the occasion his masterly three-volume history. He then planned to take the story up to 1915, and the fourth, supplementary volume was published in 1916.

In that book he surveys, field by field, the work of the CMS from the centenary to 1914–15. The Churches he writes of are of very different ages, and might be expected to show problems arising at different stages of development. What is surprising, then, is the relative uniformity of the questions which exercise them – the similarities, rather than the differences. It seems that the general spirit of the age has superceded the various regional and national tendencies. The later-founded Churches have rushed through infancy and adolescence; earlier Churches had lingered there longer and developed more slowly. Not that differences did not exist, but they were differences of environment rather than of age, and fewer than might have been expected.

The first thing one notices is that across all the different missions the Christians are still identified by missionary society rather than by Church. Even in a country like Japan, considered to have advanced rather rapidly in church organisation, with seven cooperating dioceses uniting missionaries of several different Anglican missions, the number of

Christians linked to each mission is still listed separately. A Japanese "Anglican" was still primarily "American" or "CMS" or "SPG".

But along with this runs the longing for united Churches within the one tradition, for inter-communion immediately, and for the more distant goal of organic unity across all the denominations. The period we are speaking of was to see the Edinburgh 1910 conference. It was not the first conference of its type, and the CMS had sent official representatives to the Ecumenical Missionary Conference held in New York in 1900. But Edinburgh heralded a new spirit, a change of direction, and new hope. The leadership undoubtedly came from Dr. John R. Mott of the Student Volunteer Movement. It was the student conferences and the student organisation which paved the way for Edinburgh in 1910.

To an Anglican society like the CMS one of the important aspects of Edinburgh was the participation, at least as individuals, of "high" Anglicans. While they cannot be discussed in detail here, the actual meetings, the preliminary reports, and their publication with the discussions resulting, were all of the greatest importance. But two other results should be noted. One was the launching of the quarterly *International Review of Missions* in 1912. Another was the setting up of a Continuation Committee, which led to important follow-up meetings in various parts of the world. Edinburgh 1910 finally culminated, through the continuation committee and the world-wide conferences arranged by it, in the founding of the International Missionary Council, set up in 1921. The IMC made its British headquarters at Edinburgh House, 2 Eaton Gate, London, which was the office of the CBMS, and to the purchase of which the CMS had made a contribution. Cooperation with the IMC and the CBMS continued to be close, and J. H. Oldham at Edinburgh House was adviser and friend to many missionaries as well as to officials of the Society.

In country after country, missionaries and national

Christians, looking at the place and position of Christians in nations still largely attached to other faiths, were becoming increasingly conscious of their divisions. Intercommunion was the first answer, and the famous conference at Kikuyu, Kenya, in 1913 showed how partial an answer that still was. Organic union was clearly still far away. The first step was to unite at least the missions of the same ecclesiastical tradition into one Church – an obvious answer, but not yet accomplished in some places up to the present day (as witness the American Methodist and English Methodist Churches in Zimbabwe). The Japanese Church was one example of Episcopalians – American, Canadian, English Evangelical and English "high Church" – coming together; their dioceses were separate but united in the *Nippon Sei-Kokwai*. In India also Anglicans of varying tradition and background combined for various activities and within dioceses. And though in Africa a smaller Christian population had earlier kept the problem from arising, Kikuyu 1913 showed clearly that there also the question of inter-communion and organic unity must be faced.

A further tendency observable across many of the mission fields was the rising level of nationalist consciousness, with resentment of external rule or external influence, and the wish to be responsible for one's own destiny. It is likely that missionaries became aware of this sooner than most government officials, since they usually spoke the vernaculars and were in touch with the "grass roots". The First World War, when it came, and earlier the deaths of Queen Victoria and of King Edward VII, called up much patriotic loyalty to the British Crown, which was of great comfort to the missionaries. Easy as it is now to be cynical, the persons of the British royal family did provide a focus of real feeling for people reared in traditional societies with a royal family. But depths of the new nationalism still underlay the pro-British expressions of loyalty.

Right across the whole range of missions, certain issues

were commonly seen as problems and challenges. One was the "threat" of Islam, seen to be advancing rapidly and posing a real danger to Christian expansion. In view of what actually took place, it may now be asked whether Islam was as strong as many missionaries then thought. The areas of most concern were not of course the solidly and traditionally Muslim regions but the "pagan" areas which were seen as potentially Christian. There was much resentment of the protection of Islam in places like northern Nigeria, the Sudan, Egypt, and parts of India. Friday was decreed the weekly holiday "both in Egypt and the Sudan . . . quite a needless concession, as no Moslem objects to working after his attendance at mosque". In India the tolerance of the British administrators to other religions in general was seen as exceeding the bounds of necessity.

The position of women in changing societies likewise provoked concern. Even where laws had changed, customs changed more slowly, and the women, conservative, not always literate, might well hold back the progress of a whole Christian family. The example of the lives lived by the women missionaries themselves, whether wives, widows or single women, was doubtless as important in influencing the Christian women as any teaching given by such missionaries.

As far as the Churches went, there was much appreciation for the faithful leadership and service of many national clergy. But, overall, self-support was a problem, and the missionaries were far from knowing how to increase giving from peoples more accustomed to receiving. Many Christians were seen as nominal only, and there was great longing and prayer for Churches made up of live and active members, not just "cradle Christians". As the Churches grew, so the need for shared responsibility through some form of synodical government was also felt. In many areas the actual problem was growth – too many catechumens to teach thoroughly; too few catechists and clergy to undertake adequate teaching.

Around the world the number of communicants had continued to increase. Sierra Leone was now reckoned to be over one half Christian, and the influence of the Christian schools was important. In Nigeria the pressures of Islam were greatly felt, and in addition the British Government seemed to support – or, at least, did little to prevent – the liquor traffic which fuelled much social evil. Though after Bishop Crowther's death no other African had been appointed as a diocesan bishop, there had been three African assistant bishops. One of these three was a Nigerian; the two others were Sierra Leoneans returned to their ancestral home.

In East Africa the Church was expanding rapidly, though less rapidly in German East Africa than in the other two territories. Circuits of primary schools were of great importance here, as in Sierra Leone and Nigeria.

In the Sudan, Egypt, Palestine and Persia it was medical work which continued to be the main link between missions and people. This was also so in the northern – Islamicised – provinces of India. In India as a whole, primary schools continued to be of minor importance, except in parts of the south and in tribal "mass-movement" areas. But the Christian higher-level boarding schools and the hostels for Christian students associated with day schools continued to provide a trickle of converts important beyond their number. Special ministries to leprosy patients, to the blind, for orphaned girls and for widows were continued. In 1912 the first Indian bishop had been consecrated – V. S. Azariah of Dornakal. He had been groomed for leadership through student work – in his case the YMCA – and had made a notable contribution as one of the comparatively few non-missionary delegates at Edinburgh 1910. There was to be no other Indian diocesan bishop until the 1940s. The CMS was the largest missionary society in India, in terms of missionary numbers, and the adherents of the Churches set up by the various Anglican societies made up the largest Protestant Church.

In China the political unrest continued almost unabated

until 1911, when after the "Great Revolution" the Republic was proclaimed (1912). The so-called Boxer Rising of 1899–1900 saw over two hundred missionaries and members of their families killed in the Shansi massacre, and a score of others were killed between 1897 and 1906. The opium issue was finally settled in 1913, when Britain agreed to forego the last agreed imports of opium into China.

By far the largest denominational grouping in China was Presbyterian, and after that, Methodist. North American missionary societies accounted for very large proportions of both groups. The China Inland Mission, which commenced only in 1865, had achieved remarkable growth, being the fourth largest in terms of adherents, and the first in numbers of missionaries.

The follow-up work of the Edinburgh 1910 Continuation Committee was especially influential in China. Meetings were organised by Dr. Mott, and he and Sherwood Eddy of the Indian YMCA also led several missions for university students. On the side of the Anglican work, the conference of bishops organised in April 1907 a conference with delegates from each diocese, which in effect set up a general synod for the *Chung Hua Sheng Kung Hui*, as they named it. It first met as a general synod in 1912. Some schools, hospitals, and opium addiction centres were run, but work directly related to evangelism was more important in China than educational or medical work.

Japan had proved a disappointment to its missionaries in relation to early high hopes. From 1899 the legal and even social disadvantages of Christians became very much less, and the numbers of adherents was rising (from 25,000 Protestants in 1888 to 83,000 in 1912). But one problem noted was that of leakage. In a relatively mobile and increasingly urbanised society, a large number of baptised Christians (estimated as close to 30,000 in 1900) simply failed to transfer their membership when they moved, and just disappeared. Missionaries considered also that the number of people ethically influenced by Christianity was very much greater that the number actually baptised. Another problem, as well as leakage, was the spread of Unitarian theology which appealed to many sophisticated Japanese. But there were, however, a number of politicians and men prominent in public life who were known as Christians. In Japan also Dr. Mott held important meetings, especially among students. The Anglican Church in Japan, with American, Canadian and British missions participating, was more highly organised than in some other countries with a longer Christian history. Social, medical and educational work continued to be of minor importance in Japan, except for the English language classes which were a primary source of contact. Japan, like Palestine, was an area where the contribution of women missionaries was particularly marked.

All these fields were ones where the CMS saw a continuing role for itself in the foreseeable future. At first that role might even be, in many respects, an increasing one; eventually it would decrease. But there were already places where the decrease was well under way.

The CMS work in Mauritius, and in the more northern Seychelles, in the Indian Ocean, had never really taken on, although encouragement had been received when Tamil-speaking catechists from Mauritius received theological training in India, and went back to minister to their own communities. The SPG had worked there also, and from 1907 the CMS began to withdraw from these islands.

New Zealand had been one of the CMS's earliest and most favoured fields in terms of the interest it aroused. But from 1840 it was increasingly clear that New Zealand was to become a primarily white colony, and that the position of the Maori Christians would be as minority members of a larger Church. From 1883 a gradual withdrawal of CMS involvement had been taking place, though at the centenary the CMS was still supporting about twenty people, including the widows of missionaries. Seven of these were members of

the Williams family who gave so much to the cause of Christ in
New Zealand. In 1903 the final transfer of the mission to the
control of the Anglican Church took place. A Maori Mission
Board was formed, and financial arrangements were made to
support the ongoing work.

At the same time, the Church Missionary Association of
New Zealand was growing as a sending body. In 1913 it was
supporting fifteen missions in several overseas locations and
in New Zealand. And so as Stock says (he had visited New
Zealand) "We bid farewell to perhaps the most romantic of
all the C.M.S. missions." As he wrote in 1914 it was at the
time that the centenary of the first preaching of the Gospel in
New Zealand was being celebrated.

The other area from which the CMS was making a gradual
and phased withdrawal was Canada. Few new missionaries
were being sent out, and it was hoped to make a transfer to a
Canadian missions board, as was done in New Zealand, but
with less vigorous interest on the Canadian side there were
difficulties. The small population and the vast distances
made any kind of outreach and supervision difficult; it was
only to be perhaps in the era of the light aircraft that rapid
and effective contact would be possible. The separate British
Columbia mission presented different problems; in the face
of continuing opposition Bishop Ridley rebuilt the work at
Metlakhatla, and in 1907 when the jubilee of the work in
British Columbia was celebrated, two CMS missionaries
visited New Metlakhatla in Alaska and established friendly
contact with William Duncan, who stayed there until his
death in 1918 at the age of 85.

The 1913 Kikuyu conference and mission cooperation

It remains to say something more about the 1913 Kikuyu
conference, which excited such passion in England. British

East Africa, soon to become Kenya Colony and Protectorate, had received an influx of missions, including a number of small American organisations, with the building of the Uganda Railway. There had been a great need of comity agreements among the missions if wasted work and confusion was not to result. The CMS work in the far west of Kenya had been initiated not from the east, but from Uganda, and so Bishop Willis, Bishop Tucker's successor in Uganda, was involved in discussions with the head of the Church of Scotland Mission on the kind of arrangements which could be made to minimise the problems between these Protestant missions, which had so much in common. In June 1913 about sixty missionaries, serving in eight missions, met at Kikuyu, the CSM station not far from Nairobi. A "Proposed Scheme of Federation" for a "Native Church" was discussed, but it was not that which caused the uproar. It was the United Communion Service led by Bishop Peel of Mombasa, held in the Scottish Mission church at the end of the gathering, when missionaries of different denominations were invited to take Communion. The Communion itself was a regular Anglican service, and it is a sign of how far opinions have moved that we cannot easily appreciate the feelings of Bishop Frank Weston of Zanzibar when he protested against the conference. He appealed to the Archbishop of Canterbury (he himself was not a participant) and the fat was well and truly in the fire. Two CMS missionary bishops stood accused of "propagating heresy and of committing schism".

Discussion ran on for months in national newspapers and in Church-related publications – and even in *Punch*. The *Church Missionary Review* gave month-to-month reports of the progress of the controversy, and in July 1914 the consultative body appointed by the Archbishop of Canterbury met to discuss the whole group of issues raised by Bishop Weston. Their report, and the archbishop's comments, were not published until April 1915. As might have been expected, neither the non-conformists nor the high-Churchmen were much pleased by the very moderate conclusions on intercommunion – but a world war was now raging and the issues became overshadowed by others more urgent.

In Kenya no very dramatic results were seen, and no "united Church" resulted. Relations between the principal missionary societies continued to be good; a continuation committee was set up which led to the foundation of an "alliance of missions", and later to the Kenya Missionary Council (ultimately to become the National Christian Council of Kenya). The decisions on inter-communion were important for the CMS, since it was for a long time the only non-Catholic society with churches in the cities of Nairobi and Mombasa, and inevitably Africans coming from other missions became adherents while working in the city. The chief result of the alliance was, in Kenya, the founding of Alliance High School, which was to have so marked an influence on the educational and political development of the colony.

The World War 1914–1918

Meanwhile, in August 1914, the World War had been declared. It affected the CMS (and all missionary bodies) through the recruitment of individuals into the armed services, and through the dangers of and restrictions on travel. But in some fields there was greater disruption. This was principally in German colonies where British nationals were working, and in areas in British and French colonies where German nationals worked. The missionary societies as a whole felt under obligation to give help to the Churches and societies affected in this way. So, for the duration of the war, work in many parts of the world did little but mark time, and in some cases slipped backwards. But there were cases where the removal of missionary supervision led to the emergence of local leadership.

The lack of new missionaries and the slow return of those on leave were the first negative results of the war, since sailings were soon cancelled; the transfer of funds was also affected and eventually the amount of money available also dropped. A number of male missionaries, chiefly laymen, volunteered for active service; some ordained men became chaplains. A few missionary bishops became chaplains, including Bishop Gwynne of Khartoum, who became Deputy Chaplain-General; Bishop Taylor Smith, another CMS missionary, formerly of Sierra Leone, was Chaplain-General.

In West Africa British missionaries in the German colonies of Togoland and Cameroon were interned and deported, and the numerous German missionaries of the Basel Mission in the Gold Coast were also affected. British troops eventually occupied the German colonies, and captured German civilians were cared for by missionaries. In East Africa the long boundaries of German East Africa marched with both Uganda and Kenya, and also the Belgian Congo. The British missionaries of the CMS and the UMCA were interned at Tabora and on the whole well-treated. The whole of the eastern Mediterranean area was the object of concern, since Turkey was aligned with Germany and these countries were, like Turkey, Muslim. It was feared that the lives of British Christians might be in danger. But, in fact, open support for the British cause was often displayed, and most missionaries were offered safe passage out. In India the fields operated by German-based missions, like the Gossner mission in Chota Nagpur, were severely disrupted by the internment of missionaries. The CMS still had a few German missionaries, like Paul Zenker of north India, in Anglican orders and resident in India since 1866. At the age of seventy he was interned and eventually repatriated to a Germany he hardly knew. It was a sad end to a long and faithful service, for he died in 1920.

There were two German women, also elderly, in the same situation. The Roman Catholic missions, in India and in Africa, were much more severely affected, for their personnel included many German and Austrian nationals. French and Belgian men were recalled to their home countries to be conscripted, and funds for their missions dried up. The Edinburgh Continuation Committee, under J. H. Oldham, was able to send some funds to the continental missions, and in most places missionaries in adjacent areas took on the extra task of helping to supervise what were known as "orphan missions". And the national clergy rose to the crisis and congregations continued to meet for services.

The effect of the war on national Christians (and others) in the colonies is more difficult to document. The spectacle of Christian nations fighting one another was not easy for missionaries to explain away; there had been much self-righteous criticism of "bloodthirsty savages" who seem by comparison peaceful peasants. But the righteousness of the British cause was still an axiom to most British Christians.

From British East Africa (Kenya), to take an example, a long and hard campaign was fought across the plains of "German East" even down into Nyasaland, the British forces in pursuit of the elusive and talented German commander, Von Lettow-Vorbeck. The already-enlisted units of the King's African Rifles were involved, and further recruitment was not for fighting men but for porters. The Carrier Corps was formed, and over the course of the war thousands and thousands of Africans were conscripted for service. Probably as many as 350,000 "unarmed porters" were used, in addition to 14,000 native soldiers. Over 42,000 died, mainly of disease, though the official death-toll was under 24,000.

When it became clear that many young Christians would be recruited (by force), Dr. John Arthur of the Church of Scotland mission put forward the idea of a Kikuyu missions volunteer corps, which was raised in 1917 from adherents of the missions in the alliance, mainly in Kikuyu and Kavirondo. Missionaries became the officers of this corps, which comprised 2,000 men, and which had a very much better record for survival. One of the officers who went to German East

Africa with the volunteers was Handley Hooper, only son of
Douglas Hooper, who had gone to his father's old station,
Kahuhia, just before the war. The close relations forged in
that period stood him in good stead in the 1920s, when young
Kikuyu Christians began organising themselves into a
political association. The Great War had taken them into
new places and brought them into contact with a wide variety
of people and, especially, had shown them that even the
white men were vulnerable to hunger and thirst, disease and
bullets. Certainly in Kenya relations between the administration and Africans were never the same after the war, and
this was true over a much wider area.

10 RETREAT AND ADVANCE
1918–1942

Introduction

The World War ended on 11 November 1918, and there was
a slow return to normality, if a world could ever again be
normal which had in four years seen almost ten million men
die in battle, without reckoning the wounded, the refugees,
those who died of disease. The pan-epidemic of influenza
prolonged the suffering well into 1919. It was not only the
countries of Europe and the Middle East, scene of the main
hostilities, which suffered. A missionary doctor in the Kikuyu
area of Kenya reckoned that deaths among the Kikuyu alone
from war service and the diseases and famine which followed
amounted to 120,000. Casualties among Indian troops were
particularly heavy, though few Indian Christians were
involved. Missionaries had volunteered or been called up as
chaplains or medical doctors. Furloughs had been missed;
missionary families were separated. A return to the pre-war
situation was not likely to be rapid; in fact, it was never going
to be the same again.

For it was a changed world in which the CMS and other
mission agencies were now called to work. The war had seen
violent revolutions sweep away governments, as in Russia; it
had – possibly – also prevented violent revolution in other
places, such as Ireland. New forces of nationalism and self-
determination were working, and in part at least they had
been unleashed by the missionaries who had preached justice
and equality and established schools and colleges where such

theories were taught. In the years before the war missionaries were constantly being exhorted to encourage the development of self-supporting, self-governing and self-expanding Churches. The period of rapid missionary expansion which began in 1887 had been accompanied by the "policy of faith" with regard to finance, and by 1912 this was pushing the society to its limits. Though the problem had been tackled in an imaginative and sacrificial way, it remained a problem.

After the war, rising inflation and the heavy losses through sterling exchange rates magnified the financial problems, and the CMS began to report a deficit on every annual budget. Only during the Second World War, when the whole mission enterprise was turned upside down – few recruits, staff reductions at home – was no deficit recorded.

From 1910 to 1923 the CMS General Secretary was the Rev. Cyril Bardsley, who left to become first secretary of the Missionary Council of the Church Assembly, and shortly afterwards Bishop of Peterborough. His successor as CMS General Secretary was, uniquely in the CMS history, a layman. He was Dr. Herbert Lankester, who had come on to the headquarters staff through his medical work, but latterly had been lay secretary in charge of finances. His appointment was by intention a short term one, and he retired in 1926. But the theological crisis which came to a head in 1922 made a lay secretary an appropriate and conciliatory appointment.

The decade of controversy 1912–1922

The CMS had never been immune to theological argument, and a number of issues had divided its supporters over the years. It had from the beginning sought to be inclusive rather than exclusive, an Anglican society rather than a party group, but inevitably it had been seen as a rallying centre for Evangelicals – a role which had not been denied. The CMS *was* an evangelical society, but it did not require of its missionary agents – or members – doctrinal commitments beyond those of the Church of England.

Some of the earlier occasions of division within the CMS now require a great effort of the imagination if we are to appreciate them. In the 1830s it was the Trinitarian-Socinian debate, which is still a matter for possible theological discussion. But later it centred on what we now see as minor issues, like the wearing of the surplice in the pulpit and (in the 1880s) the holding of a CMS service in St. Paul's Cathedral in front of a new reredos which incorporated images. The various theological innovations of the Tractarian or Anglo-Catholic movement were not in themselves a matter of debate, since Evangelicals of all shades of opinion rejected them. But if not a danger to missionaries, such views were seen as a potential danger to CMS catechists, clergy and students in overseas seminaries, colleges and universities, who had to be protected. In 1912 a group of clergy presented a memorial to the CMS committee deprecating aspects of the Society's activities, and in particular its inviting men to speak at CMS functions "who have encouraged the development of the Tractarian movement". It was in the main the more superficial aspects of the Anglo-Catholic movement which were threatening, especially as a number of Evangelical clergy found its emphasis on higher standards in church music and furnishings, and in matters of ceremonial, helpful.

But more important in the rising controversy were the divisive effects of biblical criticism. And the results of the 1910 Edinburgh Conference, which stressed comprehensiveness and cooperation, were a further threat. Cyril Bardsley was in the forefront in the development of missionary cooperation, and during his term of office he was under increasing attack by the more conservative. Although in 1914 a number of northern incumbents, led by Theodore Woods of Bradford, wrote to the CMS president expressing their "complete confidence in the leadership of our present Honorary Secretary", the criticisms continued.

In 1917 another memorial was presented to the CMS which defended and approved the more liberal views of Bardsley. It made three points which it requested the Society to affirm. The first two emphasised the comprehensiveness of the CMS and its willingness to cooperate with those of other schools of thought within the Anglican Communion. The third point was perhaps the most crucial and controversial: "The Society's position with regard to revelation and inspiration is defined for it simply by the formularies of the Church of England; and that no further restriction or definition of belief on these subjects is sought from its candidates, agents or supporters."

After receiving and discussing this memorial (in November 1917), the General Committee set up a representative sub-committee to discuss it, and to take account of "other questions raised among the Society's members and friends about the position of the Society." Before any report had been received from the sub-committee, two further memorials had been received, one countering and one supporting the first. The sub-committee met in January 1918 and discussed the issues raised in all three memorials. Their report, signed unanimously by all twenty-two members, was presented to the General Committee in February 1918. At first reading Bardsley was delighted. On all points it supported his own liberal and comprehensive stance. But, though adopted by the General Committee, it was immediately attacked in the *English Churchman* and by the council of the Church Association. Bardsley was forced to the defensive, clinging to his hope of maintaining a society representative of all sections of the Evangelical school:

There have always been Conservatives and Liberals amongst us. Again and again the Conservatives have attacked the position of the Liberals and tried to limit the Society in accordance with their own views, but such attempts have caused heart-burnings . . . Unless the principle of comprehension is accepted there cannot be peace, and the deepest life and best service in the CMS. [Letter from Bardsley, November 1918]

But the Conservatives were not satisfied, and their next assault came directly, through the CMS general committee. The organisation of the CMS made this possible in a way that would not have happened in most societies. The CMS general committee, which met monthly, was unusually open in its composition. It consisted of twenty-four laymen, elected at the annual general meeting, and of any clergy members (subscribers) who chose to attend. The total attending was usually about sixty, but there was nothing to prevent the numbers swelling to several hundreds should that number elect to come. Four years after the sub-committee's report, under the leadership of the Rev. Daniel Bartlett, this happened. Bartlett put a resolution to the March meeting of the committee. The immediate provocation was reports on a series of sermons preached by a CMS missionary in Hong Kong, said to put forward "higher critical" views of the Old Testament. Bartlett's resolution read:

Whereas the authority of Holy Scripture as the Word of God necessarily involves the trustworthiness of its historical records and the validity of its teachings; and whereas Holy Scripture claims this authority for itself, and our Lord, Whose utterances are true, endorses that claim; we, the Committee of the CMS, because we believe that the acceptance of this authority, so endorsed, is necessary to the fulfilment of the missionary ideal hitherto associated with CMS, hereby undertake neither to send out as missionaries nor to appoint as teachers or responsible officials any who do not thus wholeheartedly believe and teach.

Over 400 were at the meeting, but the discussions were inconclusive. Many present said they accepted the motion personally, but were unwilling to tie the CMS to any particular formula other than those of the Church of England interpreted on well understood Evangelical lines. It was decided to arrange a conference to discuss the issues, and this was convened by the Bishop of Chelmsford and held in June. The hope was that such a meeting might promote reconciliation, and some of those attending believed that the purpose had been achieved. But when the general committee met on July 12, and Bartlett's resolution was put again in a slightly amended form, it was obvious that deep divisions remained. An amendment to the resolution was lost, and at the August meeting the hopes of reconciliation were slender. Another sub-committee was assembled "to secure harmonious cooperation by adequate representation of all such differences of opinion both in administration at home and in service abroad". The Rev. Daniel Bartlett was nominated to the sub-committee but felt himself unable to accept.

The sub-committee met for three days and presented its report in November 1922. But even before the report was published, a group of about thirty clergy and laymen had met in London and decided to form an alternative Anglican missionary society, although they waited until the November meeting of the General Committee in the now forlorn hope that the situation might be saved. The sub-committee's statement sought to put forward a doctrinal position acceptable to all, and by now, especially in the type of meeting convened, this was not possible. After long debate and at one point an adjournment for consultation and prayer an amendment was put and accepted which made it certain that the organisation of the new missionary society – the Bible Churchmen's Missionary Society (BCMS) – would go ahead. What had been threatened and feared for so long had now occurred. It was a heavy blow.

But the results for the missionary work of the CMS were less devastating than might have been feared. Only two missionaries, a couple in India, resigned over the issue.

Within Britain a number of supporters and subscribers were lost, and three vice-presidents resigned, with four honorary governors. The staff in London, and association secretaries, had a difficult time for the next few years, since the CMS was publicly accused of rejecting the trustworthiness of the historical records of the Bible by the vote in the November committee. Explanations and defence were difficult, and the line taken was to present not a defence but an active and positive account of what was being accomplished. This policy was continued, and gradually much of the bitterness was absorbed and, if not forgotten, ignored. The BCMS went on to do excellent work in a number of areas, usually complementary to the CMS and often in a pioneering role. In the mercies of God the tragedy of the division became something used for his glory. The CMS was able to remain as a comprehensive evangelical society, and a number of men and women who would not have been able to work within the structure of the CMS went on to serve in another organisation which had the same aim – of glorifying God and bringing men and women to faith in his Son.

The Ruanda Mission

It was not really to be expected in the decade after the ghastly tragedies of the World War that the CMS would take on a totally new field of work. At this stage it was more likely that fields would be given up – another society consolidating work, or a developing Church taking over responsibility. The CMS had begun, and left, work in Australia, South Africa, the West Indies, the Seychelles and Mauritius, and in New Zealand and Canada had been able to hand over to a locally constituted mission board.

But in the purposes of God a new field was now taken on, which was to be a source of great blessing to the CMS and to the universal Church. The Ruanda Mission has written its own story well, and only the barest outline can be given here. It begins with two young English doctors, Algernon Stanley Smith (son of the Stanley Smith who went to China with the Cambridge Seven) and Leonard Sharp, already close friends at Cambridge and acknowledging a missionary call, who during the War were sent to Uganda. They were located to Mengo Hospital, Kampala, which was being used as a military hospital. From their vantage point within Uganda they were able to survey the land, and their gaze was directed to the almost legendary twin kingdoms of Ruanda and Urundi, to the south of Uganda. Previously part of German East Africa, they were to be under mandate agreements, administered by Belgium.

The two doctors found some support among CMS Uganda missionaries, including Bishop Willis, but there were obstacles at every turn. Many suggestions for alternative fields for a pioneer medical mission were made; they could still be profitably used at Mengo. But at the end of 1916 they obtained a permit from the Ugandan government (in error, it later turned out) and set off by motor-bike to the extreme south of Uganda and then on by foot into Ruanda. Every hope they had was confirmed, but they had to go back and work on at Mengo for two more years. Then, in 1919 they returned to England. Now they had to persuade a missionary society which could hardly staff and finance existing work to commence a new mission, and that the most expensive, a new medical mission, in a non-British colony.

To complicate things further, both young men promptly married. Stanley Smith's wife was Zoë Sharp, sister of Leonard Sharp. Sharp himself married Esther Macdonald. The CMS, through its Africa Secretary, the Rev. G. T. Manley, listened to them and caught the vision. By June 1920 the new venture was officially approved. But there were two important provisions: "the consent of the Belgium authorities" and the raising of funds specifically for the new work.

Money was received in ways that confirmed God's calling, and permission to go to Urundi was received from Belgium. In November 1920 the two couples (the Stanley Smiths now with a young baby) set out. Before they left Europe they heard that the Belgian government had withdrawn permission to enter their territory. But they were sure enough of their call to go on and wait for further guidance.

They were assigned by Bishop Willis to Kabale in Kigezi district, bordering on Ruanda, and started work there. Many people from Ruanda lived in the British territory, and a start with language study could be made. African Christian volunteers went with them and so, once again, we see the Gospel being brought not only by the foreign pioneers but also by locally prepared Christians. Houses were built, treatment of the sick commenced and soon also a school. The Stanley Smiths, who had been separated till a suitable dwelling for Zoë and the baby was ready, were together again, and Esther Sharp had her first baby. But little Robin Sharp died at the age of eight months. Still the work went on and by 1924 the first hospital buildings were opened. Built of sun-dried brick with a roof of papyrus reed, the new hospital had 125 beds.

Difficulties were by no means over. This was a pioneering work, with languages to be reduced to writing, Bible translation to be undertaken, and the missionaries were not yet in Belgian territory. Physical conditions were primitive in the extreme; roads were almost non-existent, and there were serious famines and epidemics. Nevertheless, in 1925 Geoffrey Holmes settled in his tent at Gahini, on Lake Muhazi, well within the Belgian mandate, and the next stage of the work had begun.

This advance gave impetus to the need within Britain to rationalise the organisation. The CMS could not take full responsibility and now the early support group, the "Friends of Ruanda", gave way to a Home Council which, as an auxiliary of the CMS, was to direct the Ruanda General and

Medical Mission. The new departure came in 1926, only four years after the controversy which had led to the formation of the Bible Churchmen's Missionary Society (BCMS). The Ruanda Mission contained in its foundation constitution principles which guaranteed its operation on "Bible, Protestant, and Keswick lines". Thus it retained for the CMS (in general at least), the support in prayer, in giving and in offers of service, from Anglicans who might otherwise have transferred their allegiance to the BCMS or to non-denominational societies.

The work developed rapidly in Kigezi, in Ruanda and, from 1934, in Urundi. New hospitals, boarding schools, networks of village schools, leprosy work – all helped to contact people and build up the Church. The medical work was especially important in the Belgian territories where, because of the Roman Catholic missions' close connections with the administration, schools could not be as freely established as in Uganda. African missionaries from Uganda continued to give vital help with the work. One of these was a young man surely prepared by God for his future service. He was a Tutsi from Gahini district whose family had moved to Ankole, in Uganda, in his childhood. He was educated in the best Uganda schools, finishing at King's College, Budo, where in 1924 he heard Dr. Stanley Smith appealing for volunteers to go as missionaries to Ruanda. So young Kosiya Shalita went back to his own country, and later pioneered in Urundi. Much later he was to be diocesan Bishop of Ankole, the country where he had been brought up.

Revival in Ruanda: the beginnings

We have seen how the vision of the young English doctors, Stanley Smith and Sharp, brought into being a new CMS field. This came at a time of financial difficulty, of theological controversy, and the new field was, moreover, in a non-British colony, which posited further problems. But the Church was established, prospered and expanded, and in the mercies of God there came from it a movement of the Spirit of God which was to bring blessing to the Church in the whole of East Africa, in the Sudan, and much further afield. Some missionaries who have lived through the troubles of those countries in the 1950s, 1960s and 1970s as colonial rule came to an end, and as the problems of independence have surfaced, wonder whether the Church would have survived without the new life that came, humanly speaking, through Ruanda.

Humanly speaking, again, the immediate source of the revival was the coming of yet another young English doctor, John E. (Joe) Church, who arrived at Kabale in 1927. His fellowship with African fellow workers, especially Yosiya Kinuka and Blasio Kigozi, were the sparks that kindled the flame.

But Joe Church came out as a CICCU missionary – his support guaranteed by the Christian Union of Cambridge, and its prayers surrounding him. The influence and teaching of Keswick was strong too. So influences going back directly to the late 19th century – the Moody and Sankey missions, the holiness teaching that led to the Keswick convention, and the enthusiasms of those Cambridge students which had led so many other students to offer as missionaries – were all with the young doctor as he took up his work, briefly at Kabale and then at Gahini, in Ruanda.

He arrived at a desperate time, for a severe famine was gripping Ruanda (then, as now, a fertile country with a very dense population). The tensions caused by the famine, with helpless men, women and children literally dying on their doorstep, made relationships doubly difficult for the two young missionary bachelors (the second was the Rev. Herbert Jackson), trying to cope at Gahini. Joe Church was further disturbed by the success of his own attempts to publicise in England and Europe the famine and the need for relief; he feared this might lead to trouble with the Belgian authorities.

In 1929 as the famine situation improved, the hospital and church staff, African and European, were exhausted with the strain, lack of good food, and the aftermath of the terrible period they had passed through. The hospital staff were especially discontented. At this time Dr. Church began to work closely with his senior hospital assistant, Yosiya Kinuka, on studying and teaching the Bible in a way that could be understood by the local people. From the middle of 1929 the whole station – pupils, workmen, hospital patients, staff – came together for a daily hour of Bible teaching. This they later saw as the foundation for the revival. Kosiya Shalita took over from Yosiya Kinuka as Joe Church's helper when Yosiya had to go back to Kabale.

Other missionaries beside Joe Church were concerned about themselves and the young Church. Growth was rapid – so rapid that baptisms and confirmations took place with insufficient teaching and with little or no follow-up for the new Christians. And missionaries realised that lack of love and unity among themselves harmed the witness. There was also the racial division between African and European, taken for granted at that time. Most of the missionaries, with public school and Cambridge education, came from the same background as the administrators, and followed the same social conventions.

But the Ruanda mission from the beginning had its innovators, eccentrics some might call them, who took little account of convention and followed, even if stumbling, the Calvary road. One of the greatest was the Rev. Harold Guillebaud, who came in 1925 with his wife and four of his children. He was God's gift to the Church as its first Bible translator (and two of his daughters followed him in this). He brought another gift to the Church in the breaking down of social and racial barriers – he invited Africans into his own home for the family's Sunday night hymn singing. It was first their house servant, but soon others also; a small thing seemingly but the beginning of something great.

Another of God's early gifts to CMS Ruanda was the Rev. Jack Warren who also came to Kabale in 1925. His service only lasted for four brief years, during which time he married and saw a baby daughter born, who still in 1984 serves God in Uganda. In January 1929 he died in England, of TB contracted during his earlier war service. But his work of love has not been forgotten. He saw the great needs of the growing Church and appealed for prayer. "Pray until it hurts, that the mighty indwelling, keeping power of the Holy Spirit may be experienced by the Christians." (In a letter written in 1926.) He did not live to see the answer to the prayers, his own and those of many in England, but answered they were.

At Gahini, in the same year that Jack Warren died, rapid development in the hospital, church and schools was combined with the continuing sense of failure and the belief that God had a better way. Joe Church, on holiday in Kampala after the humiliation of failing his first language examination, met a prosperous, well-educated Muganda, Simeon Nsibambi, who, like himself, was seeking the secret of the spirit-filled life. Joe Church had been longing for an African partner in this search. Together the missionary doctor and the African civil servant read the Bible, kneeled and prayed. They claimed the gift of the Spirit, and without ecstatic signs believed they had received the gift. (Simeon shortly resigned his post to become a full-time evangelist.)

When Joe Church arrived back at Gahini he shared his new insights with his African friends, especially Kosiya Shalita and Blasio Kigozi, who was the younger brother of Nsibambi. Blasio had come during 1929 as a schoolteacher, conscious of a missionary call. He became right-hand man to Dr. Church in the following months, up to and after Church's marriage in the cathedral in Kampala in May 1930 to a young doctor who came from England, Decima (Decie) Tracey. Yosiya Kinuka was still standing aside from Joe and Blasio in the spiritual quest, and indeed was thinking of leaving the hospital work to go back to Ankole. But he went on holiday to Kampala, stayed with Nsibambi, and was challenged by him to recognise the sin that separated him from his brothers. He came back to Gahini a changed man. Now the four, Joe Church, Blasio Kigozi, Yosiya Kinuka and Kosiya Shalita worked, studied and prayed together, the first of many "teams" of the revival. From that beginning of simple acceptance of forgiveness which each had received came acceptance and forgiveness of one another and of their colleagues in the mission community. Former enemies became friends and brothers, relationships were healed, and from Gahini many went out preaching.

While this new life was springing up the work of the mission was extending rapidly. New stations were established on new sites in Ruanda and Urundi; the hospitals at Kabale and Gahini flourished; a leprosy centre was set up on an island in Lake Bunyoni; school and boarding hostels were extended; new missionaries arrived; the Lunyaruanda New Testament was published. It was just ten years since the first beginnings. A little later, in September 1933, the Ruanda mission met in conference, and among other things discussed the role of lay people in the Church. This was to be an important (and sometimes divisive) factor as revival spread.

Even more important, in the long run, was a convention held at Gahini after Christmas 1933. On the last day there was a breakthrough, as African after African stood to confess hidden sins and to testify to new life received. An immediate result was that the number of Africans offering to go out to new stations and outschools as medical assistants, teachers and evangelists was more than could be accepted.

In 1934 Joe Church's doctor brother Bill Church, who had arrived at the end of 1931, took over much of the hospital work, and Joe was freed for more continual evangelistic and teaching work away from the main station. He embarked on a new project, sending teams out on safari for about one week a month, medical and evangelistic staff together. Camping in one place — usually a church/school centre — there was intensive preaching, teaching and simple medical work, with the teachers and evangelists from the little outschools and churches participating and receiving themselves help and training. Those working together were continually learning about the way of fellowship; one practice which developed among them was that of "keeping short accounts" or "walking in the light"; bringing up immediately small differences, tensions, misunderstandings, asking forgiveness of Christ and of the brother or sister involved, and leaving the sins there. This became a special mark of the revival fellowship as it developed.

In 1932 the young teacher Blasio Kigozi had gone back to Uganda for theological studies. He returned to Gahini in 1934, now ordained as a deacon. In that year a great evangelistic thrust into Urundi was made, with two new stations settled. But there was still a spiritual battle raging and Blasio, now pastor in charge of the Gahini parish, was in the centre of it. The church teachers accused him of preaching too much about sin. But soon many of those accusers came into the new blessing and withdrew their complaints, working instead with Blasio. In September 1935 a convention led by Yosiya, Blasio and Joe Church was held at Kabale, and Simeon Nsibambi came from Kampala. Despite the need to use four languages (and so three interpreters) there was great blessing.

But 1936 was the crucial year. It began with what superficially appeared to be a great tragedy. Blasio Kigozi was back in Kampala on a visit during which he was (though only a deacon) to speak to the Uganda Church synod. He became suddenly ill and died on 25 January, of tick fever. The news was a stunning blow at Gahini, but new leaders appeared, and what might have been the work of one gifted man now clearly became the work of the Spirit. The three points he had intended to raise in his address to the synod were passed on and discussed, ending with the question: what must be done to bring revival to the Church of Uganda?

Now begins a period when details can no longer be given, so rapidly did the movement spread. Teams went out in all directions, small meetings and larger conventions were held, and wherever the message of sin, repentance, turning to Christ, and confession was preached, results were seen. Indeed, the "signs following" became a rock on which the young movement nearly foundered. There was crying out, weeping, whole congregations praying, trembling and crying out all night; reports of dreams and visions. There was also restitution of money and goods stolen, restored relationships, changed lives. It was in the hospitals and boarding schools that the violent outward manifestations of revival presented the most difficulties. Missionary head teachers and hospital sisters found their entire institutions disrupted while dancing, drumming, singing and praying went on all night. But "in most cases, as the fierce almost hysterical emotion passed, there arose something from the dust and ashes that no missionary could gainsay, a love and zeal that glowed and burned and must testify." (Patricia St. John, 1971, p. 127.)

Revival: the crisis in Uganda

"Revival", or "the Ruanda Revival", as it was already being called, was now entering a crisis period in the fullest sense of that word. There were dangers and great opportunities. The theological and administrative difficulties brought the movement (and, perhaps, the CMS Ruanda Mission) close to breaking off from the Anglican Church. And there were the ongoing difficulties of the revival signs – the weeping, crying, all-night singing and drumming – which alienated a number of missionaries who would have wished in most ways to be a part of the movement.

The CMS Ruanda Mission had preserved and perpetuated the more conservative aspects of the parent society, but organisationally it was a part of the Church of Uganda, with which more theologically liberal missionaries might be working. The ordinands from Ruanda's sphere were trained at Bishop Tucker Theological College at Mukono, where problems could and did arise. Missionaries themselves had some reservations about Anglican liturgical forms, and even about the sacraments. Like many missionaries from many sending Churches, they were hoping to see formed in the new environment a Church which avoided the faults of the one they had come from. Infant baptism was in itself questionable to some of them; Holy Communion seemed to be too easily open to abuse, and especially in the circumstances prevailing when hundreds of semi-literate men and women had been baptised and confirmed in a short time. There was thus a wish to "fence the sacrament" beyond what was normal practice.

At the centre of these very real problems was, on the one hand, the Bishop of Uganda, the Rt. Rev. Cyril Edgar Stuart, who had succeeded Bishop J. J. Willis in 1934, and, on the other hand, the CMS Ruanda Field Secretary and the missionaries like Dr. Church who were leaders in the new movement. The severest church test came in 1941 when a number of young and promising ordinands left the theological college and so gave up their hope of ordination and leadership in the Church. One of these students was William Nagenda, who was to become the apostle of the revival, though never ordained. A few were reconciled and returned. Bishop Stuart, despite great provocation, showed immense patience and love. He recognised that there were "faults on both sides". In other areas there were misunderstandings and deep tension. But there was also much prayer and much love, and in the end there was no split, no organisational division.

While there were ongoing meetings and discussions to try and solve these divisive issues, the revival also continued, leaping like a bush-fire from place to place. Sometimes it was carried by purely informal contact; sometimes by small teams where three or four went to another mission to preach for a weekend; sometimes it spread by the larger conventions which were to become such a feature of the revival. Missionaries who come from the same society and the same country have wide links through their education and training and often through marriage. They visit one another on holiday and their children are at school together. African networks are likewise extensive; all these means were used by the Holy Spirit. In 1936 the Burundi churches were really touched; in 1937 Kenya was effectively reached, first through meetings at a CMS station near Nairobi where Dr. Church's brother, the Rev. Howard Church, was working. By 1938 the far north of Uganda (where the Africa Inland Mission provided missionaries) and the Southern Sudan were involved. In 1939 it was the eastern Congo. In 1938–39 the message went to Tanganyika, first into the Bukoba area, or "West Lake", long in close touch with Uganda Christians, and then eastward into central Tanganyika.

Even further afield, three missionaries went overland to South Africa in 1944, and preached to white and black. After the end of the war, when overseas furloughs were resumed, European countries were touched, and in particular Switzerland. That connection brought not only prayer and financial support to the CMS Ruanda Mission, but also some excellent French-speaking missionaries to strengthen their staff. Later still teams went to India and the United States of America.

What did this particular ongoing revival mean in the churches? First, without doubt, hundreds and thousands of conversions, many of baptised, nominally Christian men and women who had never really comprehended the new life in Jesus. But in the particular circumstances of East Africa there were other results. It broke down the racial and social barriers between black and white, even in Kenya where an informal apartheid was the rule in settler areas, and had spread to missionaries. It likewise broke down barriers between

Africans of very different groups, at a time when educational barriers were beginning to reinforce tribal differences.

It also brought missionaries of different societies and nationalities together in a new way – American Mennonites, Swedish Lutherans, English Anglicans, Scottish Presbyterians. They found an active fellowship and unity previously lacking. Likewise the leaders of young and growing Churches, without becoming involved in drawn-out theological conferences, found themselves working together in the conventions that were an aid to, and not a substitute for, the Churches' own programmes. Patterns for conventions grew up – frequent meetings at a local level, less frequently on a provincial and national level, and every five years or so an East African convention when thousands came together from all over the three territories, with international visitors as well, to praise the Lord and learn new lessons. No one who has been to such a convention can forget it – the spontaneous praise, the joy, the orderly way in which physical needs are cared for, and the simplicity which is sufficient. Usually a short verse becomes a motto for the convention, and a message to take back at its end. So at one conference the motto was "Jesus satisfies", and at the same place, a number of years later, it became "Jesus satisfies?"

Thus, when trouble came – to Kenya in the late 1940s and 1950s, to the Sudan from the mid-fifties through to the 1970s, to Uganda, to the Congo/Zaire in the flare-up after independence in 1960, to Tanzania in the long-drawn-out difficulties of that lovely but poverty-stricken nation – there was a strong Church ready to meet difficulties, torture and even death. Nowhere was this shown better than in the nations of Ruanda and Burundi themselves, when, after independence had been granted, civil war flared up and thousands were killed. Kenya, Uganda and Ruanda have given their martyrs to the Church universal; Sudan also. The message of revival, of brokenness, walking in the light, confession, has been a gift to Christians everywhere.

The revival message did not, however, penetrate all the Protestant Churches of East Africa equally. Strangely, it was strongly opposed, and mostly rejected, in the more evangelical missions and Churches. The reasons are complex and not yet fully explored, and it may be that some of the criticisms which were brushed away at the time should have been listened to more carefully. For it seems that in success and freedom the "Revival Christians" have been more open to sin and division than in times of persecution and troubles. The story has not yet ended; it is still being lived out and added to.

11 NEW PARTNERS IN WAR AND PEACE

Australia takes up the challenge

The 1920s were difficult years for the CMS on many fronts. There were the adjustments to the post-war world, a declining economy, and the theological rift that led to the founding of the BCMS. We have already noted the continuing financial problem that led to deficits being reported each year. In 1919 two small missions had been closed, partly for financial reasons. In Turkish Arabia (Iraq) only five missionaries remained after the war, and all could be reassigned to other work in Arabic-speaking areas. In Mauritius no new missionaries had been sent out after 1907, and CMS grants were gradually reduced so that by 1919 the SPG had assumed full responsibility for Anglican work in the island.

But the savings thus made were small; further savings could only be made at the expense of holding back workers who were urgently needed. One particularly needy area was the newly British mandate of Tanganyika, formerly German East Africa. It was a large and poor country, and still handicapped by the wartime internment of British missionaries and national Christians, and then by the removal of the German missionaries after Britain and Belgium took over. It was not known when the Lutheran and Moravian missionaries would be allowed to return. The CMS work was still ecclesiastically controlled from Kenya, where the Bishop of Mombasa had recently moved his headquarters from Mombasa to Nairobi. It was hard for him to give adequate help to such a large and remote area.

So there was talk of the CMS work being transferred to the UMCA and thus coming under the Bishop of Zanzibar. But the difference in theology and especially in churchmanship made this a very unwelcome suggestion. Then, with the founding of the BCMS, another possibility opened up. On the Church side this was more acceptable, but the BCMS was not willing to give assurances about the maintenance of educational work.

A third possibility was then suggested – that the Australian CMS should take over the responsibility for Tanganyika, with a new diocese and an Australian bishop. The Australian CMS had been established in 1916, but it brought together groups with a long-standing interest in the CMS. It replaced Church missionary associations in New South Wales and Victoria, which had been founded in 1892 and themselves replaced earlier auxiliaries – that of NSW going back to 1825. The 1892 reorganisation took place when the English CMS sent out a delegation consisting of the Rev. R. W. Stewart, an Irish clergyman from the CMS Fukien mission, and Eugene Stock, the editorial secretary of the CMS. As had happened in Great Britain, the expanding Keswick movement was being used not only to encourage deeper consecration among Christians, but also to arouse interest in missions. A Keswick "missioner" who had been sent out to Australia reported back on the possibilities. From 1892 the Auxiliaries organised meetings, raised funds and took responsibility for seeking, training and supporting missionaries, but their location was still fixed by the parent society, as the British CMS now became known.

The first missionary, Miss Phillips, was sent to Ceylon almost immediately. In the years up to the founding of the Australian CMS in 1916, almost 130 men and women had been sent out. Many went to China, for Mr. Stewart had created much interest in that field by his writings as well as his personal contacts. In 1893 two young sisters from Melbourne, Harriete and Elizabeth Saunders, joined the

Stewart family in the Fukien mission. They were with the Stewarts in August 1895 when the holiday party was attacked by the "Vegetarians", and were among the eleven who died. So the Australian Church Missionary Auxiliary had its first martyrs, and although deaths were few compared with the early days of the CMS, there were others who died overseas.

By 1926–27, when Bishop Heywood of Mombasa was discussing the question of the new diocese with the English CMS and CMS Australia, there were seven Australians serving with the CMS in Tanganyika. The most senior was Archdeacon Doulton, the second man sent out by the NSW association, who had arrived at Mpwapwa in 1894. Another long-serving missionary, Miss Katie Miller of NSW, arrived in 1905; she did not resign till 1944. In 1927 the total number of missionaries in the CMS sphere was only eighteen, and in so large a country with extremely poor communications this was far too few, even for the section worked by the CMS.

The man chosen to become the first bishop was the Rev. George Chambers, Rector of Holy Trinity, Dulwich Hill, NSW. The details of the new diocese were worked out when Bishop Heywood visited Australia in 1927. The new bishop went to England for his consecration (November 1927) and incidentally formed a very active diocesan association in England, helped considerably by the family of his English wife, whose father, Canon Talbot-Rice, was Vicar of St. Paul's, Onslow Square. As Canon Hewitt writes of him, he proved "an excellent first choice as the first bishop of a missionary diocese. He had confidence and enthusiasm, and he was unusually gifted both as a recruiting-sergeant and money-raiser." He went back to Australia to recruit and raise funds there, and arrived in Tanganyika in November 1928. During that year sixteen new Australian missionaries arrived there, in addition to the bishop and his wife. One was a young Welshman, William Wynn Jones, whom Chambers had encouraged to emigrate to Australia some years before. Now with a university degree, and ordained, he gave outstanding service from the beginning, and was eventually to succeed his patron as second Bishop of Central Tanganyika.

Under the new arrangements the diocese expanded rapidly. Work on earlier stations was consolidated, and with the fresh government initiatives in education, the Church was able to cooperate with mutual benefit. The boys' school which eventually became the Alliance Secondary School (in partnership with the Moravian Mission) was moved to its permanent site at Kikuyu, outside Dodoma, in 1929. In 1933 the Cathedral of the Holy Spirit was consecrated in Dodoma.

Bishop Chambers made use of the connections he had to expand and improve the medical work of the diocese. At Kilimatinde and at the neighbouring leprosy centre of Makatupora there were greatly improved physical facilities. A little later the hospital at Mvumi began the expansion which was eventually to make it the leading hospital in the diocese. The girls' boarding school at Mvumi was also expanded and built up.

Bishop Chambers also took special note of the needs of Europeans living in Tanganyika, and did not neglect a ministry to them. In practical terms an important step was assisting the administration in running a boarding school for European children in Arusha. Further pioneer work, in the more usual sense of the work, was the expansion west to the borders of the territory, along the shores of Lake Tanganyika, where the first worker was Lionel Bakewell, who came in 1929 and literally walked hundreds of miles contacting people and patiently building up the small congregations which would eventually become a strong Church. With him was an African pioneer, Yohana Omari, whose home was to the east of Dodoma, but who with his wife worked for ten years in the remote west. He was to become the first African in the diocese to be consecrated bishop.

Bishop Chambers resigned in 1947, after twenty years. There were then almost eighty missionaries where there had been eighteen; and twenty-eight African clergy where there had been two. In the west there was a church of 10,000 adherents where there had been nothing. Bishop Wynn Jones (who had been consecrated in 1943 as assistant bishop) was installed to lead the diocese, but died suddenly after only two years. His successor was another Australian who had been serving in Kenya. Alfred Stanway possessed many of the gifts of recruiting personnel and raising funds which George Chambers had possessed; he and his wife were also fluent speakers of Swahili, and the diocese, despite plenty of difficulties, continued to expand. Independence was granted to Tanganyika a little earlier than to her northern neighbours, and virtually without any kind of violence, and Mwalimu Julius Nyerere, the first president, a practising Roman Catholic Christian, was a leader who called forth respect and affection.

Other Commonwealth partners

From the 1890s, the British CMS benefited from a number of missionaries from the "white colonies", who were recruited by the Church missionary associations and supported by them, but located through the parent society. A Church Missionary Association for New Zealand was formed in 1892–93, at the time of the English Deputation, and two women were sent to Japan in 1893. A small but steady number went out from New Zealand, and eventually a Church Missionary Society of NZ was formed (1916). Although missionaries were sent to different fields, as need and their training directed, NZ CMS eventually came to take a special role in NW India – the later Pakistan. In the Church of the Province of New Zealand a board of missions was formed as the official fund-raising agency, and NZ CMS has worked happily within that relationship, unlike Australia, where the Board of Missions has acted separately from CMS.

In Canada a Church Missionary Association was also

formed, but a little later, in 1895–96. Previously a sending group had been organised around the theological college in Toronto, Wycliffe College. The Wycliffe College missionaries had become responsible for a section of the Anglican work in Japan; in 1895 this was handed over to the CMA and so added to the CMS staff in Japan. Between 1895 and 1899 twenty-five men and twenty women went overseas from the colonial associations. As we have seen, in Australia and New Zealand independent and flourishing societies were eventually established.

But in Canada the Domestic and Foreign Missionary Society of the Church eventually superseded the CMA, and Canada today has no Church Missionary Society, although there are of course missionaries serving overseas from that Anglican Church.

Involvement in education

From the earliest days of the Society, missionaries had disagreed about the depth of their involvement with education. About basic literacy there was little argument; all those who enquired about baptism should be taught to read if they were physically able to do so. But after that? Was it the business of the missionaries, part of their calling, to conduct more advanced schools? Or even high schools and universities?

By the 1840s missionaries in India were receiving grants-in-aid for schools which they supervised, and in Sierra Leone, from an early stage, the missionary societies were practically responsible for all education. In Sierra Leone also the Society made one of its earliest forays into higher education, and even though there were difficulties and disappointments Fourah Bay College largely fulfilled the hopes centred on it, producing a good number of educated and dedicated pastors and teachers. In India there was rather more ambivalence on the part of many missionaries. In Sierra Leone, and in Nigeria as it opened up, almost all the children and young people attending mission institutions were at least *potential* converts; in India it was clear that the majority of pupils were not. The Presbyterian missionary Alexander Duff (as Max Warren points out in *To apply the gospel*, p. 184) held to a vision of Western education in mission schools "changing the minds of Indians and preparing them for the gospel," regardless of the individual conversions witnessed. Most of the Anglicans were less clear on this point. In fact, however, a number of notable leaders came into faith and later leadership in the Indian Church through the schools and colleges, out of varied backgrounds – Hindu, Muslim, Sikh, Parsee.

In many of the CMS fields, such as Canada, New Zealand and Japan, the involvement in education was limited and specific, and decreased as the government took over responsibility. In Africa, on the other hand, it was apparent from a very early stage that education could not be limited to simple literacy; that the people wanted further education for their children, including the teaching of English; and that only the missionaries were in a position to organise such education. As mission work in Africa extended – as far as the CMS was concerned in Uganda and in British and German East Africa as well as in Nigeria and Sierra Leone – the role of the missions and Churches was extended. Other missionary societies – American and continental – faced similar problems in other parts of Africa. These problems could be magnified by language and nationality differences, such as when an American mission was working in a French (and French-speaking) colony.

Protestant missions world-wide, and not least the CMS, owe a great deal to the secretary of the International Missionary Council (IMC), J. H. Oldham, for his part in guiding them in developing popular education and in smoothing and facilitating relations with the colonial administrations and with the Colonial Office. From the time of the 1910 Edinburgh Conference onward Oldham's political and spiritual wisdom was used in many ways. He was a secretary, from 1912, of the Conference of Missionary Societies of Great Britain and Ireland (CBMS) and through that cooperation a number of programmes were enabled to go ahead. Some of these were concerned with higher education – the Women's Christian College in Madras (1915) and medical schools in China. It was clear that no one society acting alone could initiate and maintain that level of institution, but cooperatively it was possible.

The CMS responded to the CBMS with financial aid towards the purchasing of Edinburgh House, 2 Eaton Square, in 1920. It became the headquarters of the CBMS, and in 1921, after the IMC had been formed, its British head-quarters. Oldham became one of the two secretaries of the new world body. One of the areas where the missionary societies required guidance and stimulation was in this matter of education. Even where grants-in-aid were offered there was often considerable hesitation over accepting them. The case of eastern Nigeria can be taken as an example. Between 1910 and 1914 the mission executive committee debated and rejected grants. They feared the so-called "conscience clause", giving parents the right to withdraw children from religious instruction, the government preference for English rather than vernacular instruction, and the effects of govern-ment inspection, standards and the administration work which would be required. It was not till 1919 that it was agreed to accept grants for a limited number of elementary schools, under protective clauses, and not till 1922 that a grant for a training college was applied for. In this situa-tion the mission executive had been in opposition to the bishop, the parent committee of CMS, the local mission education board and, without a doubt, to the vast majority of African Christians. Obviously it was the missionaries themselves who needed to gain a vision of what could be achieved through cooperation with governments in education.

Oldham therefore called a conference, which was held in Le Zoute, Belgium, in September 1926. It was an international conference with the title, "The Christian Mission in Africa". It dealt with much more than education, but a careful reading especially of Oldham's own contribution shows that his major concern was to have the societies accept a new educational role in Africa. It was not long since the members of the Phelps-Stokes commission had passed on their mission through Africa, and Canon Anson Phelps-Stokes and the director of the Phelps-Stokes Fund, Dr. Jesse Jackson, were consultative members of the conference. Oldham was able to call on the help of academics and administrators at the highest level. Lord Lugard was there — and Belgian, Portuguese and French administrators. The recommendations of the conference on education called for cooperation among missions, cooperation with government, and emphasised the special responsibility of the missions with regard to village, central and secondary schools, and in the training of teachers. But higher and technical education "should, under present conditions, ordinarily be conducted by the Government". Financial assistance from the government should be such as to enable mission schools to attain the same standard of efficiency as similar government schools.

One result of this new emphasis on participation in education related to the grants-in-aid being received, was that the proportion of missionaries in different fields changed. There was a continuing shortage of staff to send overseas, from the point of view of the missionaries in each field, who felt pressures, saw unfulfilled needs, and came to believe that the suitable recruits always went elsewhere! Now with the increasing educational needs in Africa, and with grants-in-aid to pay staff, it was not surprising that suitably qualified men and women went to Africa. In 1910 there were 253 CMS missionaries in Africa and 479 in India and Ceylon. In 1942 the numbers were almost reversed — 450 in Africa and 259 in India and Ceylon. Most "educationists" entered with enthusiasm into their specialist roles, but there was ongoing frustration at the busyness which kept them from participating fully in the life of the Church, and even handicapped pastoral and evangelistic work among their own students. This was a problem which did not go away.

Medical missions

In the period after the war, as the Society's role in education changed, there were also gradual changes in the medical outreach. From 1904 the Medical Mission Auxiliary (MMA) (founded in 1892) had been responsible for fund-raising, and had carried on an existence somewhat separate from the rest of the Society. The amount of money raised was considerable, increasing to as much as £70,000 a year in the later years of the period we are discussing, and the missionary education through exhibitions and literature was also considerable. There was in the early years a popular method of fund-raising whereby a church or a church society supported a hospital bed, for which they gave money. But the emphasis in medicine, and especially the role of missionary health workers, began to change. In many countries the government was increasingly providing the hospital care; the Church contribution was changing to mobile medical teams and preventative medicine. So the fund-raising shifted to a five pound share scheme, which provided a more fluid income not tied to institutions. In 1942–43, despite the war, the jubilee of the Medical Mission Association was celebrated. A widely-read book, *The Wholeness of Man* (1943) by Phyllis Garlick, was published to mark it. The title expresses the new emphasis in medical work – an interesting emphasis when forty years on (1983) a new Holistic Medical Association for Great Britain has only just been launched.

The new emphasis extended to structures, and early in 1943 the MMA became the Medical Missions Appropriations, with the same initials, but integrated fully into the CMS. The MMA secretary at headquarters became a full secretary of the Society, but the activities of the MMA continued as before.

12 MAX WARREN'S PROPHETIC VISION

General secretary 1942–1963

It has been remarked earlier that the CMS was a missionary society without any famous founding figure. During its first hundred years the most important and influential personality was an administrator, the clerical secretary from 1841 to 1873, Henry Venn. For that long period he was the hub about which the Society turned. He coped with all aspects of the work – personal dealings with missionaries, committees, relations with government officials, deputations for churches. And, perhaps most important, he wrote the minutes on the organisation of the native Church, which were to direct the thinking of Church and mission leaders so influentially for decades to come.

In the second century of its life, the leading personality of the CMS was, once again, an administrator. Max Warren, born in 1904, took office as general secretary in 1942, just a hundred years after Henry Venn. He remained in office till 1963, and in those twenty-one years he took the Society through the ending of the Second World War, and through a shaking of the foundations which might have brought to an end the Anglican Church overseas as the British colonial empire came to an end. That this did not happen was due in no small part to his leadership and to his prophetic vision.

So the story of the CMS in the last forty years must start with the story of this one man. Like Henry Venn, he was born into the CMS. His father, an Irish clergyman, was a CMS

missionary in India, and although he was born in Ireland he
went to India as a baby and lived there till he was eight. In
that period white children were normally sent "home" even
earlier; his father was in 1914 appointed an assistant Home
Secretary in the CMS headquarters, and so the Warren
family stayed in England.

Max Warren went to Marlborough and from there in 1918
to Jesus College, Cambridge, where he read history. His age
saved him from service in the war, in which one older brother
had died and a second was wounded and gassed. He was
already thinking in terms of a missionary vocation, and this
vision carried him on after his father's sudden death in 1920.
While at Cambridge he and some friends made an offer to go
to northern Nigeria under the CMS when they had qualified.
Having taken his degree, he took a further year to prepare for
ordination, without at that point intending to be ordained.
By 1927 he was ready to sail for Nigeria, as a layman, with
what was now being called "the Hausa Band".

In the event, what Max Warren hoped would be a lifetime's
service in northern Nigeria turned out to be less than one
year's. In December 1927 he landed at Lagos. In October
1928, with both lungs affected, he was sent back to England
with "bovine" tuberculosis. Three years in bed followed,
but he emerged healed, although with scarred joints and
one eye removed. In 1932 he was married, ordained, and
started on the road which was to lead to the CMS General
Secretary's chair, and to an incomparable role in the
Anglican Communion and in the ecumenical world
Church as well.

Already we have seen the first major divergence between
Henry Venn the 19th century leader and Max Warren the
20th century leader. Henry Venn never served overseas as a
missionary. Warren's term, short as it was, gave him an
insight into the problems of a raw recruit which served him
well. The second difference in their careers was soon to be
made clear. Venn never visited any overseas mission field

(although it would have been difficult, some of his contemporaries in other societies, like Rufus Anderson of the American Board, made such visits). Max Warren, on the other hand, was constantly travelling. Building on his wide contacts inside and outside the Churches, and with an unsurpassed gift for friendship, he was God's man to lead the Society through those difficult years. His writings stand today as relevant and helpful as when they first appeared. If one could sum up his complex message in just one phrase, it would be that of the importance of a *related* Christianity. Always he showed how the work of the Holy Spirit relates the believer to the world as well as to God. So for twenty-one years he gave himself to the task of relating mission to the Church at home, to the Church overseas, of government officials relating to Church leaders, of men and women of one culture relating to men and women of another culture – and all in relation to God.

Max Warren came to this task at a uniquely difficult time. He succeeded Dr. William Wilson Cash, who became Bishop of Worcester in 1941. Dr. Cash had served as General Secretary from 1926, and for three years before that as Home Secretary. So he had borne the burden of the theological controversy which had divided the Society in the early 1920s. Max Warren paid a warm tribute to him in his autobiography:

I came into office with a very deep respect for my predecessor. What attracted me above all was the spirit of the man. Throughout a large part of his time as General Secretary he had been occupied with an unhappy theological controversy in which the society was involved. What profoundly impressed me, as it did many others, was that he never allowed controversy to dirty his soul. Bilious comment he always refused to respond to with bile. This was the gentleness not of a weak man but of a very strong one . . . From Dr Cash I learnt that it is possible to disagree without bitterness even about the most deeply held

convictions: to disagree and yet to remain in spiritual
fellowship.

Again, I was fortunate that Dr Cash's far-sighted
statesmanship had ensured that the Society entered the
war years in a financial situation which was basically as
sound as possible; that of being out of debt.

(*Crowded Canvas*, pp. 115–116)

The financial situation was indeed serious in 1942, and was
only saved from being disastrous because during the war no
recruits (or virtually none) could be sent overseas. So the war
helped – at least to balance the budget. But meantime
missionaries were unable to take long leaves; stations stag-
nated with no replacements; in some areas (as in Tanganyika)
the depleted missionary ranks had to lend staff to Lutheran
churches and schools whose German staff had been interned.
The withdrawal of missionary leadership did of course call
forth local leadership, but medical doctors, and men with
advanced theological and academic training, cannot spring
forth overnight. There were gaps which could not be filled.

Meantime Max Warren was finding his place in Salisbury
Square and among the secretaries, where he was *primus inter
pares*. Some sections of the secretariat had been evacuated to
Chislehurst, the former men's training centre just outside
London. As he writes, the secretaries were tired; no end to
the war was in sight; and the end of the war would bring back
"a great many desperately tired missionaries returning from
long-extended terms of service abroad".

So, in some senses, the remaining years of the war were, for
the parent committee, a marking of time and a preparation
for the crises ahead. In 1943 Max Warren sailed by the *Queen
Mary* to New York to attend the jubilee celebrations of the
Foreign Missions Conference of North America. But more
important became his encounter, on the journey, with a
delegation of American and British trades unionists (and
ultimately with many other passengers) with whom what is

now called "a meaningful dialogue" took place. Warren listened to them; they listened to him. And that journey in many ways set the direction of his future work.

> Somehow, as I saw it, I had to share my understanding of the context in which the modern missionary had to work, help the missionary to understand it, and go on understanding it better myself. At the same time I had to try, as far as possible, to help the devoted and dedicated members of the Society at home to welcome the brave and strange new world in which the Gospel had to be interpreted,
>
> (*Crowded Canvas*, p. 114)

One way in which he communicated, with missionaries and with the Society's members, was through the *CMS News-Letter*, which had been started by Dr. Cash. Dr. Warren (and his successors) have kept up an important medium of communication, and the letters, written often in response to current events, can still be read with profit – and delighted interest – many years later.

As the years of the war were obviously drawing to a close, the Society used a newsletter format to communicate its thoughts for the future to the same people – missionaries and members. In autumn 1944 Max Warren on behalf of the secretaries submitted an "Inquiry" to the committees of the Society. After discussion it was remodelled, and finally a twenty-four page pamphlet was printed and sent out (in February 1945).

It is a remarkable and a prophetic document, and worth recalling both for its content and for the way it sets the scene for the future. It puts the Church and the missionary task within the changing world context. Warren mentions first the growth of the social service State, as surely as if he had seen already the results of the 1945 election. The tensions which will arise between Christians and the State he sees clearly also, but without fear. "An awareness of this tension, and the acceptance of the suffering and misunderstanding it will involve, is absolutely essential if the missionary task of the Church is to be maintained in our time." (p. 4)

He goes on to speak of the new nationalism "coming to its full flowering after the long revolt against the medieval synthesis in the West", and of his belief that the forces making for nationalism will impede the trend towards a standardised economic order. He looks at the world-wide Churches and draws attention to the emergence of the indigenous Churches, related to the missionary movement, and of the probable growth of autonomous Churches which must inevitably draw away from their founding Churches and societies. Then in some detail he speaks of the inadequacy of missionary personnel, and relates this to the financial resources available, and likely to be available in the near future.

He sets out very clearly the situation in which the Society will find itself at the end of the war, including a clear analysis of the harm as well as the help likely to result from larger government grants (as in Africa, for educationalists).

And, having dealt in some detail with financial matters, he returns to close with a message from the Spirit, and in the Spirit. There are two factors which must not be left out of account – if God calls a man to his service He provides the means, and the incalculable possibility of a revival of spiritual life first in the Church and then in the nation.

Seeing then that we cannot dictate the course of events in any case it would seem the path of wisdom at least to envisage the Society not as some rigid organization hard bound by the rules and precedents of another age, but as an organic fellowship of men and women who are seeking to be obedient to the calling of God in this generation, and who will be willing to make precedents as well as to follow them, and who will remember that the rules of the Society were at one time adventurous innovations and that what has happened once can happen again. (p. 23)

The way ahead was in every way as difficult as Max Warren and the secretaries had envisaged. He followed up the earlier Inquiry with three shorter letters: *A letter of interpretation to all missionaries* (March 1946); *Invitation to danger* (January 1947); and *The will to go on* (January 1948). From the last:

The title of that last letter, *Invitation to danger*, has been more than justified by the event. Unparalleled economic distress over a large part of the world, increasing political unrest in almost every country, the replacement of ordered government by the forces of anarchy, these are the commonplaces of our contemporary situation. (p. 2)

He writes frankly about the very difficult financial situation and the probability of rapid and necessary changes in the pattern of work overseas. In part these letters are dictated by his great sensitivity to the feelings of the missionary on the spot. He or she sees so clearly the opportunities opening – *if only* there is money and new staff; he or she sees so clearly the disasters if no help comes. And it always seems that some other field, some other diocese, some other country, is receiving the help instead. How much trust is needed!

During the immediate post-war period Max Warren also helped to bring the Society firmly into the mid-20th century by the appointment of two men who came out of the commercial and business world to advise and help the CMS at a most opportune time. One was Leslie Stubbings, who became Publicity Director. The other was Bernard Nicholls, who became Public Relations Officer. Max Warren paid warm tribute to them both in his autobiography (*Crowded Canvas*, pp. 126–128). They were especially valuable as they worked with Leslie Fisher, the Home Secretary, on the "Third Jubilee Programme" in 1948–1949.

It is perhaps less surprising that men like John Drewett and Douglas Webster should have served as successsive

Education Secretaries, for one expects more from a missionary society in the realm of theology and education than in publicity and public relations. But how fortunate when both can be advanced together! The Society again owed much to Max Warren for his courage and discernment in making appointments.

India and Church Union: to 1947

In the difficult days after the war, as Churches and missions struggled back on their feet, the eyes of the Anglican world turned on India. For it was there that nearly thirty years of committee meetings, conferences, minutes, published schemes, and many, many books and pamphlets were leading to a climax. In 1947 occurred the inauguration of the Church of South India, and it was the largest and most complex re-union of Churches to take place up to that time.

India held a place of high affection in the hearts of Anglicans. So many English Christians had personal and family ties there. It would, but for the rules of the East India Company, have been the Society's first field. It was always a complex mission area, combining as it did pioneer work to illiterate peasants and colleges for wealthy and sophisticated aristocrats, ministry to expatriates of the Army and Civil Service and to mixed-race Christians, and contacts with an ancient Orthodox Church.

It might have been expected that in India, rather than West Africa, the Church would have pioneered with national leadership and seen the development of the *three selves*. One reason why it lagged behind was because in India the CMS related to an established Church, tied to the British Crown, and not wholly free to develop as an *Indian* Church. When in 1930 the legal constraints were taken away, the strong psychological constraints remained. A great advance was made in 1912, when a young Indian from Tinnivelly,

V. S. Azariah, was consecrated bishop. He became technically assistant bishop in the diocese of Madras, whose bishop, Henry Whitehead, had sponsored and encouraged him. But he was given full jurisdiction in the Telugu-speaking area of Dornakal, where the Indian Missionary Society, which he had founded, was working. Dornakal and its neighbouring territory, included in the area over which Azariah was allotted jurisdiction, were in the realm of the Nizam of Hydrabad, and therefore problems relating to the established Church did not arise.

V. S. Azariah was a remarkable man; his chief fault, as Bishop Stephen Neill points out, was that in a sense he spoiled the market by his very greatness. He was the son of a village pastor in Tinnevelly; he worked for thirteen years as a YMCA secretary in southern India, where he learned to take leadership, to cooperate with Christians of many denominations, and also to work in friendship and equality with Western colleagues. When he himself decided that he should join the mission team working in Dornakal, Bishop Whitehead helped and encouraged him in reading for ordination.

But before Azariah became bishop, only a few months after his ordination as priest, in 1910, he was present as a delegate (one of the very few from the "younger Churches") at the 1910 Edinburgh Conference. He presented a paper entitled "Cooperation between foreign and native workers in the younger Churches." His tone was moderate and conciliatory, but there was an implied criticism in his conclusion, in words that have been quoted often enough to become famous. "Through all the ages to come the Indian Church will rise up in gratitude to attest the heroism and self-denying labours of the missionary body. You have given your goods to feed the poor; you have given your bodies to be burned; we ask also for *love*. Give us *friends*."

Edinburgh was important to him not only for his exposure to the leadership of the world Protestant Churches, but also for the follow-up in the continuation conferences. The National Missionary Conference which commenced in 1912 became by 1922 the National Christian Council of India.

The climate of India, politically and in the Churches, was ready for the discussion of any scheme which emphasised Indian leadership and control. But the Christian emphasis was much more than an appeal for independence. Continuing mass movements were bringing large populations into the Churches, and there was a need to utilise all possible workers to the best advantage. Although the Churches had grown they were still a tiny proportion of Indian society, and the divisions were a scandal. Indian Christians were as a whole exceptionally mobile, and often moved to work in areas where, because of mission comity agreements, they could find no church of their own denomination. The cooperating Christian colleges of higher education made young Christians both conscious of, and impatient with, the varying denominations. Nationalism was in the air; in a soon-to-be-independent India should there be these Western-made divisions? And among missionary leaders there were many able men who saw these issues clearly, who were willing to listen to others, to change, to risk their own status, in order to see something better in India than they knew in their home countries.

So, in south India, the first steps were taken that ultimately led (in 1947) to the Church of South India. Later, in 1970, the Church of North India and the Church of Pakistan were inaugurated. Just as the mission-founded Churches of East Africa brought a gift to the world-wide Church in the movement known as the East African Revival, so the mission-founded Churches of the Indian sub-continent have brought the gift of visible organic unity. As a second gift they have enriched the liturgies of other Churches, as they themselves were enriched in using the liturgical resources of their re-uniting churches in their new liturgies.

It is not possible to trace the complex and long-drawn-out

negotiations which occupied nearly thirty years. There was already in south India a united Church – the South India United Church (SIUC) – formed from a union of Congregational and Presbyterian-founded Churches. The other elements were the Anglican Churches in the four dioceses of Madras, Travancore, Tinnevelly and Dornakal, and Methodist Churches. The influence of the CMS was strong throughout the four dioceses, and all were in a deep sense Evangelical. But Anglo-Catholic missions were also present.

The movement toward union could hardly have begun if the Anglican dioceses had not, in 1930, become part of a free self-governing province of the world-wide Anglican Communion. With neighbouring British colonies included, these dioceses were no longer controlled ultimately from outside (by Canterbury) but were now "The Church of India, Burma and Ceylon". In 1930 Bishop Azariah was still the only Indian bishop, though two Indian assistant bishops were consecrated in 1935 and 1937 (Tarafdar in Calcutta and Bannerjee in Lahore).

The first formal step on the way to the CSI, after much informal discussion, was a meeting at Tranquebar, chaired by Bishop Azariah, in 1919. There, thirty-three people, members of the Anglican Churches and the SIUC, discussed the possibility of wider union. All but two of those meeting were Indians. They concluded with a call to union, based on the so-called Lambeth Quadrilateral.

The Lambeth Quadrilateral, which had emerged from the Lambeth conference of 1880, laid down four cornerstones which were required if any union discussion could go forward. They were (1) the Holy Scriptures of the Old and New Testaments, as containing all things necessary to salvation; (2) the Apostles' Creed and the Nicene Creed; (3) the two sacraments of baptism and the Lord's Supper; (4) the historic episcopate, locally adapted. It was clear, from the beginning that "the historic episcopate", with all that it signified in authority, ordination, and inter-communion, would be the most difficult item. And so it proved.

In 1920 the Churches involved at Tranquebar appointed members to a joint committee to continue the discussions, and in 1925 the Methodist Church in south India joined in. (It should be remembered that although the SIUC and the Methodist Church were not divided like the Anglicans with the CMS and SPG elements, they were divided by missions coming from Britain and the United States, which brought with them very different views on leadership and authority.) In 1929 a Scheme of Union was published; subsequently discussed in the most minute detail within India and overseas, it was changed, modified and presented again in 1941 for final approval. The negotiating Churches had to consider their continuing relations with their "mother Churches" and missionary societies. The world war prevented a conference, but in the case of the Anglicans every province world-wide was consulted. In January 1945 the CIBC gave its consent for the four south India dioceses to leave it and enter the new Church. A difficult but vital part of the Scheme was the "pledge" – by which the united Church promised not to impose on any congregation forms of worship, or a minister, to which they conscientiously objected. Last-minute difficulties arose here, and the final affirmative decision was made in January 1947. With the Methodist Church and the SIUC also consenting, the Church of South India was inaugurated in Madras Cathedral on 27 September 1947.

It was a propitious year, since in that same year India – divided into the two nations of India and Pakistan – became independent dominions. But there was sadness that Bishop Azariah was not there to see the consummation of all he had worked for. He had died at the age of seventy in 1945.

If the discussions had been confined to south India – even with the participation of missionary leaders – the process might have been much more rapid. In fact, some British

Anglicans fought doggedly against the Scheme, and pages of *The Church Times* and *The Times* testify to this intense concern. The sending societies of the Anglican Church were inevitably involved. The CMS was in general favourable to the Scheme. The SPG was wary and although its secretary behaved very correctly in not seeking to interfere in the affairs of independent dioceses, he sounded warnings over "too comprehensive an outlook on inter-communion and equal ministries" (Sundkler, p.141). In the event, after much heart-searching SPG grants to the uniting dioceses ceased at the end of 1947, and missionaries and Indian clergy who became members of the CSI had to give up their formal connection with the SPG. The Archbishop of Canterbury, Dr. Geoffrey Fisher, intervened in a difficult situation to help set up a south India separate account to aid former SPG missionaries and the work within south India formerly funded by the SPG.

Dr. Warren pays tribute to Archbishop Fisher's contribution to the mission of the Anglican Church overseas when he describes the books which he called into being on Catholicity. One – the first – was written by a group of known Anglo-Catholic theologians; the second by those of Evangelical tradition; the third by Free Church scholars. Max Warren himself was a contributor to the second volume, and he wrote, "I was particularly glad to be associated with this enterprise, as it served to demonstrate that the emphatic position taken by CMS as to continuing support for the Church of south India was based on theological principles which could not be lightly dismissed."

(*Crowded Canvas*, p.167)

Missions leave China; the CMS opens in Malaysia

In 1947, when India achieved her independence, Max Warren was travelling in China, and he went with Canon Harry

Wittenbach to pay his respects to the Indian embassy in Nanking. It was ironic that at such a point India – nation and Church — was embarking on a new journey of voluntarily chosen co-endeavour, while in China a forced cooperation in the Church was coming, and a long period in the wilderness as far as the rest of the world Church was concerned.

China had been a relatively late field for the CMS, and never of quite the same importance as India. The highly disturbed conditions which prevailed in the 19th century continued into the 20th century. In 1911 the Manchu dynasty at last fell, and on New Year's Day 1912 Sun Yat-sen assumed office as provisional president of the Chinese Republic. The change-over period was not without its dangers, but no CMS missionaries (and indeed, comparatively few, whether Chinese or Western) lost their lives.

However, the hopes for a democratic republic did not last long. By 1913 Dr. Sun was in exile, and General Yan Shih-ki was seeking control. The years from 1916 to 1925 are head-lined "The years of chaos" in the CMS History. Warlords again fought for control of provinces; there was a rising tide of nationalism and an appeal from Dr. Sun (in desperation, since the West had failed to help) to Russia. Missions and missionaries were sympathetic to Sun, and believed his protégé (and brother-in-law) Chiang Kai-shek to be a man they could cooperate with. Chiang Kai-shek succeeded Sun at his death in 1925, as leader of the Kuomintang (Nationalist) Party. But without a strong central government there was little anyone could do.

The years from 1925 to 1928 may be labelled "the second revolution". Starting with a student-led demonstration in the International Settlement in Shanghai there were violent anti-foreign strikes and demonstrations throughout China. Rifts between the Chinese Communist Party and the Kuomintang became apparent. Most missionaries in the inland of south and west China had to leave their posts, going at least to the coast and in some cases taking overseas leaves or going temporarily to Japan. When the IMC Jerusalem meeting opened in April 1928, it appeared to many there that the day of the foreign missionary in China was over. But God granted them another twenty years; by the end of 1928 many of the evacuated missionaries were back on their stations.

From 1928 to 1937 Chiang Kai-shek was virtually the dictator of China. But the Communists were gathering strength, and Japan was mustering her forces for full-scale invasion. The Japanese threat brought the two factions together; the expected war broke out in July 1937. By 1939 the country was effectively divided; the coastal areas were almost totally under Japanese control. Thousands of people – including whole educational institutions – went west as refugees into "free China". Missionaries stayed on under the Japanese in the coastal regions, working fairly normally, until 1942 when they were interned or deported. Those in the west continued to give practical help and to evangelise among the refugees, but for the political parties – as for the missionaries – it was now a long wait till the World War should end, as it did in August 1945.

Despite all the turmoil the Church in China had continued to grow. By 1930 the Anglican-related section, now formed into the *Chung Hua Sheng Kung Hui*, had twelve dioceses. In 1936 there were about six thousand Protestant missionaries in China; nearly half of them came from the USA and Canada. This was a decline from a high of nearly eight thousand in 1924. Although the number of foreign missionaries had dropped, the number of communicants was rising. Between 1914 and 1936 the numbers doubled, even allowing for those at one time members who "disappeared" from Churches into the mass of people in the huge and still sparsely evangelised country.

Protestant Christianity was deeply involved in education in China, especially at secondary and university level. From the late 1920s government regulations affected Christian schools, and there was a general tendency towards secularisation. Missionaries, especially from the USA, made notable contributions as professors and teachers, but often could only give a personal and individual Christian witness. Nor were these large institutions, heavily subsidised from overseas and often managed by inter-denominational boards, easy to pass over to national control. The same applied to the excellent hospitals set up and maintained by missions. Despite the contributions of many fine Chinese staff, they remained very much missionary institutions.

The twelve dioceses of the *Chung Hua Sheng Kung Hui* related to several different founding missions. Three dioceses were connected to the CMS; two others were connected to the CMS and also to other societies. These dioceses were along the southern and south-eastern coasts of China, except for western China (Szechwan), where the CMS had shared work with an Anglican section of the China Inland Mission.

As in other countries, the aim was always to see the mission grow into an independent self-governing, self-supporting, and self-propagating Church. Perhaps the progress was slower in China than in some other parts of the world. Among many factors, we can note that in China there were no bodies of ancient Christians to strengthen the hands of Western missionaries, and no mass movement occurred. The Churches grew one by one, or at best family by family. Of the young men who passed through the Christian colleges into the Christian universities comparatively few felt called to align themselves with the "foreign devils". Though many missionaries were personally dearly loved, they remained for the most part representatives of much-hated foreign powers in the eyes of the Chinese people. However, by 1918 there was a Chinese assistant bishop in Chekiang, and in the 1920s also in Fukien diocese and in Szechwan. The missionary bishops proceeded with plans to hand over control and property to diocesan bodies. All this continued despite ongoing disruptions and violence on an immense scale. In 1923 two male missionaries were kidnapped and murdered in Fukien. In 1925 Howard Mowll (soon to become bishop), with his wife and eight other missionaries, were taken from a holiday home in Szechwan and held for over three weeks in the mountains, but were all released. The wonder was that any work continued, and faithful teachers, catechists, clergy and hospital staff proved their commitment to Christ by their steadfast devotion.

The end of the war between the Allies and the Axis powers did not mean an end to fighting in China. Missionaries were released from internment; passages home were arranged for them. A few were able to go back and assess the situation. As well as material damage and incredible suffering – refugees and orphans in millions – they also found evidence of the faithful service of Chinese Christians. In Peking, for instance, a Chinese clergyman, the Rev. Timothy Lin, had continued services at the cathedral without a break.

Slowly more missionaries returned and began the task of rebuilding. But a civil war was raging between the Nationalists and the Chinese Communists. The armies of each group had raced to take over the Japanese-held territory, the one being given help by the USA, the other by the USSR. The outcome was by no means a foregone conclusion. But by the end of 1947 a Communist offensive was under way, and the Communists' military successes were supported by widespread popular approval. Finally, on 1 October 1949, Mao Tse-tung, in Peking (now to be capital) proclaimed the People's Republic of China. The years following, 1949 to 1952, were years of reconstruction and consolidation, when a war-weary nation struggled to rebuild and regroup for the future.

Even at this point, in late 1949, many missionaries hoped to stay on. At a slightly earlier date they were being actively encouraged by Church leaders to return to China. In 1948 the Bishop of Hong Kong asked Canon G. K. Carpenter and his wife to return to Canton for theological teaching. But by the time they reached Hong Kong, towards the end of 1949, no entry visas to go inland were being received.

Still, work continued. In Fukien a very successful youth camp was held in September 1950, during which over thirty young people were confirmed. There were baptisms in a number of places; Bibles and Testaments were distributed and received eagerly. But by Christmas 1950 the change in atmosphere was obvious, and it was realised that those Christmas services would be the last, at least in the tradition which had been known. Missionaries were now being refused permission to travel locally, and they realised that their presence might endanger the Chinese Christians. It was time to go. Most applied for exit visas, which sometimes took months to come through. Christians showed great love and put themselves in danger to support the missionaries. It was reported that at Sia-Pu, in Fukien, when at the end of February the missionaries left under escort, the pastor led prayers, and that large numbers of Church members, hospital staff, students and teachers from the Church schools went out with them to the city gates and along the road. They knew the danger of possible reprisals, but were willing to risk it.

In June 1950 there were just over fifty CMS missionaries in China. A year later, all but seven had left. And in June 1952 there was just one. Dr. S. D. Sturton was professor of radiology at Chekiang Medical College, and the authorities regarded him as essential to its work, and refused him an exit visa. Other missions also had only the one or two exceptions left in China. After just over a hundred years of work, the foreign missionary presence in China was over.

So, by the middle of 1951, a number of missionaries were, either in their home countries or in Hong Kong or Singapore, waiting for relocation. One such couple were the Carpenters who, after ten years of home service following seventeen years in China, had left their family and gone back. Their hope was to proceed to Canton. In fact, they were never able to go beyond Hong Kong.

It soon became clear that China was closed to outside workers. Some missionaries were relocated to completely new cultures – such as Dr. David Milton Thompson and his wife Beatrice, who were to serve in Kenya for another thirty years. But was there no sphere where the particular experiences of the "old China hands", especially their hard-gained knowledge of a very difficult language, could be used? There was, in Malaya.

Malaya had been under British influence, direct and indirect, since the 1860s, and Anglican work there had been initiated first by chaplains (sent primarily to the British officials and settlers) and then by the SPG. Of the peoples living in Malaya, the Malays were strongly Muslim, and evangelising among them was practically forbidden by the administration. There were two large immigrant populations. The south Indians – Tamil-speakers for the most part – had come to work on the rubber plantations. Some of them were Christians on arrival. The Chinese came initially to work in the tin mines, but many became prosperous through commerce. From the Chinese and the south Indians came most of those who became Christians.

The Japanese conquest of Malaya in 1942 was rapid and brutal. About 166,600 British soldiers lost their lives. Europeans, including missionaries, were interned. The peoples of Malaya were treated in very different ways. The Malays were employed in positions of responsibility; the Indians were encouraged to form an army which would help to free India from British rule; the Chinese were persecuted and brutally treated. There already existed a Communist Party among Malayan Chinese, and in the jungles was organised the Malayan People's Anti-Japanese Army (MPAJA). Many Chinese labourers fled away into the jungle to join it.

When the war ended and the British came back, it was not

so easy to go back to the pre-war situation. The Malays were now pressing strongly for independence. But the guerrilla bands which had fought the Japanese were now disrupting the economy and seeking to bring in a Communist régime. The guerrillas could not survive in the jungle without food coming in from outside, and this was supplied by their relations and friends in the villages. In 1948 when the Communist Party rose in open revolt, a state of emergency was declared.

Very slow progress was made in the struggle to eliminate the Chinese guerrillas from the jungles. Finally, in 1950, it was decided to bring all the Chinese squatters into large, guarded "new villages", where they would not be able to communicate with the Communist bands or give them food. So, in a very short time, 420 "new villages" were formed and thousands of Chinese were uprooted from their homes and transported for shorter or longer distances to rebuild a home and a new way of life.

Obviously the Bishop of Singapore saw the opportunities, as well as the problems, of these new population centres. His diocese had never been well-staffed; now the needs were even greater. And not far away were experienced missionaries, already speaking Chinese languages, asking for assignments. Needless to say, he invited them in.

The CMS agreed to send and support ten missionaries. The Carpenters, already in Hong Kong, were asked to prepare the way. They arrived in Kuala Lumpur in July 1951. By the end of that year there were fourteen CMS missionaries in Malaya; the original ten had been increased by some from the NZCMS and Australian CMS. The CEZMS and the Australian branch of the Overseas Missionary Fellowship – the new name of the old CIM – were also invited to send former Chinese missionaries, and they accepted.

The main task for the newly arrived missionaries was to establish a presence and a witness in the new villages, and to build up a church in each one. On the whole the method adopted was to send a team of two women, usually one missionary and one Chinese nurse, to start a clinic, where welfare work could be centred. The women would live as nearly as possible like the villagers, breaking down the suspicion which would inevitably arise. Play groups, school classes, women's groups, would follow. It was desirable for the first attempts to be made in villages fairly near Kuala Lumpur, so that the Chinese priests already working there could come out for services and baptisms. After delays permission was given for clinics to be established in Sungei Buloh, Jin Jang, and Salah South, all quite close to Kuala Lumpur, and later in more distant villages. The first witness came when the villagers saw the workers living together as friends and colleagues.

Missionary clergy and senior women were able to travel from a central spot giving help and encouragement. Kathleen Carpenter, who did just that, wrote moving accounts of this new work. Her first book is titled *The password is love*. And it was the love of Jesus seen in the nurses and others which drew many Chinese men, women and children into the fellowship of the Church, while they lived as semi-prisoners behind the barbed wire of the villages.

Gradually the fight for the country was won. An anti-Communist but also anti-colonialist Chinese party, the Malayan Chinese Association, joined forces with the Malay Nationalists, and in 1955 their alliance won almost all the seats in the legislative assembly. In 1957 the British Government handed over the government of the country to the local leaders. The emergency did not end till 1960. Singapore gained full self-government in 1959, and in 1963 Malaysia was established as a separate nation, leaving Singapore as another country of the Commonwealth. The work in the "new villages" continued as the emergency measures were gradually withdrawn. The number of CMS missionaries in Malaysia increased to over twenty, and some were assigned to work other than in the villages. But the

churches established in the villages put down roots and
continued. So out of the closing-up of China to CMS
missionaries came the opening-up of Malaya, and in addition
contributions from ex-China missionaries in many other
parts of the world.

Changes in the Anglican Communion

Truly, the end of the World War had not brought to an end
war in the world. In continent after continent, in nation after
nation, wars, however disguised in the language as liberation
struggles, guerrilla bands, isolated terrorist attacks or whatever, were breaking out. In the ten years after the end of the
world conflict, the CMS was close to the battle lines in place
after place. China, Malaya, Kenya, Uganda (although as yet
no fighting there), Egypt, Sudan. The struggle in Korea did
not touch the CMS so closely, but it did touch the Anglican
Communion, for American Episcopalians and English
missionaries of the SPG were deeply involved.

As we have seen, it was the case in several countries
that missionaries were expelled, and even before the edicts
were passed they came to feel themselves an embarrassment
to the national Churches. For a long time missionaries had
been talking about a self-governing, self-supporting, self-
propagating Church. Now, more than ever, it was necessary
to turn talking into reality.

Many changes had been made which helped a smooth
transition. For example, when the missionaries, mostly
medical personnel, had to leave Old Cairo Hospital in
1956, there were already joint mission-Church boards and
committees set up as early as 1950, and so the trained
Egyptian staff were able to carry on.

The CMS secretaries in England, needless to say, were in
favour of such developments. Their task was not easy. In
many respects they stood in the middle, between a Christian

constituency which still saw mission in personalised terms – "our own missionary" – and the serving missionaries overseas who, however much they agreed in theory and in principle with the ending of dependence, were still emotionally attached, somewhat threatened, and saw the local difficulties so clearly that they felt an exception needed to be made in their particular case. Max Warren foresaw the difficulties bound to arise in the change from fairly direct CMS involvement in the affairs of overseas dioceses to a time when, although individual CMS missionaries would still be present and serving, the participation of, say, a CMS local secretary would no longer be welcome. In addition, the missionaries would no longer be serving in colonies of their home country, dealing with administrators with whom they might easily have been at school or college, and who, in more than one sense, spoke the same language. Now they would be foreigners and aliens, dealing with officials who, consciously or unconsciously, wished to underline the fact that the missionaries were there on sufferance.

It seems best to let Max Warren speak for himself on this point.

For me, and for my colleagues, it seemed an urgent matter for the C.M.S. to be put in a posture where it could be of maximum service in the coming new political situation. Already such machinery as we possessed abroad was very simple, a corresponding secretary with an office. Conferences of missionaries, where they survived, were rapidly ceasing, or had ceased, to be the centres of power they had been in an earlier day. But even greater simplification was now being demanded. To this end we proposed a regional secretariat for East Africa which would be able, over a wide area, to relate the needs of the several dioceses to the strictly limited resources of the Society. It was as simple and innocuous an idea as that. However, we badly miscalculated the reactions of 'the man on the spot'. He, whether Bishop, Archdeacon or Mission Secretary, all of them English, together with many a missionary, interpreted this as an insidious attempt to establish control from Salisbury Square. Our purpose, in point of fact, was to abandon every vestige of such distant control as might still appear to exist. And we wanted to do this before all positions of authority were held by Africans, who might think that we were withdrawing support. But the presentation of our case was unconvincing. No doubt there were personality problems which were complicating factors. Furthermore, the 'man on the spot' saw only the 'spot'. Nowhere was he seriously facing the imminent end of colonial rule – I write of the late forties. In the sequel, the chance was lost of creating a really adaptable machinery which would have helped to smooth the early years of that provincial development which the Archbishop was soon to initiate. We did, indeed, establish a regional framework but it was only given grudging local support. When provincial autonomy was established the necessity for just such provision was belatedly recognised as essential. But a great opportunity for a smooth transition had been thrown away. (*Crowded Canvas*, pp. 169-170)

Regional secretariats were set up in West Africa, in East Africa (for Kenya and Uganda) and in India. Undoubtedly they did help the transition, and it is now impossible to see how much more they might have accomplished if the preparation and the acceptance had been different.

At almost the same time important changes were taking place in the organisation of the world-wide Anglican Communion, helped generously by the then Archbishop of Canterbury, Dr. Geoffrey Fisher, to whom Warren pays warm tribute.

Someday, so I believe, it will come to be recognised that the single most farsighted piece of statesmanship during his archepiscopate, was his steady and deliberate diminution of the metropolitan authority of the Archbishop of Canterbury. The decisive step which he took in this connection was the hastening of the creation of new Ecclesiastical Provinces which were to enjoy virtually complete autonomy. (*ibid*, p. 169)

Before the creation of the Provinces came the consecration of more national bishops, at first as assistant or suffragan bishops. Many, many Africans still remember with great joy the day in May 1955 when Archbishop Fisher, in Namirembe Cathedral, consecrated four men for such positions in the dioceses of Sudan, Mombasa, and Central Tanganyika.

In 1950 there was only one Anglican archbishop in the whole of Africa, and that was the Archbishop of Cape Town. The next province was that of West Africa, inaugurated in 1951 (and, sadly, with the diocese of Liberia outside it for other than religious or theological reasons). Next, in 1960, came the two East African Provinces, Uganda, and the Province of East Africa which included Kenya and Tanganyika. That province was in 1970 divided according to the national boundaries. Further south, the Church of the Province of Central Africa came into being. So by 1970 there were six Anglican archbishops in Africa. Several were at first white missionaries, but soon African nationals held these positions also, and the unusual thing was to find a white bishop.

Needless to say, Max Warren was much involved in the behind-the-scenes happenings in both the ecclesiastical and the political developments. He was often the go-between for Church leaders in trouble spots and politicians and administrators back in Britain; likewise he was often the archbishop's chief adviser in a matter of choosing a suitable itinerary or in the setting-up of a new provincial constitution. But his routine work had to be continued, including the writing of the monthly *CMS News-Letter* and other articles and books. Committees also continued – Warren would have been the first to admit how much he owed to his fellow Secretaries and secretaries. And above all, he was "in journeyings often". From that wartime journey across the Atlantic on the *Queen Mary* he travelled every year, renewing old friendships, and making new friends, personally and for the CMS and for the Church. He travelled to the places where the missionaries were, and the places from which their support came.

Many of his journeys were connected with that great secular and religious phenomenon of this century, the world conference. Both the world-wide Anglican Communion and the world-wide ecumenical movement engaged his time and attention. In the ecumenical world the CMS stood in a peculiar and important position. Although manifestly a Church mission, related to and serving a State Church, it had many features in common with conservative faith missions and with inter-denominational and "non-denominational" missions. There were therefore occasions when CMS personnel could act as intermediaries. Churches related to the CMS joined local and international groupings which were taboo to many, especially American, Churches and missionary societies. Anglo-Catholics, for different reasons, also felt unable to participate in many ecumenical gatherings, and here their fellow Anglicans in the CMS could be mediators.

In 1948, after the long preliminary period in which the conferences on "Life and Work" and "Faith and Order" prepared the way, the World Council of Churches came into being at the first assembly, Amsterdam. Max Warren was not present then, but he was at the second assembly at Evanston (outside Chicago) in 1954. In the same year he attended the Anglican Congress at Minneapolis, and in 1963 that at Toronto. For the 1958 Lambeth Conference he was chairman of the important commission on "The Family in Contemporary Society", and also contributed one of the major study documents, "Missionary Commitments of the Anglican Communion."

But perhaps Max Warren's most important and crucial contribution came in relation to the International Missionary Council (IMC). The IMC was a third section parallel to "Life and Work" and "Faith and Order", in the pre-Amsterdam developments moving towards an ecumenical organisation. But at Amsterdam the IMC remained outside as an independent, yet closely related body. WCC was a council of *Churches*; the IMC was a council of councils and missionary societies. But there was a joint-committee, of which Max Warren was early a member. It also met separately, at Whitby (Canada) in 1947, at Willingen (Germany) in 1952, and at Evanston in 1954. Pressures began to build up to bring the IMC into the WCC. In this move Warren's part was crucial. He began by strongly opposing the move, and his argument (given in his autobiography on pages 157 to 159) should be studied in full by those who are interested in an important issue as considered by one who had thought and prayed over it for years. He concludes his case by saying:

At the joint-committee I was courteously allowed once again to state my case which I developed mainly on the ground of the need for maximum flexibility in the Missionary enterprise. Dr Helen Kim of Korea warmly supported me, but we were overwhelmingly outvoted. As far as I was concerned I thought this was the end of the matter. I had persevered in stating my case, had been given a fair hearing, and had failed to carry conviction. Knowing that the I.M.C. Conference to be held in Ghana in the following year would be asked to endorse the decision of the joint-committee, I intended to remain silent on the issue at that conference. (*Crowded Canvas*, pp. 158-9)

But the matter was not allowed to rest there. Max Warren found that at the Ghana meeting (1957) a number of delegates, especially Germans and Scandinavians, fully agreed with him, and wished him to present their case because of their own inability to do so adequately in English. Despite his reluctance to speak, he was in fact asked to do so by the chairman who, "having discovered the wide measure of resentment in the conference at the way the issue of Integration had been presented as a *chose jugée*, asked me to speak, knowing the line I would take, hoping that this would redress the balance somewhat." (*ibid*, p. 159)

As he describes it, he spoke with "fear and trembling". But he succeeded in defusing a tense situation, and he explained why he would vote for integration, because "things have gone too far for the Assembly to turn back". He adds, "This was my swan-song as far as the I.M.C. was concerned, but not so far as the Ecumenical Movement is concerned. That, in the mercy of God, is not wholly engrossed with structures." (*ibid*, p. 160)

The union was formalised in 1961 at the New Delhi assembly of the WCC, when the IMC became the Division of World Mission and Evangelism of the WCC (DWME), and the Commission on World Mission and Evangelism was set up. It was that section which was responsible for the great conference in Melbourne in 1980. So the work continues, and Max Warren's contribution is not forgotten. Nor is he. He was to a vast number of people throughout the world a friend, a guide and a philosopher, a leader under God for whom they still give thanks.

13 TENSIONS IN AFRICA

Emergency in Kenya

After an emergency in Malaya, an emergency in Kenya.
After "new villages" in Malaya, "villagisation" in Kenya.
Those in control in Kenya consciously took over and adapted
helpful aspects of the anti-guerrilla campaign in Malaya, but
the two situations were not really so similar. In the case of
missions, the CMS was already deeply involved in Kenya,
and could not escape being caught up in the emergency.

This section is largely about the period of "the
emergency" in Kenya, and cannot do justice to the growth
and development, in Kenya as a whole, and in the Anglican
Church, since independence. But this crisis was important to
the Society, both in itself, and as the last time where the
Society was deeply involved with those in Britain who formed
policy. In Kenya today this period is seldom spoken of, but
the "roots of bitterness" as well as the "roots of freedom" lie
there, and we need at least to attempt understanding.

J. L. Krapf had commenced his residence on the East
African coast in 1844, but until the coming of the Imperial
British East Africa Company and the building of the railway
it had remained a small and geographically confined mission.
From the turn of the century things were different. Missions,
everywhere commencing with primary schools, spread
rapidly, and the number of Christians rose. The CMS worked
in three main areas, and had three different conferences and
councils: coast, highlands and Kavirondo. The work among
Europeans was separate, and only the bishop really brought
the two sections together.

For Kenya was a divided country. With a large and largely progressive African population it had also a strong and vocal white settler population, with many upper-class members used to leadership and command. Dukes, members of the House of Lords, baronets, retired officers of the armed services, a considerable proportion of former members of the Indian Civil Service – all were found in Kenya. From the first period of settlement their spokesmen were Lord Delamere, Lord Francis Scott, and Colonel Grogan. Such men (who, like Grogan, often had ties with South Africa) introduced a *de facto* apartheid system into Kenyan life. Not that the treatment of African employees was necessarily hard and cruel. It was often kind and humane. But an African, even a well-educated man who had studied overseas, was excluded from hotels and restaurants; schooling was rigidly divided on racial and ethnic lines; the tiny minority of mixed-race children were an embarrassment to the education department, for they fitted nowhere. This situation brought difficulty enough to the missionaries who were there to preach a gospel of love and equality in the eyes of God. But the deepest problem in Kenya, as both white settlers and Africans saw it, was land.

Kenya combines areas of high rainfall and high fertility with larger tracts of semi-desert where even cattle-keeping is hazardous. The agricultural peoples of the central high-lands, who also kept cattle, sheep and goats, were confined by the mountains and the semi-desert to a relatively limited area where they could live in the way they preferred. The Kikuyu and their cousins the Embu and Meru were of this group, and they were also among the first to accept Western education and the Christian message. They were sturdy individualistic people, gifted traders, and they held their land in clan groups with very definite rules of transfer and use. They did not live in village settlements, but in small homesteads on their own land. And land was the basis of the family, of the clan, of all life. It could not be alienated. And land was also what the European settlers wanted, and obtained. The "White Highlands", which included much of the great Rift Valley, came into existence, in fact and in law. In the White Highlands Africans could be only labourers and squatters on land they still thought of as their own.

The First World War was a turning point for many Kenyan Africans. Probably over a third of a million served as soldiers and porters for the British forces in German East Africa, and thousands died. Those who came back had travelled, undergone new experiences, and realised the human vulnerabilities of the whites. They were gaining confidence; a few were travelling to Europe and America. There were certainly injustices about which to protest, and, most of all, the loss of land. The white settlers now had representatives in the legislative council which advised the governor, and they pressed for an elected representative government which would inevitably mean white control. In the year when such agitation came to a head, 1923, the colony of Southern Rhodesia was granted such self-government, and the years of UDI and civil war might have happened in Kenya also if the agitation had been successful. But the Colonial Office stated, in effect, that Kenya was an African territory and was not to become primarily a white colony.

This statement from the Colonial Office, known as the Devonshire Declaration (since the Duke of Devonshire was colonial secretary), owed a good deal to Christian leaders in Britain. Dr. J. H. Oldham, secretary of the CBMS, with the then Archbishop of Canterbury, Randall Davidson, had consulted with missionaries in Kenya and drafted an important and influential memorandum which seems to have influenced the White Paper of July 1923 from which the Declaration is taken.

In Kenya there were sharply divided land rights, the different ethnic groups being treated very differently. Only whites could own land in the so-called White Highlands (which also included coastal areas). Asians, a large minority in Kenya, mainly traders, could settle and buy land only in designated towns and townships. African rights were confined to "the Reserves", areas reserved by the Crown for members of certain ethnic groups. Once the boundaries had been laid down by law, no change or expansion for a growing population was possible.

The Kikuyu, Embu and Meru of the central highlands, north of Nairobi, east of the Aberdare Range, and around Mount Kenya, responded in several ways. They accepted eagerly the Western schooling offered by the missionaries, and through it found it possible to get work with the administration and in commercial enterprises in Nairobi and Mombasa. They travelled widely as traders. And many, especially from the higher, colder, less fertile lands just below the Aberdare forests, went over the mountains and became labourers and squatters in the Rift Valley on European estates and ranches. They were paid little, but retained the right to cultivate a piece of land and to keep some cattle, goats and sheep. There were others, especially west of Nairobi and around Thika, where the white lands went deep into traditional Kikuyu lands, who became day labourers on the coffee estates, or who lived and worked on the huge sisal plantations. They managed to support themselves, but did not progress in education like those who stayed in the Reserves. Nor did many become Christians. Education was primarily carried on by missions at this stage, and the missions were largely limited to the Reserves; there were few doing Christian work among town Africans, and even fewer in the White Highlands.

The Kikuyu and their neighbours, who have no traditional chiefs or headmen, are organised into named age-grades (*mariika*) according to the date of circumcision-initiation, a ceremony which all adolescent boys passed through. The men of one *riika* are always afterwards brothers and comrades who may call upon one another for mutual help and defence. It seems that a group of such circumcision brothers, *Aanake wa Forty* – "The young men of [nineteen] forty" – may have been the leading organisers of what became known as Mau Mau. I write "became known as" advisedly, because an organisation claiming that name, or the meaning of the name, has never been precisely identified, and it was not used by the participants.

The Kikuyu, among whom witchcraft is of minor importance, traditionally make use of oaths, whereby the suspect affirms his innocence, and by which people band themselves together for mutual purposes. Some time between the ending of the war in 1945 and 1950, people in Kiambu district (the nearest Kikuyu reserve to Nairobi) and the Rift Valley began taking an oath of unity, which at some point became an oath committing those who took it to organised violence in order to regain the land from the whites. It is difficult at this early stage to disentangle the movement of "forest fighters" generally known as Mau Mau from the activities of two political organisations, the Kenya African Union (KAU) and the earlier Kikuyu Central Association (KCA) which were also involved. Participation in all three overlaps. It seems to be established that the earliest area of mass oath-taking was at a place in the Rift Valley called Olenguruone, a tract of land where Kikuyu whose land in Kiambu had been alienated had been resettled as a result of the recommendations of the Carter Land Commission in the early 1930s. Over the years following the end of the war armed robbery and violence were on the increase, and there was very strong resistance to such government measures as compulsory terracing of land (against soil erosion) and cattle dipping. In 1950 and 1951 violence became even more widespread, but it seems doubtful whether any strong central organisation was in control. Certainly criminal elements became involved. The movement, through oathing, spread quickly from the towns to the countryside, for most town workers were men living alone, visiting when possible, perhaps once a month, their families back on their land in the Reserves. During this period some changes were made in the administrative structures of

Kenya – an appointed African supplemented a European who represented African interests in the legislative council in 1944. However, more radical changes which might have softened or at least slowed up African demands were opposed completely by the Europeans, who not only had good representation in the legislative council, but who also had fairly direct access to politicians of influence in Britain (some of them were members of the House of Lords).

So what chances there may have been of a peaceful solution to the problems raised by land, labour, wages, and political demands were lost. A militant group among the Kikuyu were able to convince their fellows that only violent means could achieve their ends. The oathing took place on an ever-increasing scale. The governor had in 1950 outlawed the Mau Mau Association (probably having been informed of KCA activities), but this made little difference. The *de facto* Kikuyu leader was Jomo Kenyatta, a charismatic personality who had twice been sent to Britain by the KCA as their representative, and who the second time had stayed in Europe for a number of years (1931–1946). On his return he became president of the moderate KAU, as the more radical KCA had been proscribed. He endeavoured to build up a popularly-based mass political party, but outside Kikuyu country there was little real interest. Whether the future president of the Republic was actually involved in the organisation which came to be called Mau Mau will probably never be known. However that may be, oathing and acts of violence escalated. In early October 1952 Senior Chief Waruhiu, a respected personality and a leading Christian in northern Kiambu, was assassinated. That action precipitated the declaration of a state of emergency and the coming of the security forces. The legal implications were that the "Government and its officers" were granted special powers "for the purpose of maintaining law and order". Those powers included arrest and detention without trial, special passes needed for travel, and many other restrictions. At the same time Jomo Kenyatta and five other officials of the KAU were arrested. Four of the six were Kikuyu. All were brought to trial accused of managing, assisting to manage, and being members of "an unlawful society . . . commonly known as Mau Mau . . ." In April 1953 the judge delivered his verdict; all six accused were found guilty and sentenced to seven years' hard labour.

This trial and the declaration of a state of emergency probably precipitated greater violence than was as yet planned. On the Government side thousands of Kikuyu working in towns and in the Rift Valley were rounded up and sent back to their areas of origin where many, especially the Rift Valley squatters, had never lived and where they retained no land rights.

From this point confrontation followed. British regiments were brought into Kenya; whites were conscripted; the police force and the Kenya Guards were augmented. The government forces had every resource of technology available at that time – radio links, land rovers, arms and ammunition. The Kikuyu had almost no back-up; they retreated into the forests of the Aberdares and Mount Kenya poorly armed and dependent for supplies and food on what could be brought to them from the Reserves. In fact, it was largely women, the tough and all-enduring Kikuyu women, who carried in what they needed. Government powers of detention without trial put thousands behind barbed wire, women as well as men. Home Guards were enlisted from the local population, and Home Guard posts were built, with ditches, drawbridges and watch-towers. From the forests gangs of forest fighters made excursions into the Reserves, and into the settled areas, often to kill as well as to steal. Within the Reserves groups acted for the forest fighters, and re-oathing as well as the spread of the first oath went on. To cut out the food supplies going into the forests, and also for protection, a policy of compulsory "villagisation" was embarked on. The scattered inhabitants of the homesteads along the ridges were moved into large, fenced and fortified settlements. It caused a good deal of hardship, as some of the women had to walk many miles to the gardens they had to cultivate for their livelihood.

Slowly the Government gained the upper hand, as was almost inevitable given the unevenness of the opponents. Over 11,000 Kikuyu had been killed by the end of 1956, over 1,000 captured wounded, and close to 30,000 were in detention. Throughout the emergency a total of 124 Europeans and Asians were killed, including those killed in raids, and 175 wounded. About 2,000 Africans in the security forces were killed. There was a slow relaxation of regulations and detainees were released (77,000 by the end of February 1959). First those who had confessed and had been "cleansed" came out; later, even those who had not confessed. The Emergency Regulations were finally lifted in 1960, the year that Jomo Kenyatta and his associates completed their term of imprisonment. However, he was then restricted, and with the country-wide cry for his full release another phase of Kenyan history began.

So in all this, what of the Church? It may seem a long introduction to the central topic, but without some background Mau Mau cannot be understood. And indeed it is my belief that it was not well understood by the missionaries who were the men and women on the spot.

Kikuyu society can be seen as divided in several ways. A basic division was (and is) male/female; another is between generations; yet another between literate and illiterate. The last division is often transposed into Christian/traditional, since nearly all who attend school are baptised and become at least nominal Christians. If one looks at the group of Christians one might divide it into nominal/active and, at least among the Protestants (Anglican, Methodist and Presbyterian) an inner group of saved or revived – those who were identified with the East African Revival Fellowship. Those who supported Mau Mau were in general the young and middle-aged men and women. It was mainly young men

who were in the forests, and on the whole the illiterate or
the barely schooled, though this was not true of the leaders.
Many old women were strong supporters, but many old
men who were conservative and held to traditional Kikuyu
values would have nothing to do with the movement. However it was the Christian group, and especially the Revival
Christians, who were the strongest and most cohesive
opponents of Mau Mau. And since one aim of the oath was to
ensure unity among the people, a group who refused the oath
and who held together among themselves were a real threat
and danger. Some hundreds of Christians were killed, largely
because of the denial of unity which they represented. It was
not only that Mau Mau was anti-Christian; it was also that
the Christians – *these* Christians – were against Mau Mau.
They were *against* an oath which (even if not often as obscene
as the early accounts represent) was associated with pre-
Christian rituals, which used blood, which put another unity
before the unity with Christ and with one another. They were
against violence and, in fact, most took a pacifist stance
stemming from their own reading of the New Testament, and
refused to join the Home Guard or to carry arms. (Almost all
missionaries also refused to carry arms, but pacifism had not
been actively taught.) What the Kikuyu Christians were not
against, and this is where most missionaries failed to follow
them, were the aims of the movement. They could not join in
the armed struggle, and they could not join in a general
hatred of whites, but they were for its ends – the end of
colonial rule, the end of white domination, the end of racially
biased land laws, the end of settler Kenya.

It was not until Mzee Kenyatta was released from detention
and had gone home to Gatundu, that missionaries began to
grasp this fully. Groups of people from all over Kikuyuland
travelled to Gatundu to greet him, in fact to pay him homage.
The Christians (including Revival Christians) went along
with as much enthusiasm as anyone else – he was *their* leader,
too.

So during this period of trial – the worst years were 1953 to 1956 – though from the Kikuyu Christians came martyrs and confessors, there were few prophets. We can remember today with great thanksgiving men and women like Ganthon, Rebecca, Andrew, and Ernest, who died, many others who were beaten and lived; many more who were willing to face death rather than deny their Lord. But there were virtually no Christians – certainly no Revival Christians – among the leaders of the KAU, among the trades union leaders, among those who had public influence. There were a few Revival Christians who were members of the local African district councils; they were known and respected for their personal integrity but they took little initiative in seeking positive change.

What could the missionaries have done? It had not always been like this. In the 1920s it was young Christians, especially around Kahuhia, the CMS station in Fort Hall, who had founded the Kikuyu Central Association and helped to run its paper, *Muigwithania*. The missionary at Kahuhia, Handley Hooper, coast-born son of the pioneer Douglas Hooper, had helped and encouraged them, at some risk to his own reputation with the administration. It was in the 1920s that Archdeacon W. E. Owen risked his reputation with settlers and administrators in defending African rights in Western Kenya. Hooper left in 1926 to become Africa secretary of the CMS, a post he held until 1949. If he had stayed, and retained the same vision, would things have been different? The missionary leaders included many good and able men, but there do not seem to have been many who felt the burden of Max Warren's vision, that our Christianity should be related to the whole of life. For education there was great concern, for social problems some concern, but for encouraging and supporting African Christians in political action there was little concern. Fine African leaders did emerge, but their concerns were for spiritual matters rather than for the dangerous ways of politics. Perhaps if there had been a more holistic emphasis, the position of the Churches in Kenya today might have been better, and they might be winning more respect from today's youth. For it must be said that in many ways the Revival Brethren acted better under persecution than they have in prosperity. The close fellowship between Christians of different denominations, of different areas, and of different generations, is now less close than it was in the days of persecution, and in the Kenya of today corruption of various kinds continues scarcely challenged by Church leaders.

This is not to deny the great contribution of the Revival Brethren. In that time of terror they stood fast. "They overcame by the blood of the Lamb, and the word of their testimony, and they loved not their own lives unto the death." But perhaps if the missionaries of Kenya, CMS and others, had been able to teach earlier a more related faith, Mau Mau need not have happened.

One small note: in all that time, when a number of settlers were attacked and murdered in their homes, no missionary was attacked or harmed, whether Roman Catholic or Protestant. In only a very few cases was an atttack made on a mission station, and unarmed missionaries travelled freely in their work, as school supervisors and the like, without trouble. Probably the very lack of arms protected them. Certainly much prayer was offered for the Kikuyu Church, and that prayer was honoured.

It is only fair to add a tribute to what missionaries and Church leaders, of other denominations also but in many respects led by the CMS, did to keep at least a semblance of justice in the darkest days. The young white Kenyans who became specially gazetted district officers and police superintendents may have known Swahili, but they had a great deal of power, little supervision, and their attitude towards the Kikuyu was that "the only good Kyuke is a dead Kyuke." It was very hard for whites, outside a very small number, to believe that a "good" Kikuyu — i.e., a Kikuyu who had not taken the oath – existed. There were beatings and brutality during arrests, during interrogations, and in the detention camps, culminating in the deaths at Hola in early 1960. The Emergency Regulations were not only severe, they were interpreted severely. In less than eighteen months from the imposition of the Emergency Regulations, about 820 Kikuyu had been hung. Only 250 of these were actually charged and convicted of murder. The other 570 were charged with offences like "consorting with terrorists" (which could mean as little as sharing a meal with a brother who was a terrorist) and possession of arms and ammunition. Given the general situation and the fact that in a number of respects Mau Mau was also a Kikuyu civil war, it was only too easy for miscarriages of justice to result.

The Christian Council of Kenya (CCK) and the Bishop of Mombasa, Leonard Beecher, from the first made private and personal representations to the governor and to senior administrators. But they refrained from public protest. The first person to break this conspiracy of silence was the Very Rev. David Steele, minister of St. Andrew's, Nairobi (Presbyterian). In January 1955 CMS London published a four-page pamphlet: *Kenya – Time for Action*, which quoted Steele's sermon and brought a number of misgivings into the open. Bishop Beecher immediately and publicly repudiated the publication, believing that such public protests hindered the administration in their task. The fat was well and truly in the fire! There was a basic difference between the views of many Christian observers in England and those of the "men on the spot". In Britain leading newspapers and politicians, from the Secretary of State downwards, became involved. The CMS information secretary, Bernard Nicholls, received much of the blame – which was applause for some.

But looking back over those almost thirty years, it would in Kenya and in many other places be agreed that the view at CMS headquarters would today be more acceptable. It is hard now to remember the strength and vehemence – and power – of white opinion at that period in Kenya, and so to understand why there were such inhibitions. This is not to discount the great services rendered by missionaries as the emergency continued, to bring atrocities and injustices to the attention of the authorities in Kenya and in England. The work of Leonard Beecher, Peter Bostock, Willoughby Carey, S. A. Morrison, at a central level should never be forgotten; nor the work of Carey Francis, Cyril Hooper, Alan Page and others at a local level. A Kikuyu politician, one of Mzee Kenyatta's "prison mates", wrote in his autobiography that "all the Christian churches openly supported all actions, including atrocities, committed by the British forces and the home guards against the 'Mau Mau'." This is not true; it can be shown to be not true; and I believe that the man who wrote it knew it to be untrue. There are reasons for shame, to be sure; but the CMS (and other societies) can be proud today that their missionaries did not run away; that they did not seek to protect themselves with arms; and that they did speak out against injustice, even in high places.

Crisis in Uganda

The Uganda Mission was in the late 19th century the glory of the CMS. Its first bishop had become a martyr; there was an early influx of young converts, some of whom after persecution were also martyred; the growth of the Church continued under the leadership of the third bishop, Alfred Tucker; a Church which was meeting many of Venn's "three-selves" requirements was emerging. A synodical system was early established; African evangelists were the pioneer evangelists in outlying areas; there was generous giving on the part of the young Christians. The only other missions of any significance were those of the Roman Catholic Church; that Church likewise had seen growth, martyrdom and a strong body of believers steadily increasing. This continued well into the

20th century, with the added factor, on the Anglican side, of
the East African revival. Weaknesses there were, without
doubt, but by the early 1950s Uganda was (except perhaps
for Lesotho) the most Christianised nation in Black Africa.

The Anglican Church, by then, was divided into two
dioceses, both with missionaries as bishops. One diocese,
that of Uganda, had its centre in Kampala, and covered the
south and west of the country, including the Belgian trust
territories of Ruanda and Burundi. There were three assistant
bishops; two were Africans and the third a missionary with
special responsibility for the work of the Ruanda mission.
The other diocese, for the north-east and north, was the
diocese on the Upper Nile. Missionaries of the BCMS and
the Africa Inland Mission worked within that diocese, but
with and for the same Church.

Uganda was not, like Kenya, a colony, but a protectorate.
There were very few white settlers and it was essentially an
African country in mood as well as in law. There were several
kingdoms – Buganda, Bunyoro, Toro, Ankole – whose rulers
did in fact *rule*, with advice from a British resident. In areas
where there were no traditional rulers, colonial-appointed
chiefs often had considerable power, but the administration
was carried on mainly, as in Kenya and most of Tanganyika,
by district commissioners and district officers.

Many Ugandan Africans, especially the Ganda, but also
others, had become prosperous through the growing of cash
crops, chiefly cotton and coffee. There were good schools and
colleges, and in general the wealthier Ugandans, often coming
out of a traditional aristocracy, were sophisticated people
who felt themselves to be the equal or indeed the superior of
any other tribe or nation, including Britain. In Buganda the
king, or *kabaka*, who had inherited in infancy, had been
brought up as an Anglican. He was a handsome and able
young man who had studied in England, and he was regarded
by his subjects with a reverence difficult for outsiders to
comprehend.

In Uganda the missionaries had preceded the colonial administration. Indeed, it was partly through the intervention of Bishop Tucker and the CMS that the British protectorate was ever declared. The Imperial British East Africa Company, which had entered the area, was losing money and was about to withdraw. This left open the strong possibility that Buganda, and what later became known as Uganda, would be annexed by Germany. British missionaries regarded this as dangerous for their work and for the future of the people whom they saw as under their tutelage. Money was raised in Britain to keep the Company operating till the British Government could make up its mind about taking over, which in the end it did. Buganda developed as a semi-independent entity within Uganda and the bishop became one of a triumvirate with the Kabaka and his Prime Minister (*katikiro*), both of whom were always Anglicans. The governor also continued to consult with the bishop, who usually had a longer knowledge of the territory and a closer acquaintance with its leading citizens.

The Anglican Church in Uganda grew steadily through this period, and especially in the kingdoms. All of them had rulers who were traditionally Anglican, and often in fact active Christians. In these societies each ruler had a "royal mother" and "royal sister" who stood in a special relationship with him, and such women when devout Christians exercised a strong influence. The village schools were under the management of the churches; the secondary schools, where missionaries still taught, were of great importance. Missionaries also served in the Bishop Tucker Theological College at Mukono, where Africans were trained for the ministry. The colonial government established in Uganda the first post-secondary college for the three territories — Makerere. It began by training higher-level teachers, and though it took students from all of East Africa, the exceptionally good secondary schools run by both Roman Catholic and Anglican Churches, together with its site near Kampala, began to give Uganda a lead in the "development stakes". This naturally led to an expectation of early self-government.

But tensions were always present. In the economic sphere they existed between the peasants and the large land-holders, especially with the kingdoms. The people of the non-kingly societies, especially in the less prosperous north, sometimes felt themselves neglected by both Church and State, and the growth of the Church was slower in those societies.

Within the Church there were the tensions brought about as the "saved ones" – those now part of the East African revival – challenged what they saw as the nominal Christianity they found round about them. At one point, in 1941, as we have discussed in the section on revival, the differences led to a number of young ordinands leaving their training, some for good.

From the very early days of mission in Uganda, Ugandans, and especially Christians from Buganda, had gone as missionaries to the unevangelised parts of their land. One such Christian, Apolo Kivebulaya, had even gone further, into the Belgian Congo, to work among the pygmies and others in a pioneer ministry. This outreach continued, and it was stimulated by the East African revival. We have read of the Ugandans who as partners of the missionaries prayed for and received a great blessing from the Holy Spirit. One young and well-educated teacher from southern Uganda, Festo Kivengere, went for many years as far away as Dodoma, in the diocese of central Tanganyika, to teach in the Anglican secondary school there. It was a real sacrifice for him, and an even greater one for his young wife, living in an unfamiliar climate and with neighbours culturally very different from themselves. But they did it happily as a service to the one who had saved them.

But as the leaders in the various parts of Uganda began to look towards self-government for their country, another tension became obvious. The colonial government, after the Second World War was over, saw one way forward through a closer relationship between the three territories. And this was totally unacceptable to Uganda. In Uganda the power of the white settlers had always been feared. They dominated Kenya, and even in Tanganyika there was a strong settler lobby which could make its voice heard. So Ugandans opposed programmes which linked them in any way to Kenya, even for sensible financial and commercial reasons. (Even in Church matters the same argument was applied.) And there was another tension within Uganda, as independence and self-determination were being demanded. It was between the rulers of the kingdoms, who wanted to retain *their* independence, and who were looking for a federation-type constitution for Uganda in the future, and those, led by the governor, who wanted to see a modern unitary state. The governor in the 1950s, Sir Andrew Cohen, had previously been involved in the setting-up of the ill-fated and unpopular Central African Federation. That did not increase confidence in him, and opposition was especially strong in Buganda.

In September 1953 the Ganda parliament (the Great Lukiiko) passed two resolutions calling for Buganda's complete independence at an early date, and expressing their opposition to East African federation. They also asked for matters relating to Buganda to be transferred from the Colonial Office to the Foreign Office, on the grounds that when the first treaty was made it was the Foreign Office with which they dealt.

The governor had several discussions with the Kabaka and his ministers over these demands. But there was no yielding on either side. The Ganda wanted immediate and complete independence for themselves without taking the rest of Uganda into consideration. The governor on his side was determined that only as a unitary state would Uganda gain independence. Finally, on 30 November 1953, the Governor gave the Kabaka an ultimatum. When he refused to cooperate the governor signed a prepared deportation order, and within a few hours the Kabaka was on his way to exile in England. A state of emergency was declared in Buganda.

Bishop Brown was recalled to Kampala from safari, by a message to go to see the governor at Entebbe (the administrative capital). He heard the news with astonishment and dismay, and gave the governor his opinion that the Ganda would never agree to elect another Kabaka in the place of Edward Frederick Mutesa.

Buganda was stunned. That the Kabaka should be abruptly taken away like this was incomprehensible. The country, literally, went into mourning. Leslie Brown, then Bishop of Uganda and later Archbishop of the new province, describes how he came home one day and found about two hundred women sitting on the lawn. "Many were pillars of the Mothers' Union, but they were almost unrecognisable with their hair fuzzed up and wearing old tattered clothes to show they were in mourning." (Brown, p. 104)

The bishop was inevitably involved in the bewildered anger of the Ganda people. It was hard for them to believe that he was not party to the governor's action. His social contacts with the governor were well known, and in the past he had often been consulted. But in this case the governor had been particularly careful to keep the bishop in ignorance, for he understood the implications. As Bishop Brown recounts, "Attendance in our churches dropped dramatically. Those who came did not hide their anger in the church meetings we always held after services on my safaris. There was a revulsion from European things and a revival of paganism. The bataka (the heads of the clans) urged a boycott of the Church, but this failed." (Brown, p. 104)

In the short run the situation was saved when the British government sent Sir Keith Hancock to undertake a revision of the 1900 agreement between Britain and Buganda. Hancock was an Australian, an academic with a deep knowledge of Africa. He was a guest of the bishop for the three months that he worked with Ganda representatives on the draft of a new agreement.

In November 1954 the draft agreement was put to the

Great Lukiiko. The alternative of electing another Kabaka, in place of Mutesa, was also given, but it was never seriously considered. The new recommendations were accepted, and on 17 October 1955 the Kabaka came back from two years of exile. He brought with him a number of guests to celebrate his return, and among them was Bishop Stuart, Bishop Brown's immediate predecessor, and Mrs. Stuart. From the airport the whole party went straight to the cathedral for a service of thanksgiving. Despite changes and tensions, the Anglican Church was still an integral part of Ganda life and affairs.

Internal self-government was finally granted to Uganda in March 1962. What followed takes us beyond the bounds of this chapter. Uganda's independence has not been a happy one, and it might have been expected that the links between the Anglican Church and the Ugandan people might have been strained to breaking point. But this has not proved so, and despite manifold difficulties (including the murder of their archbishop), the Church in Uganda continues to grow, and to value its links with the CMS in Britain.

The CMS exodus from Egypt

Egypt had never been one of the CMS's larger missions. In 1956 the missionaries numbered seventeen, and most were working at the Harpur Memorial Hospital, Old Cairo. One nursing sister was at Menouf Hospital, forty miles out of Cairo; some women missionaries were centered on the Boulac Community Centre, in a densely populated inner city section of Cairo. There were only two men among the number: Jesse Hillman, the hospital administrator, and Tony Chase, a doctor. And there were six young children belonging to the Hillmans and the Chases.

The country was in a state of unrest and transition. Severely affected by the Second World War, which had

made it a battle theatre, it was still reaching towards true
independence and nationhood, though it was of course
technically independent. In 1952 occurred the coup led by
the "Free Officers" when King Farouk was deposed.
Gradually one of the group, Colonel Gamal Abdel Nasser,
took over leadership. The Suez Canal, and its control by the
British, had exercised the emotions of the Egyptians for
many years. In 1954 a new agreement was signed between
Britain and Egypt, whereby Britain was to evacuate the
Canal Zone, with certain safeguards in emergencies. The
last British troops left Egypt in June 1955. But ownership
remained in British hands and resentment simmered.
Finally, in July 1956, Colonel Nasser announced the
nationalisation of the Suez Canal, and expropriated the
Company.

Other nations became increasingly nervous as Egypt flexed
her muscles. Israel felt threatened by her large Muslim
neighbour, no longer under the control of Britain. France
was alarmed at the support which Egypt was giving to the
revolutionaries in Algeria; Great Britain was in general
resentful of the new policies, especially concerned about the
loss of the Canal Zone, and distrustful of Egypt's ability to
work the canal.

For several months in 1956 the tension between Britain
(with France and Israel) and Egypt heightened. The administrator at the Old Cairo Hospital, Jesse Hillman, became
aware of it when the officials at the British embassy began to
call in British citizens in positions of responsibility to discuss
what actions would be taken in any future "troubles". Finally
it was suggested that women and children should be evacuated. That would leave only the two CMS men in Egypt.
Hillman refused. The embassy contacted the English bishop
(who was not a missionary society member) and he also
applied pressure. What does a missionary do in such circumstances, under pressure from Church and State? He prayed
and took advice from his Egyptian colleagues – and refused

to order evacuation. It has long been a general CMS principle – when in doubt, sit tight!

Finally, on 29 October 1956, Britain and her allies attacked Egypt and the "Suez Crisis" was an actuality. The staff of the British embassy all had to leave immediately, and so also the bishop. Before the invasion the missionaries had been offered passages on what would be "the last ships." They refused. Now they had to register as "enemy aliens" and were put under house arrest. A police officer with whom Hillman had previous warm contacts told him politely and regretfully that he would have to put an armed guard on the front gate of the hospital compound. This he did, but he knew, and the missionaries knew he knew, that the compound had five other gates! The missionary women stayed inside, but Hillman was able to move round freely, buying the necessary drugs and stores for hospital and home. The staff of the hospital were called on to help in civil defence, and here the missionaries, with experience of air-raids and blackouts in England, were able to be of much assistance. But there seemed something strange about an English missionary reassuring a frightened Egyptian patient during an air-raid being carried on by one's own country. Who was the enemy?

The Egyptian Christians were supportive, but after the war was officially over (7 November 1956) Hillman began to wonder if the presence of "enemy aliens" might not be an embarrassment to the Church. He put it to the hospital medical board, who replied that they wanted to keep up the witness shown by Egyptians and British continuing to work and worship together. So they stayed on, trying to work as normally as possible. Meredith Sinclair, who had been at Menouf, had to come in to Old Cairo; a rumour was going round the rural population of Menouf that she was passing information to low-flying British planes. The social workers at Boulac came in too, and ran a school for the six missionary children whose English school was of course closed. They made inventories of stores and equipment against the inevitable day of going, and began to pack. Their radios and telephones were not interfered with, and they even received Arabic-language information handouts from the Government. On many sides the missionaries received back in kindnesses the gratitude felt for the hospital's services over many years.

Finally, the secret police came and gave them ten days to leave. Exit visas still had to be applied for, and there was much filling-in of forms. But how to go? The airport had been bombed (by the British); the railway line south was fully booked for weeks ahead; few steamers were calling. Eventually some planes began to fly in again, and Hillman was able to get the missionaries, in two parties, on SAS shuttle flights to Rome, and so on to London. The second party left on 29 November 1956, having stayed exactly one month from the start of the brief Suez war.

Three years later Jesse Hillman went back to visit Egypt and preached at the cathedral. He received back the mission property taken over in 1956, and of course handed it over to the Church. Church leaders asked for several missionaries, including Hillman, to return, but the CMS parent committee decided against it in his case. That would have been a backward step, for the Church had shown it could cope. A few missionaries did return, and others, like the Hillman family, went on to give service elsewhere; in their case, in Kenya.

The Anglican Church in Egypt remains small, and it has faithfully tried to avoid proselytising among Coptic Orthodox Christians. But it has built up connections of friendship and goodwill with them, and indeed with Muslims also, and in the mysterious ways of God that short and unjust war in 1956 helped rather than harmed the process.

Civil War in the Sudan

CMS mission work in the Sudan naturally commenced from the north, and the first missionary, L. G. Gwynne, who arrived in Cairo in 1899, was not allowed to enter the Sudan for a year. Britain was maintaining the policy of protecting Muslim areas of her overseas possessions from any kind of proselytising, a policy which had annoyed CMS missionaries in India, northern Nigeria, and other places.

Gwynne, with Dr. Harpur of Cairo, was finally given permission to go to Omdurman, on condition that they did not attempt to evangelise Muslims. In 1905 a party of six, led by Gwynne, left for the southern Sudan. This first attempt ended largely in failure, but Gwynne was not one to give up, and a second party resulted in a Church being planted among the black fishermen, farmers and herdsmen of the south – the Dinka, Nuer, Azande, Bari and others.

The Church in the Sudan inevitably developed unevenly. In the Muslim north there were missionary institutions – the CMS concentrated on schools for girls – and chaplaincies for expatriates. In the south, the work was much more like that in East Africa, with village churches and associated primary schools, central stations with boarding schools and teacher training classes, and dispensaries. In 1920 Egypt and the Sudan became a separate diocese under its pioneer missionary, now Bishop Gwynne, and in 1945, after an experiment in which the southern section was administered within the diocese of the Upper Nile, in Uganda (1926–1935), the whole of the Sudan became a diocese separate from Egypt.

In many ways the growth of missionary work in the south (where Italian Roman Catholics and American Presbyterians were also active) contributed to the increasing division between north and south. Without their presence the "pagan" tribes of the south might well have become wholly Muslim, as many individuals of course did. With Islam went Arabic; those who became Christians were educated in their vernaculars and English, with Arabic, if at all, as a third language.

These divisions were reflected in most Sudanese institutions. In the army the officers were usually northerners,

Muslim and Arabic-speaking. But the other ranks were largely southerners, "pagan" or Christian. Naturally tensions resulted. Then in August 1955, in an almost spontaneous explosion, the troops in Equatoria province rose in mutiny. On one terrible night the mutiny spread from station to station, and officers, their wives and families, and other outsiders like Greek traders, were murdered. This was the first major incident of a civil war which continued until 1972.

At the time of the mutiny the Sudanese pastors in the south, and the missionaries, stood fast at their posts. In many places they were able to limit the bloodshed and check looting, and in some cases were able to save the lives of those who might otherwise have been killed, giving the wives of northern officers and administrators shelter in their own homes.

The Mutiny itself was soon over and the Church's work went on fairly normally. Unfortunately a few missionaries were deported, mainly through misunderstandings. The bishop, Oliver Allison, who had succeeded Bishop Gelsthorpe in 1953, was generally able to carry on with his pastoral and confirmation visits in the south, and this continued, but tensions increased. There had always been pressures on southern Christians to convert to Islam; these were intensified. For a while the weekly public holiday, for the south as well as the north, was changed to Friday. Some restrictive laws were passed in 1962, and finally, in 1964, all missionaries, Catholic and Protestant, were expelled.

What followed takes us beyond the dates of this section; there was to be much suffering, and the young Church in the south was to have her martyrs, and see the deaths of many innocent Christians. But the roots were strong enough, and it was to pass through and come out purified into a new era.

14   GROWING PARTNERSHIP IN CHANGING CIRCUMSTANCES

Continuity and change under John V. Taylor 1963–1975

Max Warren's period as General Secretary started in the middle of a world war and ended, after twenty-one years, as the colonial era came to an end. He had lived in India as a child during the high tide of empire. In 1948 he saw India and Pakistan become two independent nations. He had travelled to begin work as a missionary in northern Nigeria in 1927, and in 1957 was an official CMS visitor when the Anglican Church on the Niger celebrated its centenary. At the end of the 1950s and in the first years of the new decade colony after colony emerged as an independent nation: Sudan in 1956; Ghana (the Gold Coast) in 1957; Nigeria in 1960; Tanzania in 1961; Sierra Leone in 1961; Malaysia in 1962; Uganda in 1962; Kenya in 1963. The two Belgian trust territories of Ruanda and Burundi also became independent in 1962. As we have seen, one of the major developments during Warren's period as General Secretary was the growth of autonomous dioceses and the setting up of new provinces, especially during Geoffrey Fisher's time as Archbishop of Canterbury.

In 1963 Max Warren retired from the leadership of the Society. He had given two years' notice, and his successor was already on the headquarters staff. He was John Vernon Taylor, Africa Secretary from 1959. Like Max Warren, he had grown up in a tradition which prepared him for this post. Son of the Bishop of Sodor and Man, he was educated at

St. Laurence's, a school attended by the sons of many CMS missionaries. After reading history and theology at Trinity College, Cambridge, and St. Catherine's, Oxford, he attended Wycliffe Hall, and was ordained priest in 1939. A few years in parish work followed, until in October 1944 (aged thirty) he was able to sail for Uganda – not an easy thing at that stage of the war. He was assigned to the theological college at Mukono in Uganda, named in honour of Bishop Tucker. He spent two terms of service there, and perhaps it was through pictures of the passion play which he conceived and directed, performed by Ugandan students in the college chapel, that he first became known to a wider group of CMS supporters.

Max Warren, because of illness, had spent less than one year overseas as a CMS missionary. John Taylor's first gift as the new leader was a deep understanding of an African missionary/Church situation, acquired in that period in Uganda. Something even deeper was to follow. He was asked by the IMC to take part in a study of younger Churches. So for three months he lived in a small mud-built house in a Ganda homestead, and stayed also in other villages. From that experience came his book, *The growth of the Church in Buganda* (SCM Press, 1958), which is certainly one of the major books written by any missionary in this century, and an important study of the Ganda people. To that in-depth knowledge of the Ganda he added a study of the church in an ecumenical urban-industrial situation when he wrote (with Dorothea Lehmann) *Christians of the Copperbelt* (SCM 1962), after spending nine months in Northern Rhodesia (now Zambia).

After this period of secondment to the IMC (1954–1959) he came to CMS headquarters as Africa Secretary and of course continued to travel. In 1958 he was a delegate at the IMC conference in Ghana and at the All Africa Conference of Churches meeting in Ibadan, Nigeria. In 1961 he was a CBMS delegate at the WCC New Delhi assembly which ratified the absorption of the IMC into the WCC. So he came to his new position with a wealth of relevant experience to add to his singular talents. Max Warren wrote:

> His appointment as General Secretary of the C.M.S. was the one for which I had hoped. I was sure that the Society needed a new style of leadership. And John, with the sensitiveness of a rare imagination, provided it. The moment of euphoria in Africa and Asia, where so many countries had obtained political independence, was bound to pass. The tumults which follow upon the disillusioning discovery that true freedom is a spiritual, and not a political, reality, was to test the statesmanship of rulers everywhere. As a servant Society this was bound to be the new context for the C.M.S. in both Church and State overseas. John had the gifts for this new phase. (*Crowded Canvas*, pp. 226–7)

The tumults and the testing were to begin soon. Though Kenya had entered her independence with a goodwill and in a peace which would have been impossible to predict ten years earlier; though India and Pakistan had recovered from the agony of partition; though Malaysia was now prospering and peaceful; conflicts continued or were to flare up in other territories where the CMS had long worked and where Anglican Churches had been established.

Max Warren's last official engagement for the CMS was his attendance at the Anglican Congress, Toronto, in August 1963. Before the congress, missionary executives of the Anglican Communion met, and then the Anglican Council on Missionary Strategy met at Huron College to prepare for the Congress. John Taylor was at the Huron College meetings, and so the retiring and incoming general secretaries were able to overlap.

It was out of the Toronto Congress that the keyword for the next years of Anglican world mission came: MRI. Max Warren gave the theme address for the opening session of the congress: the Church's mission to the world. He spoke of the religious frontiers which present radical challenges to the Church, and of the other frontiers which contribute to the increasing complexity of the task. True to his life-long vision, he emphasised the unity of all parts of life – in one sense, a world with no frontiers for the Christian – yet a world deeply divided by class, wealth, belief systems, culture, where the Church must seek to cross frontiers. In this world – one, yet divided – "mutual responsibility and interdependence" was, if a clumsy title, a prophetic phrase. In this post-colonial age new challenges were to be met. "MRI" was to dominate Anglican thinking for some time.

Back in Britain, as John Taylor took over, the necessary call was to interpret "mutual responsibility and interdependence in the body of Christ" for the men and women in the pews of the Church of England. Some saw the document, and the appeals for new financial aid which arose from it, as just asking for yet more money in a round-about way. So the MRI Lent Campaign, in 1965, centred on a study entitled "No small change". Whatever the failures or limitations, that study, in which the CMS participated, reached an unusually large number of parish study groups, and was a real attempt to communicate to both lay people and clergy the truth that mission must be central in the life of the Church, and not just something done "over there". More, that mission must be one of mutual responsibility, of interdependence, and of receiving as well as giving.

Change, in a very real, physical sense, was coming to the CMS headquarters. In 1813 the committee had rented a house in Salisbury Square which became the headquarters, and through moves, extensions and rebuilding, Salisbury Square, off Fleet Street and not far from St. Paul's, had remained the fulcrum of the Society for 152 years. But the site was expensive: a building hard to heat and with very high rates. In 1952 the decision was taken in principle to sell and move. It was some years before a suitable site was found – on Waterloo Road, south of the river, and in the same area as the Old Vic theatre. So "157" replaced "Salisbury Square"

A working group to consult with the architect was set up, and by 1964 ideas were taking shape, for John Taylor wrote one of his earlier newsletters on the topic "Except the Lord build" (January 1964). Characteristically, he looked at the theological implications of a Church-related office building, and especially one containing a chapel. "For this recovery of a living church architecture springs essentially from a concern with the Church's mission to the world." So the Chapel of the Living Water became the centre of the new, long, six-storey building, "not cut off from the rest of the building . . . The city's street is, in fact, always in sight through the window which runs, almost at floor level, round two sides of the chapel: the Waterloo Road, filled with the commerce – and the casualties – of the city of this world. It is there that the water of life must flow; is flowing, in fact."

And if the staff with offices on the ground floor sometimes feel that the architect might have been wiser to make the windows a little smaller, a little higher and a little less accessible – well, usually they smile ruefully and sweep up the broken glass.

Outside on the great lintel-stone is the text of Mark 16.15, which was also used in Salisbury Square – but in the version of the New English Bible. "Each generation needs a new translation and a new pattern; but the Commission is unchanged."

Presidents of the Society

The position of patron of the Society was long reserved for a member of the royal family, but since 1812 there has always been a working president and never merely an honorary figure-head. The first two, Admiral Lord Gambier (1812–1833) and Lord Chichester (1834–1886) held office until their deaths. The next president, Captain the Hon. Francis Maude, who was eighty-seven years old when appointed, died within the year. Sir John Kennaway (1887–1917) and Sir Robert Williams (1917–1943) both served long and useful terms, but resigned their office. When filling the vacancy at Sir Robert's retirement, it was decided to appoint future presidents for five-year terms.

But this was renewable and in the event the next president, Sir Kenneth Grubb, served for five terms – twenty-five years. Max Warren has paid generous and warm tribute to Sir Kenneth in *Crowded Canvas* and he has written his own remarkable story in *Crypts of Power* (Hodder and Stoughton, 1971). The General Secretary could have had no better guide through the maze of negotiations with Anglican and ecumenical bodies, and with Civil Service and government agencies, than this man, a former missionary, who was a gifted administrator, a man of affairs, and a dedicated and far-sighted Christian. He laid down his office in 1969, and his successor was appropriate for the times, since she was a woman, bringing special gifts of grace and warmth to her own administrative work. Dame Diana Reader Harris, only the seventh president in 170 years, had been a well-known head-mistress, and had chaired the CMS Executive Committee. She remained in office until 1982, and as well as all the work done for the Society within Great Britain, she proved an incomparable ambassador on overseas visits, including one to the sister societies in Australia and New Zealand.

Her successor is again a layman, David Bleakley, of Belfast, Northern Ireland. He has himself served in Africa, and has long been involved in the front-line of the "troubles" in Ireland, surely a remarkable perspective from which to view the one world in which mission is carried out.

Training of missionaries

Canon Gordon Hewitt in his history of the CMS, 1910–1942 (vol. I) has given a useful summary of CMS training of missionaries from its beginnings (pp. 454–460). One point he makes is that training of missionaries has been consistently one of the first areas to suffer when financial cuts have had to be imposed. Whereas some individuals cope well and give excellent service without training, others fail after extensive training, and with external factors like wars to consider, it has often been difficult to follow even a firmly-decided policy.

It was not until 1946, following wartime disruptions, that training for men and for women was able to recommence at the two houses: Liskeard Lodge at Blackheath for men and married couples; Foxbury at Chislehurst, Kent, for single women. In 1952 a house for men's training was purchased near Foxbury and also given the name of Liskeard Lodge. Staff could now be easily shared and some activities undertaken together; surely a wise move when men and women would be working closely together overseas. The two houses at Chislehurst had the great advantage of being within easy reach of London, both for headquarters staff to visit and for those in training to visit headquarters.

It had been the question of distance from London which seemed the greatest obstacle when the possibility of moving training to Selly Oak, Birmingham, was brought up. But the facilities offered at the Selly Oak colleges, and the need to bring training firmly into the modern era, not least through working closely with other Churches, won the day. In the autumn of 1969 training was discontinued at Foxbury and Liskeard Lodge, and reopened at Crowther Hall, a CMS college joining the federation of Church colleges at Selly Oak. The new principal after the transfer was the Rev. Simon Barrington-Ward.

"Crowther" offered training for men and women in purpose-built houses. There were bed-sitters for singles, flat-lets for the married couples, special play rooms for children. All this was on the Selly Oak campus, within reach of the colleges of other denominations and of the educational and recreational facilities of the central college, including its splendid library. The distance from London was the only serious drawback – and perhaps the expense, for fast train travel had brought the journey down to less than two hours.

But Foxbury was not yet closed down completely; rather, it underwent a change of use, and became a community house for the Society. There were hopes that it would become the centre for a community of commitment, part of a vision of John Taylor's for the Society. With John and Helena Parry for the first wardens, followed by John and Dorothy Lowe, Foxbury was used by missionaries on furlough for rest and recreation, for mid-week courses, for candidates' weekends, and so on. It was also used by the "church-at-large" – by parochial groups, study groups, for ordination retreats and for many other activities. Richard Handforth, who was chaplain there and later became Home Education Secretary for the CMS, wrote:

> . . . in the wisdom of God we are never quite what everyone would have expected. Foxbury, the way it has been for the last seven years, probably failed to fulfil everybody's ideal of such a community house. . . . But as its pattern of happenings waywardly evolved we saw in it the Spirit's power to shape our neat array of conferences and meetings to his own ends. (*Yes*, July–September 1976)

In the end, finances as well as use patterns impelled thought about change. Finally it was decided to move the centre of returned missionaries' "on-furlough" training to the Selly Oak site also. This took place in 1976. Another purpose-built house came into being next to Crowther Hall, with a flat and office for the warden, bed-sittingrooms, kitchens for snacks, a quiet room and a meeting-room lounge. Those who stay at Leasow House share many meals, prayers and evening activities with the missionaries-in-training and CMS bursars, and all three groups can give and receive from one another.

The training now offered at Crowther Hall can use all the special resources of the central college, which can in turn call on the staff from all nine of the federated colleges. The staff as well as the student body are international; there are several further Special Resource Centres, such as the Centre for the Study of Islam. As well as the Selly Oak library, students can also use the resources of the University of Birmingham, only two kilometres away.

But the emphasis in training at Crowther Hall today is not primarily academic. The emphasis is on the training of the whole person, "through life in community, through worship, prayer, study and participation in common tasks . . ." Certainly academic courses are available, but there is much more. Cross-cultural communication is one important area; topics of special relevance for work overseas are discussed in Mission Forum; "College Time" is periods set aside for each community to concentrate on their own special needs. At Crowther Hall task groups are emphasised and students are assigned to a local church for one half-day a week. They work on special projects for witness and service, mainly in inner-city areas.

Candidates have been interviewed and accepted *before* training begins (which has not always been the case). But often they must go through their training without knowing their future location. This makes detailed area studies somewhat difficult. Each student is allocated to a tutor who can advise on studies and on the kind of work experience which would be useful.

Volunteers (who were once short-service workers and for a few years part of a youth service abroad scheme) are a category of worker increasing in number. Although on occasion a volunteer is sent to Crowther for a term, the usual method of preparation is a three-week orientation course. These courses are held using the facilities of Crowther and Leasow, and of Selly Oak in general, twice a year. Volunteers offer to serve for two to three years, and a few return for a second term. Some re-offer as missionaries; most return to life in this country but with their outlook radically changed as a result of time in another culture.

From 1975: change and interchange

In 1975 a new General Secretary took office, as Canon John V. Taylor moved to become Bishop of Winchester. The Rev. Simon Barrington-Ward had never been a CMS missionary himself, though his links with the society were deep and strong. Born in 1930, and educated at Magdalene College, Cambridge, he spent a total of ten years as chaplain and later fellow of his old college. But during this period he went to the University of Ibadan, Nigeria, as a lecturer in the Department of Religious Studies, and so saw at first hand one of the Churches which had developed out of CMS work. It was in Nigeria that he met his wife Jean, a doctor who was serving with the CMS there.

After returning to Magdalene in 1963, he went on in 1969 to become principal of the CMS training college at Selly Oak, Crowther Hall. It was from Crowther Hall that he moved to 157 Waterloo Road at the beginning of 1975.

Under Canon Barrington-Ward's leadership the CMS is continuing a policy of reorganisation and reassessment which will enable the Society to go on serving in a radically changing world. He has brought a gift of informality which is suitable for the time, warm compassion, and a desire to listen and understand what the Churches are saying.

One of his contributions (worked out, of course, with his colleagues) came in the clarifying of the aims of the Society, formally adopted by the general council and articulated in a filmstrip produced in 1980, *Aiming to share*.

The three circles emphasise the overall concept of sharing in "interchange" (represented by the outer circle) or what Canon Barrington-Ward called a "gift-exchange" between

Churches in different parts of the world. The CMS had never claimed, and would not now claim, a uniqueness in the mission task. The sharing is expressed in evangelism, in renewal, and in the search for social justice. These aims look to an integration of the Gospel and the world which is a growing emphasis in many Christian circles. Not spirituality and renewal *or* social action, but spirituality and renewal *and* social action, with the Cross central to all.

Within the administration of the Society major changes have been made – perhaps the first really substantive changes since Edward Hutchinson, almost a century ago, introduced the concept of regional responsibility. Perhaps the greatest change is seen in the adding of the "Britain region", symbolising as well as actualising the new conception of Britain as a missionary region, together with the new emphasis on interchange visitors from overseas.

Another major change has been in the introduction of members' councils.

Members' councils, general council, and standing committee
The CMS has been from the beginning a membership society. When it had no paid staff, no office, not even any agents –

overseas missionaries – it was already active in the persons of members who formed its committee, spoke on its behalf, and subscribed to its funds.

Over the years since these first beginnings membership has meant different things. There was a long period when *all* clerical members (subscribers) were automatically entitled to a seat on the General Committee. This has ceased to be the case, and for some years a General Council of some 200 representatives of members at home and missionaries abroad have met annually to define broad policy lines. From the associations, and from other groupings of members gathered together in given areas, representatives have gone to the General Council. The council's Standing Committee deals with the implementation of the General Council on behalf of the Society as administered by the officers and secretaries. Going back as far as 1919, the dioceses of the north have been organised in a Northern Council which has held an annual Northern Congress which has led to sustained interest showing itself in giving and in offers of service.

This ongoing commitment gave an indication of a possible way forward for the whole Society to recover grassroots interest and commitment. Following discussion at the 1982 meetings of General Council, two area secretaries, Jack Greaves and Geoffrey Goswell, were seconded as the General Secretary's representatives to help with the setting-up of six regional councils. These councils were to lay a greater emphasis on the participation of members in the life and work of the Society, so involving them in the interchange of mission. The councils were also to coordinate the work of the membership across the region in the constituent dioceses, and to be responsible for the election of representatives to the General Council.

The General Council is now a smaller body than before, and eight members of Standing Committee are to be elected from it. In this new arrangement the distance between the individual members and the decision-making bodies will be reduced. At the time of writing the interim members' councils have begun the process of holding annual meetings where the representatives to the General Council, and the members of each permanent members' council, are being elected. The first of these was held in February 1984, and was felt to be a great success. There were about 400 members present, and in worship, fellowship and business they felt themselves involved with one another and the Society in the ongoing work of spreading the Gospel. It does appear a way of advance. The challenge will be to involve more individuals, more parishes, to organise more associations and other groupings, so that mission becomes increasingly not just something done "from here" to "over there", but an integral part of the Church both here and there.

Under one roof

Over the years meetings have been held, both formally and informally, to discuss the relationship of the various Anglican missionary societies. In some cases societies have come together, as with the amalgamation of the CMS and the CEZMS in 1957, and the UMCA and the SPG in 1965. The societies have worked together in Partnership for World Mission and on the Board for Mission and Unity. Is that, at this time, enough?

Discussions are still continuing about the possibility of the four general Anglican societies (BCMS, CMS, SAMS, and USPG) coming together under one roof with PWM. The separate identities of each society would be preserved, but sharing of resources (computers, perhaps) and closer contact would answer some of the criticisms and eliminate some of the problems now existing. It is a complex question and one which cannot be dealt with quickly, but the ongoing considerations continue.

As we approach the end of 1984, with the leaders of the world-wide Anglican Communion meeting at Badagry,

Nigeria, where the first CMS missionaries landed in 1843, the General Secretary has made a suggestion which follows through on the emphases of the recent past. The term "missionaries" should be finally dropped, and the term "mission partners" be used instead. This is a part of the re-evaluation of the missionary role, a part of the renewal that is being sought, and a turning more clearly to the sharing which the CMS is seeking to emphasise.

Tumults and testing: Sudan – the Civil War

Max Warren's tumults were now to descend upon the Churches in an unprecedented way. In the Sudan trouble had been brewing openly since 1955; in fact, it was building up from the first days of colonial rule. A recent study of the south speaks of "the political and cultural hot-house which the British had built for the southern Sudanese." (Sanderson and Sanderson, p. 420) Now it was shattered "with brutal speed and completeness" as "the abrupt termination of British administration in the south created an ideological and political vacuum." The more advanced Arabic-speaking Islamic north; the poorer black, partly Christianised south; the clash was bound to come, and when it did, the conflict raged for almost seventeen years.

The mutiny of the Equatoria Corps in the southern Sudan happened in August 1955. From that time the Sudan was under martial law. The country became independent on 1 January 1956, under those very difficult circumstances. During 1955 a Sudanese priest, Daniel Deng Atong, had been consecrated in Kampala as assistant bishop to Oliver Allison. But the strains and stresses of the mutiny and what followed told on his mental health and in only about a year he was forced by a complete breakdown to retire. This was a great disappointment, but God led the Church on in what might have seemed overwhelming difficulties.

For several years life in the south continued relatively normally, despite the tensions. There was even expansion and growth. In one area this was conspicuous – in the numbers of Sudanese clergy. When Oliver Allison, who had been assistant bishop, became the diocesan bishop in 1953, there were only twelve, but year by year ordinands went to Bishop Gwynne College at Mundri and proceeded to training and ordination. In 1974, when Bishop Allison retired, there were 109 clergy as well as four bishops – a nine-fold increase in twenty years.

Pressures began to intensify in 1962, with the Missionary Societies Regulations 1962, which limited missionary activity, requiring licences for almost any church-related activity. Friday was for a short time imposed as the weekly day of rest in the south as well as the north; churches were not allowed to be repaired; compulsory teaching of the Quran was instituted. Missionaries had to be registered under the terms of the new act, but the bishop found that he could legitimately refuse to register the Sudanese clergy, and they continued to preach, teach and baptise. Through personal contacts some of the more troublesome regulations were not enforced, but the Christians in the south felt that their faith was threatened. Then in February 1964 came an order expelling all foreign missionaries from the south. By that time the CMS had only twelve, of whom six were on leave. But there were more than two hundred Roman Catholic priests, brothers and sisters.

The increasing pressures from the central government met response in the south. The already existing southern resistance movement organised a military wing, known as the Anya-nya. From that time on (1963) it was an open civil war. The expulsion of the missionaries was a great shock, though fortunately the bishop was not affected, and he continued to travel into the south, at least to the provincial headquarters, for services and confirmations. Two Sudanese assistant bishops were consecrated in January 1963 – Bishop Elinana and Bishop Yeremaya. As violence came nearer so the Church was being prepared.

Bishop Allison himself describes the next stage as an explosion after a long period when the flame crept slowly along the fuse. It came in July 1965. In fact, the miracle was that it was so delayed – in October 1964 there were riots at Khartoum University and in December further riots when on "Black Sunday" over a thousand southerners were killed on the streets of Khartoum. The Prime Minister bravely organised a round table conference but little came of it; a change of government brought increased determination to stamp out opposition in the south. And so in July 1965 came the massacres which led to the dispersion of the Church in the south.

Now that reconciliation and a measure of peace has come, one almost hesitates to recount again the tragic events of that year. At Juba, over a thousand civilians killed by the army in a single day; at Wau, a few days later, similar wholesale bloodshed; at other smaller townships, similar killings. Churches, houses, schools – any building which the Army thought the Anya-nya might use was razed to the ground; hospitals were not spared. Tens of thousands of ordinary Sudanese simply took to the bush. These included the two Sudanese bishops, who escaped separately but met, in God's providence, just over the border in Uganda. They finally arrived together in Kampala. Archbishop Leslie Brown tells how he was called from his office with the unlikely story that two men, "dressed in soiled trousers and shirts, with no luggage", who wanted to see him, were bishops. It was indeed Bishop Elinana Ngalamu and Bishop Jeremaya Dotiro. This was in October 1965. The two bishops were later reunited with their wives and families and they spent the time of the "dispersion" working among their own people in Uganda, in refugee camps. Uganda received the greatest number of refugees – over 70,000 in the organised camps, but there were also large numbers in Ethiopia, Zaire, and the Central African Republic. With those living outside the camps (in Kenya as well), there were probably about 350,000 outside the Sudan.

Obviously there could not fail to be deep bitterness as well as fear and great sadness in such a conflict. As well as the tragic loss of innocent lives, southerners saw their churches, their schools, their cathedral, wantonly destroyed. But from the beginning individuals on both sides tried to keep lines of communication open. At the time of the Khartoum riots, in December 1964, Bishop Allison and bishops from the Roman Catholic and Coptic Churches made radio broadcasts at the Government's request, asking for calm and for forgiveness. Bishop Allison's long personal contacts in north and south were of great service. He had publicly defended the Sudan against misrepresentations in the English press, but he did not hesitate to publicly criticise also when this appeared necessary. The All Africa Conference of Churches (AACC) also played their part, sending a delegation to Khartoum in December 1966. At that time nothing further opened up, but their good intentions were clear.

There were those, including Christians in the south (and some vocal supporters overseas) who felt that the CMS should have come out more openly in the southern cause. Difficult as it was, the people on the spot and at headquarters tried to maintain a neutral line, and show themselves open to be mediators and bridge-builders.

Ultimately this strenuous (some would have said cowardly) neutrality paid off. But peace came about also because of the military coup of May 1969, which brought General Nimeri into power. General Nimeri had served in the south, and knew personally Colonel Joseph Lagu, the leader of the Southern Sudan Liberation Movement (SSLM), the official name of the Anya-nya. He was willing to accept a strong leadership role and to accept the mediation of the AACC and the WCC, who were trusted also by southerners.

A plane disaster played a strange part in bringing the two sides to a greater trust in one another. In December 1969 a Fokker Friendship civilian plane, flying from Khartoum to Juba, lost its way in bad weather, ran out of fuel, and crashed in the forest. Though the pilot and some others were killed, the plane did not catch fire. Some of the survivors were quite unhurt; others were injured. The local people and the Anya-nya units operating in the area helped the survivors, and ultimately got them to Mundri, whence they were flown to Juba. There is a touching account of local women breast-feeding the child of a Muslim woman who died in the crash. The story of their kind treatment spread, and Colonel Lagu was able to send a conciliatory message to General Nimeri in Khartoum. Undoubtedly this incident created a good impression in the north. An AACC delegation was able to visit the south in June 1970, and in April 1971 there was a larger AACC/WCC delegation. But in July of that year there was a coup which almost deposed General Nimeri, who escaped narrowly with his life. He re-established himself and resolved to press on with implementing peace moves, and for this was able to use the AACC and WCC channels. In November 1971 preliminary talks were held in Addis Ababa, and for this Christian organisations also assisted by paying the expenses of the SSLM delegates. In February 1972 the peace conference took place in Addis Ababa. The role of Canon Burgess Carr, the Liberian Episcopalian who was then secretary of the AACC, will not be forgotten. The emperor of Ethiopia, Haile Selassie, also played an important part. So on 3 March 1972 it was announced that a peace accord had been signed, and this was ratified by both sides. After over sixteen years of bitter conflict, peace had come, and the people came back.

The Church had grown and matured during the time of exile. Within the Sudan two new assistant bishops had been consecrated; a number of young men had been training for ordination in Uganda and Kenya; in the forests of Sudan and in the refugee camps thousands had been baptised and con-firmed. During the conflict Christian relief agencies had given much help to the refugees, and had also managed to get medical supplies into the south, mainly through Uganda. It was recognised that massive help would need to continue for rehabilitation, and so the Africa Committee for Rehabilitation of the Southern Sudan (ACROSS) was set up. Roman Catholic, Presbyterian and other missions worked together with the Anglicans, and United Nations agencies played their part.

In 1976 Bishop Oliver Allison retired, after nearly thirty years' service as a bishop. With great rejoicing, his successor was installed and enthroned in All Saints Cathedral, Juba, as archbishop and leader of a new Anglican province. He was the Most Rev. Elinana Ngalamu, one of the two men who walked out to Uganda as a refugee in 1965.

Nigeria

In Nigeria, the civil war was not so inevitable and even now one can see ways in which it might have been avoided. That was not very obvious to the participants on the two sides at the time. It was a conflict which divided families and friends far outside Nigeria. Here was no clear-cut north-south or Muslim-Christian divide, although sometimes it was presented in those terms. Christians were clearly involved on both sides, and as far as Anglicans and CMS missionaries were concerned, they were also on both sides, geographically and ideologically.

Nigeria is an immense country, and has the largest population of any African nation. During the colonial period (which started earlier here) western influences were not evenly distributed. The policy of indirect rule, whereby the colonial authorities used traditional rulers to govern under them, worked best in the north, where strong and conservative princes maintained the status quo. In accordance with this policy, missionaries, and so schools, were largely excluded from the north which was in any case strongly Muslim. In Africa, as in the North-West Frontier of India, and in Malaya, the British administrators had been protective of Islam, and either excluded missionaries or restricted them severely. In the case of Nigeria, this had effects far beyond the religious sphere. One result was that the Ibo people of the south-east, who had accepted Western education and Christian teaching enthusiastically, and who were in any case enterprising traders and travellers, moved in large numbers to the cities and towns of the north, where they dominated commerce and the civil service.

At independence (October 1960), Nigeria became a federation of three unequally sized, self-governing regions. Each one was dominated by a particular ethnic group, but with very sizeable minorities. The north was largely Muslim; there was a considerable Muslim presence among the Yoruba of the west, but very few in the east. The Roman Catholic Church was particularly strong among the Ibo of the east. Anglican dioceses were then seven, and subsequently increased to nine, with only three missionary bishops. In 1951 the Church of the Province of West Africa had been formed, and most of the dioceses were in Nigeria. In 1966 the archbishop was the Bishop on the Niger, a CMS missionary, the Most Rev. C. J. Patterson.

Political inexperience, corruption, and personal, regional, political and ethnic rivalries had by 1965 brought the large and complex nation to its knees. In January 1966 a coup d'état by junior military officers overthrew the civilian politicians. The Prime Minister (Abubakar Tafawa Balewa) and the premiers of the northern and the western regions were all killed. Major-General Aguiyi-Ironsi, an Ibo from the eastern region, took over and tried to implement reforms which would strengthen the federation.

Ironsi remained in control for almost seven months. He was an experienced officer who had commanded the Nigerian contingent in the Congo. He acted to move Nigeria from a federated to a unitary state, and inevitably there were fears, especially in the north, which did not have a reserve of trained and educated men to replace the politicians and army officers earlier killed. So a second coup came about; on 28 July 1966 Ironsi was taken by young northern officers, while visiting Ibadan, and killed. Northern officers and men then spread out and began to kill Ibo officers and men. In the north and west there was total confusion; even in the east the governor, General Ojukwu, was under threat, but he survived in safety till he was able to go back and reassert political control.

The question now was, could the federation survive? At this point it was the north, not the east, which seemed to be on the point of secession. The most senior northern officer finally emerged after days of impassioned debate as the new leader – the only hope of keeping the north in the federation. Yakubu Gowon *was* a northerner, but from a minority tribe, and he was a Christian, not a Muslim, the son of an Anglican catechist.

At this stage there was still hope. But Ojukwu was unwilling to accept the new situation. Rumour and counter-rumour ran wild; discussions about the future went on till mid-September, when what can only be described as a pogrom burst out. In the north mobs, led or encouraged by the military, turned against the Ibo. Accurate figures are hard to come by, but at least six to eight thousand Ibo, possibly many more, were killed. Several hundred northerners were killed in reprisals in the East. About a million and a half Ibo fled back to the east from other parts of Nigeria. Then Ojukwu expelled non-easterners from his region.

In January Gowon and Ojukwu met at Aburi, Ghana, supported by advisers. Ojukwu gained concessions and it still seemed possible that by moving slightly apart, the federation could survive. But the Ibo élite who surrounded Ojukwu were determined on secession, and the Aburi agreement was not really working. Finally, on 30 May 1967, Ojukwu proclaimed that, "The territory and region known as Eastern Nigeria . . . shall henceforth be an independent sovereign state of the name and title the Republic of Biafra."

This war was by its nature destined to be uneven, with the comparatively large, well-trained and well-equipped federal forces opposing the smaller and much less professional army of the "rebels", as the Biafrans were termed. (They called the federal troops "vandals".) But there were well-trained and experienced officers on both sides (both Gowon and Ojukwu had served with the Nigerian contingent in the Congo) and the Biafrans had the advantage of dedication to a cause. After a "phoney war" period of over a month, the war really began in July with fighting in the far north of the region, when Nsukka fell. The federal forces made a number of advances, also taking Bonny island off the Coast. So far Gowon was keeping up with his aim of a short sharp campaign which would rapidly bring down the "rebels". But the "vandals" were yet to be surprised. On 9 August the road blocks at each end of the Niger bridge (at Onitsha) were removed, and a mixed cavalcade of vehicles poured across from the Biafran side into the mid-west region. Ojukwu was taking the initiative, striking for the head of the serpent, and Ibo officers in the mid-west had been cooperating. The major towns fell to Biafra with very little fighting. On 17 August Biafran troops crossed into the western region on their way to Lagos. But here they overreached themselves. The two armies engaged at Ore, 135 miles from Lagos. After several days of struggle the Biafrans retreated, and within two months they had left the mid-west region also. In the wake of the retreating Biafrans there were several bloody and cruel massacres of Ibo civilians, mainly carried out, it seems, by civilians rather than by federal troops, but reinforcing Biafran and Ibo fears of genocide.

This campaign was the high point of Biafra's war. By late October Enugu, the administrative capital of the eastern region, had fallen, and Calabar was taken on 18 October. Moving north the federal divisions encircled Biafra and the enclave was under a siege which, essentially, was to last for two years.

The food shortages, the shortages of almost everything, were beginning to be felt; refugee camps and hospitals felt the difficulties early, but the whole population was soon to be affected. Ibo resourcefulness kept things running longer than would have been thought possible, but neither side made much progress. The next struggle was at the negotiating table with the OAU intervening. In August 1968 talks were held in Addis Ababa, and then in Algiers at the OAU annual summit meeting. But the end of it all was Biafra's unshakeable determination to fight on.

Where were the missionaries in this situation? The CMS followed its usual policy of letting those on the spot make their own decisions, while giving them maximum support. Obviously mothers with young children came home; most of the others stayed on till it seemed right to go – on normal leave – or when responsibilities could be handed over. Many stayed on throughout the war, going on leave and returning. Some in the north and the west were, in physical terms, little affected, but the tensions of a country divided and at war affected all. Emotions in some cases ran high; missionaries tend, all over the world, to identify with "their" people, usually those whose language they speak. Inevitably, some were more pro-Biafran than the Biafrans, or more pro-federal than the federalists. Whatever their sympathies (and most saw both sides) they endeavoured to act neutrally and to give help wherever it was needed.

Perhaps this line of neutrality was hardest for Archbishop Patterson. He was in overall charge of the Anglican Church in all Nigeria (from 1961), but he had been a CMS missionary in eastern Nigeria since 1934, and naturally had very close personal links with many Ibo. After the outbreak of hostilities he stayed for some time in the federal territories, but eventually went back to Biafra, where he lived at Alor, near Nnewi, until his resignation in 1969. During the war he continued to travel on both sides, having to go back to London to do so. Like the others who stayed, he took the dangers and discomforts as a matter of course. One simply did what had to be done. But taking a night flight from Uli Airstrip, which was nothing but a length of highway used as a runway, required a good deal of courage.

Most of the missionaries who stayed, unless involved in medical work, took on some kind of relief work. Dr. Elizabeth Edmonds worked at Iyi-Enu, the diocesan hospital, right through the war, and moved with it on two evacuations. Other medical workers were nurses, like Anne Travis and Anne Bent. Canon David Hawkins came back alone even when his wife Lois had to stay in England. Jennifer Carey lived at Alor, near the archbishop, and among various tasks cared for children who were the chief victims of malnutrition. Bob and Anne Burke, Beatrice Waddington, Mary Bunting – all of these stayed on when it would have been so easy to go, not because they necessarily agreed with what was happening, but in order to express their fellowship with their brothers and sisters who were suffering.

One CMS couple paid the price all were willing to give. A.F.C. ("Tarka") Savory and his wife Marjorie were shot and died at Okigwi on 30 September 1968. With them died two relief workers, doctors, one from Sweden and one from Yugoslavia. The Savorys had been in Nigeria since 1947, and were involved in welfare and rehabilitation work at a leprosy settlement. On 28 September, as federal troops approached Okigwi, civilians left, but on 30 September the Savorys went over and joined the ICRC team in the hospital. They were wearing Red Cross badges when they were killed, not in fighting but, it seems, by the hand of a young and excited soldier whose officer could not control him.

Neither the CMS nor the missionaries showed bitterness at the death. On 4 October Brian de Saram (Africa secretary) wrote a brave and Christ-filled letter to *The Times*. At that time the blame was being publicly laid on "drunken soldiers". But responsibility could not be assigned to any one individual – it was a total situation, including Western nations, commercial interests, and much more, which must bear the responsibility for the deaths, not only of the Savorys, but of tens of thousands of innocent Africans. Ken Gill, who was financial secretary of the Niger diocese, tells how two Ibo, one a Roman Catholic priest, saved the lives of three Westerners at Asaba as the Biafrans were retreating. The whites (one, Mark Inman, was a CMS missionary) had been taken for white mercenaries, and Biafrans began clubbing them to death. After the intervention the three men, badly injured, were taken to Onitsha and released into the custody of the CMS representative, when it was clear that they were not mercenaries. Atrocities could occur from either side.

Throughout the war, and before it, Christian groups in Nigeria endeavoured to keep lines of communication open, which might lead to reconciliation. So interdenominational consultations were set up by the Christian Council of Nigeria in Lagos, Ibadan and Enugu. Members used their personal contacts with General Gowon (who was an Anglican) and General Ojukwu (who was a Roman Catholic). Canon John Fowler, who was director of the Institute of Church and Society, and spent the war years in federal territory, wrote: "These consultations, though voicing Christian concern, were not effective in avoiding conflict; nevertheless it would have been a failure if they had not taken place." The Anglican Church did seek to maintain a neutral role, made more difficult by the support the British Government gave to the federal side. The Roman Catholic missionaries in Biafra were openly partisan, and the Pope was identified as a supporter of the Biafran cause. This meant that after the war the majority of RC missionaries were expelled and not permitted to return.

Even before the conflict ended Christian organisations had begun to think about reconstruction and reconciliation. That this took place so comparatively rapidly, that there were few killings, no genocide, and no reprisals, was in part due to this preparation. Despite all the plans, humanitarian aid was limited, in part by refusal of cooperation on the part of Nigeria. Western humanitarians, for all their good intentions, still have much to learn about how aid can be offered to a proud country which has become tired of charity and patronage. At all events, there was much less violence, and quicker reconciliation, than most had dared hope for.

A journalist who had travelled on both sides during and after the war has written:

> When one considers the brutality, the proscriptions, the carefully nurtured, immensely durable hatreds that have so often followed wars in the "civilised" West (the terrible aftermath of the Spanish civil war, fought not so long ago is one example) it may be that when history takes a longer view of Nigeria's war it will be shown that while the black man has little to teach us about making war he has a real contribution to offer in making peace. (John de St. Jorre, 1972, p. 407)

One missionary who left at the very end of the war (January 1970) was invited back ten months later, and returned. She spoke Ibo, and relates how she overheard former Biafrans saying to one another that the peace and forgiveness owed much to the leadership of General Gowon, the northern Christian who set up a code of conduct for his troops. So before, during and after the war Christians in federal Nigeria and "Biafra" were still able to see one another as brothers and sisters, and were supported by missionaries who did the same. One of the greatest goods which came out of this tragic period was the spirit of oneness between local Christians and missionaries as they worked together and faced dangers and hardships together. "When you have sheltered together in the same ditch during an attack, you see things in a new way."

EPILOGUE

In the years approaching its first centenary, the number of CMS missionaries serving abroad was steadily increasing. In 1887 it was (without counting wives) 309. Seven years later, in 1894, the number had doubled to 619. Giving was keeping pace, and the Society came to its centenary in good heart.

As the time shortens to the second centenary, the figures show something different. In 1970 the number of CMS missionaries from the UK and Ireland, *including wives*, was 617. When the missionaries sent out by CMS Australia and CMS New Zealand are added the total was about 770. But that number has been dropping year by year. In 1982 there were 350 missionaries and volunteers from the UK and 200 from the Commonwealth societies – a total of 550.

And the treasurers of the societies affirm that if the numbers had not dropped, the finances available would be insufficient. Although giving appears to have increased, in real terms it has dropped sharply. The £1,396,551 received in 1981 is £655,211 more than the amount received in 1970. But when adjustments are made for inflation, it is actually worth almost a million pounds less.

So as we face the future, looking towards the centenary, let us also face the plain facts. The CMS is receiving less financial support; fewer people are serving overseas as CMS missionaries. Is this a decline? Is the time of the voluntary missionary society coming to an end?

A former Methodist missionary in China and in Africa, who has been a friendly critic of the CMS, has called his book about Africa and the missionary *The end of an era*. Are we at the end? Or are we at the same time coming to a new beginning?

Certainly the Society finds itself in an almost entirely different context from that in which it appeared to be set at its first centenary. In Africa and Asia there are independent, self-governing Churches, mostly organised in their own provinces, with local clergy, teachers and evangelists, with many skilled leaders staffing their own institutions and with their own theology and strategy developing rapidly. They are, it is true, continuing to ask for missionaries with special skills to supplement or reinforce their work. There are still some opportunities for which no suitable man or woman can be found locally. So traditional requests of this kind are still being made.

But alongside this diminishing type of involvement a whole new area is opening up. There is now a demand, even from Churches with no actual obvious need for skills from outside, for an exchange of people ready to give, but even more to receive. There is a sense, in Churches in Asia especially, for the need to sustain sometimes tenuous relationships with the Churches in Britain. The best way of doing this is still through the coming and going of people, who may or may not be "skilled" in the old sense. Some may be going mainly to study and learn, like an English couple in Pakistan preparing to work later in Britain, or CMS volunteers in India spending two years in the Churches there essentially as students. Their actual contribution has been highly valued both in India and, on their return, in Britain.

The Church in Britain however often seems far less aware of its own need, and less sensitive to a new global interdependence, both in and beyond the Church, than Churches overseas. It still seems difficult to open up opportunities for overseas Christians to participate in the mission of the Church in Britain.

In this situation, the CMS has sought in the last decade to

re-articulate its aims and reorganise its structure. The Society has recognised itself to be, as one outside consultant put it, no longer in the role of an exporter but of a broker. In some parts of the world men and women with specific skills may still be needed and asked for in the old way. Everyone who goes must obviously still have some skill to offer, not least if such a person is to obtain a visa. But their essential task is somewhat different from what it may have been in the past. They go primarily to share in and stimulate a movement for renewal in mission which is as much needed in the Churches of the West as in those in other parts of the world. They go as mission partners. They go as part of what must become increasingly a two-way, many-way flow; without this flow Churches in the West as well as elsewhere will be the losers. The new base of world mission is not in the West but in an increasingly international Church. The urgent need now is that Christians should join in the renewal of one another's Churches worldwide. The CMS becomes one channel among others through which this renewal can flow. The Society has to make its appeal for money in order to fund a relationship. Its members and those whom it both brings and sends embody and realise that relationship. As a voluntary society it provides the best possible way of sustaining people in this task. It can still be and needs to become again a movement, a "fellowship of enthusiasts" (Max Warren), a "community of commitment" (John Taylor).

But it has also developed a much closer involvement in the other structures of the Anglican Churches of Britain. The formation in 1978 of Partnership for World Mission was the recognition, at least at the London end of the missionary societies and of the Anglican Church, of the role of the voluntary societies as an overseas missionary arm of the Church. This has been to some extent a new recognition on the part of the archbishop and the general synod.

288 PROCLAIM THE GOOD NEWS

The possibility that the four main Anglican "general" overseas societies might move together into one building, a kind of Overseas House of the Church of England under one roof, suggests a strengthening of this central operation. Alongside this development goes the inter-Church involvement of the CMS through its committed membership of the British Council of Churches' Conference for World Mission, an ecumenical body in which overseas agencies of different Churches work together. On the other side are its equally vital links in its membership of the Evangelical Missionary Alliance, with a wide range of inter-denominational evangelical agencies. The CMS has perhaps a key mediating function between these two groupings which arises out of its whole tradition both in this country and overseas.

When the CMS was launched in 1799 it was by a small and obscure group of laymen and clergy. After more than a year's wait, the Archbishop of Canterbury gave grudging assent to its existence. Without paid staff, without a regular office, without any kind of trappings, it was volunteers who started the Society on its way.

Obviously growth brings change. It is for good reasons that the last two volumes of the Society's history have for their general title *The problems of Success*. We cannot go back in time. We cannot wish for failure. But success is of different kinds. This Society is not one which looks for its own growth and aggrandisement as an end in itself. Its great secretary, Henry Venn, spoke of the euthanasia of the missionary society. Has the time indeed come for the Society to legislate itself out of existence?

It does not seem so. If anything, it is entering upon a new function for which its whole history has uniquely fitted it, namely, to become a vital part of that network of worldwide inter-Church relationships through which new life can spread from growth point to growth point. It looks as though it will and should continue as a voluntary society and will not merge with all the other Anglican voluntary societies, nor become absorbed in a official board of missions in this country. It will work more and more closely with other societies and with the overseas departments of other Churches, both in this country and abroad.

It will continue to grow smaller in the number of long-term "mission partners" sent out, but perhaps more slowly than in the recent past. It will facilitate many more kinds of mutual visit and exchange between Churches, and between the Anglican Churches of Britain and other Churches in particular in the effort to generate renewed mission worldwide. The number of mission partners who serve for two or three years will increase. So will the development of links with CMS members overseas, of visits of groups, both of young people and of representatives of congregations. So an ever-increasing number of Christians will have experienced a first-hand involvement in the world Church, and the task will be increasingly apparent as one of shared worldwide renewal and revival of Christian witness.

But what will this mean? How do we spell this renewal out? It is likely to be increasingly costly if it is to mean anything in the present, unjustly divided, conflict and famine-ridden, oppressed and tormented world, over which looms the growing threat of nuclear war. Those struggling for a new humanity in Christ in such a setting realise increasingly that it means nothing less than entering deeper into Christ's death and resurrection.

When the representatives of the Church in China renewed contact with the Church in Britain and came on a visit here, as their leader stood on the steps of Lambeth Palace Chapel he said, "We have been through a death and resurrection." Prophetic words, as those who heard him knew, summoning the Churches in every country of the world to be ready. There is going to be a cost of partnership if it is to mean this shared dying and being raised.

The Church in Iran

Perhaps the tiny Episcopal Church in Iran can stand as a symbol of what may be asked of many Churches in the future.

CMS missionaries took the Gospel to Iran – Persia – from 1869, though there had been an important earlier contact in Henry Martyn's brief visit in 1811, and through his translation of the Scriptures into Persian. The number of CMS missionaries was never large, but there were outstanding and dedicated people, and they sought above all to build up a *Persian* Church. As a rule the transferring of members from the ancient Eastern churches was discouraged, and the Episcopal Church never became large. There were converts from Islam; some also from Jewish and Zoroastrian backgrounds.

When in 1961 the English missionary bishop was succeeded by an Iranian, the prayers of many for that Church seemed to be coming to pass. He was the son of a Muslim father whose mother had become a Christian, and he eventually followed her in the faith. His wife was the daughter of the previous bishop, from a family who had served Persia over several generations. He wrote poetry in his mother-tongue and was proud of his Persian culture. The little Church had five Iranian priests of varying religious backgrounds; there were even fewer expatriate priests, some serving as chaplains to the expatriate community.

But this small and comparatively weak Church, seeking to show the love of Jesus in action, had built up a network of institutions rather out of proportion to its size. There were several hospitals and dispensaries, some schools and hostels, and especially some specialised institutions to serve the blind, including a farm to train adult blind men in self-sufficiency. The leadership and many of the workers for these projects came largely from overseas; some, though not all, were CMS missionaries. A good deal of the finance needed came from overseas. As the bishop explains, the country welcomed this. "They even helped us financially sometimes. Preaching was allowed within our hospitals and blind schools and of course no difficulty was raised over worship services in churches, whether in English or Persian." (*The Hard Awakening*, p. 24)

The missionaries tried to remain neutral in political matters, and to immerse themselves in the Iranian culture. All who knew the country well expected an eventual confrontation between the Shah and the Islamic religious leaders. "By the late 1970s oppression was universal in the country. There was no longer any doubt that we were living in a police state. The whole country was demanding freedom . . . When the Revolution came we welcomed it. But it was not long before we found that we had exchanged one form of oppression for another even more severe." (*Ibid*, p. 35)

David Paton has written, thinking about the position of the missionary in China: "In a country which is being revolutionised by the invasion of the Western world, a Christian missionary who comes from the Western world, be he as harmless as a dove, as unpolitical as Jane Austen, is in himself by his very existence a political fact." (*Christian Missions and the Judgement of God*, p. 23)

So as the Revolution – in this case a reaction to the West – built up in Iran, the missionaries were inevitably seen as agents of the West. No other reaction is, in the end, possible.

The whole world has followed the story of that small Episcopal Church since the beginning of 1979. In February of that year an Iranian clergyman was murdered. In June and July, two hospitals and the blind school were confiscated. The bishop's house and office were raided. In October an attack was made on the bishop's life and his wife was wounded.

In May 1980 the bishop's secretary, a CMS missionary named Jean Waddell, was attacked and barely escaped death. Just a few days later his only son, aged twenty-four, was shot and killed. In August Jean Waddell and two other CMS missionaries, Dr. John Coleman and his wife Audrey, were all three arrested and held without trial. Other diocesan workers were arrested; others again were expelled. By the end of 1980, of the five national clergy and the bishop who had been serving the Church at the beginning of 1979, all but two had been arrested, were dead, or had been forced to leave the country. So also all the expatriate workers.

Now, four years later, the Church in Iran continues. There are no "mission partners" from overseas; there are no longer any institutions which, as well as helping individuals, remind people of the links with an affluent and patronising West which they would rather forget. All that is left is – the Church. But that "all" is important. "Christians must learn again what Christians have always known, how to live without immediate hopes in the world." (David Paton, *ibid*, p. 57)

There were traditionally in the ancient Church two kinds of martyrdom. A "red martyrdom" was the laying down of one's life, and a "white martyrdom" a deep repentance and brokenness, a surrender of one's being through which God's love can flow to others.

Martyrdom then becomes part of "martyria", the word from which it springs, "witness". To encourage each other across the world in this witness, this life out of death, both corporately and individually, is an urgent necessity for Christians now if they are responsibly to seize hold of a moment of crucial, unprecedented opportunity for witness in every part of the globe. This may mean a breaking and remaking of our institutions, a loss of our "physical plant", our buildings, our prestige. In such a situation the Church Missionary Society and those willing to serve in its fellowship will surely have, now as in the past, a crucial part to play and find, now more than ever, a glorious fulfilment.

I am indebted to Canon Simon Barrington-Ward for his contribution to the Epilogue.

SELECT BIBLIOGRAPHY

Ajayi, J. F. A. *Christian missions in Nigeria 1841–1891. The making of a new elite.* London: Longmans 1965

Allison, Oliver. *Through fire and water.* London: CMS 1976

Allison, Oliver. *Travelling light. Bishop Oliver Allison of the Sudan remembers.* Bexhill-on-Sea: privately published, 1983

Brown, Leslie. *Three worlds: one word. Account of a mission.* London: Rex Collings 1981

Church, J. E. *Quest for the highest. An autobiographical account of the East African revival.* Exeter: the Paternoster Press 1981

Church Missionary Society. *Register of missionaries (clerical, lay and female) and native clergy. From 1804 to 1904.* Printed for private circulation

Dehqani-Tafti, H. B. (Bishop in Iran). *The hard awakening.* London: SPCK 1981

Gibbs, M. E. *The Anglican Church in India 1600–1970.* Delhi: Indian SPCK 1972

Hastings, Adrian. *A history of African Christianity 1950–1975.* Cambridge: Cambridge University Press 1979

Hewitt, Gordon. *The problems of success. A history of the Church Missionary Society 1910–1942.* London: SCM Press. Vol. 1, 1971; Vol. 2, 1977

Hopkins, Hugh Evan. *Charles Simeon of Cambridge.* London etc.: Hodder and Stoughton 1977

Hunt, Paul. *Inside Iran.* Tring, Herts.: Lion Publishing 1981

Kendall, Elliott. *The end of an era. Africa and the missionary.* London: SPCK 1978

Latourette, Kenneth Scott. *A history of the expansion of Christianity.* Grand Rapids: Zondervan. Vol. 6, 1944; Vol. 7, 1945

Neill, Stephen. *Anglicanism.* London and Oxford: Mowbrays 1958

293

Neill, Stephen. *A history of Christian missions*. Harmonsworth: Penguins 1964

Neill, Stephen. *Men of unity*. London: SCM Press Ltd. 1960

Paton, David M. *Christian missions and the judgement of God*. London: SCM Press 1953

St. John, Patricia. *Breath of life. The story of the Ruanda mission*. London: the Norfolk Press 1971

de St. Jorre, John. *The Nigerian civil war*. London etc.: Hodder and Stoughton 1972

Shenk, Wilbert R. *Henry Venn – missionary statesman*. Maryknoll, N.Y.: Orbis Books 1983

Stock, Eugene. *The history of the Church Missionary Society. Its environment, its men and its work*. In three volumes London: Church Missionary Society 1899

Stock, Eugene. *The history of the Church Missionary Society*. Supplemental volume, the fourth. London: Church Missionary Society 1916

Sundkler, B. G. M. *Church of South India. The movement towards union 1900/1947*. London: USCL, Lutterworth Press 1954

Taylor, John V. *Change of address. Selections from the CMS Newsletters*. London: Hodder and Stoughton 1968

Taylor, John V. *The growth of the Church in Buganda. An attempt at understanding*. London: SCM Press Ltd. 1958

Thompson, H. P. Into all lands. *The history of the Society for the Propagation of the Gospel in Foreign Parts 1701–1950*. London: SPCK 1951

Warren, Max. *Crowded Canvas. Some experiences of a life-time*. London etc.: Hodder and Stoughton 1974

Warren, Max. *Letters on Purpose*. London: the Highway Press 1963

Warren, Max (ed.) *To apply the gospel. Selections from the writings of Henry Venn*. Grand Rapids, Michigan: William B. Eerdmans Publishing Co. 1971

Yates, T. E. *Venn and Victorian bishops abroad*. Uppsala and London: Swedish Institute of Missionary Research and SPCK 1978

INDEX

Abel, Rev. Frederick, 68
Abolitionists, 10, 11
Abyssinia, 33, 94
Africa Inland Mission, 248
The African slave trade and its remedy, 51
Aguiyi-Ironsi, Major-General, 278
Ainu (Japan), 154
Alexander, Rt. Rev. Michael Solomon, 136
Alford, Rt. Rev. C. R., 146, 147
All Africa Conference of Churches, 260, 275, 276
Allepie, South India, 30, 34
Alliance High School, Dodoma, 199
Alliance High School, Kenya, 172
Allison, Rt. Rev. Oliver, 258, 272–3, 275, 277
Anderson, Rt. Rev. David, 86
Anderson, Rev. Rufus, 209
Anglican Congresses, 232, 261
Anglo-Catholic party, 7
Annie Walsh Memorial School, 45
Anti-Slavery Society, 35
Arthur, Rev. Dr. John, 174
Associations (of CMS), 14–15, 270–271; in India, 68; in Australia and New Zealand, 118, 170, 197, 200; in Canada, 200–1
Australian CMS, 118, 149, 196–200, 226
Azariah, Rt. Rev. V. S., 167, 215, 217, 218

Bailey, Rev. Benjamin, 14
Bailey, Rev. Joseph, 14

Bailey, Sarah (Dawson), 15
Baker, Amelia, 110
Baker, Amelia Kohloff, 65
Baker, Rev. Henry, 110
Bakewell, Canon Lionel, 199
Balewa, Abubakar Tafawa, 278
Bannerjee, Krishna Mohan, 63
Baptist Missionary Society, 4
Bardsley, Rt. Rev. Cyril, 177, 178, 179–80
Barrington-Ward, Canon Simon, 265, 268–9, 292
Bartlett, Rev. Daniel, 180–1
Basel Mission, 173
Basel Seminary, 2, 17, 28, 95
Batchelor, Rev. John, 154
Bathurst, Rt. Rev. H. (Bishop of Norwich), 16
Battersby, Canon Harford, 102
Beale, Mrs. Mary, 109
Beecher, Rt. Rev. L. J., 246, 247
Bennett, Rt. Rev. Frederick Augustus, 118–19
Bent, Anne, 282
Berlin Seminary, 9, 17
Bernau, Rev. J. H., 36
Berridge, Rev. John, 3
Bhushanam, Rev. Ainala, 63
Bible Churchman's Missionary Society, 181, 185, 197, 248, 271
Bickersteth, Rev. Edward, 13, 16, 19, 152, 153
Bickersteth, Rt. Rev. Edward, 152, 153

Bird, Robert Merttins, 69
Bishop Poole Memorial Girls School, 152, 153
Bishop's College, Calcutta, 27, 31, 62
Bleakley, Hon. David, 264
Blomfield, Rt. Rev. C. J. (Bishop of London), 40
Blyth, Rt. Rev. G. P., 138
Book of Common Prayer, 7
Borup, Kristin, 131
Bostock, Ven. Peter, 246
Bouffler, Mary, 107
Bowley, Rev. William, 66
British Council of Churches Conference for World Mission, 288
British East India Company, 9, 59, 142
British and Foreign Bible Society, 17, 37, 46, 140
British Guiana, 36
Brown, Rev. David, 26
Brown, Most Rev. Leslie, 252, 274
Bruce, Rev. Robert, 137
Buchanan, Rev. Claudius, 26, 34
Budd, Rev. Henry, Sr., 85
Buddhism, 155, 157
Bühler, Rev. G. F., 55
Bültman, Rev. Frederic, 21
Bunting, Mary, 282
Burdon, Rt. Rev. John, 147
Burke, Bob and Anne, 282
Burnside, Rev. H., 152
Butler, Bishop, 1
Butler, Rev. John, 23
Butler, Samuel, 23
Butscher, Leopold, 19
Buxton, Sir Thomas Fowell, 35, 51

Caldwell, Rt. Rev. Robert, 77
Cambridge, 2, 3, 103
Cambridge Brotherhood, Delhi, 152
Cambridge Inter-Collegiate Christian Union, 101, 102, 103, 115, 186
"The Cambridge Seven", 102-3

Canada (Manitoba), 84-8, 170
Canning, Lord, 74
Carey, Jennifer, 282
Carey, Rev. William, 4, 26
Carey, Willoughby, 246
Carpenter, Canon G. K. and Mrs. Kathleen, 223-4, 226
Carpenter, Kathleen, 227
Carr, Canon Burgess, 276
Carr, Rt. Rev. Thomas, 60
Cash, Rt. Rev. William Wilson, 209-10
Cassels, Rt. Rev. William, 103
Ceylon (Sri Lanka), 30-1, 155-162
Chambers, Rt. Rev. George, 198-9, 200
Chase, Dr. Tony, 253
Chelmsford, Rt. Rev. the Bishop of, 181
Chiang Kai-Shek, 220, 221
Chichester, Lord, 47, 263
China, 140-50, 167-8, 197-8, 219-224
China Inland Mission, 102, 111, 147, 168, 222
Christian Council of Kenya, 246
Christian Researches in Asia, 34
Christian Researches in the Mediterranean, 32
Christians of the Copperbelt, 260
Chunar, North India, 30
Chung Hua Sheng Kung Hui, 168, 221, 222
Church, Dr. Bill, 189
Church, Decie (née Tracey), 188
Church, Rev. Howard, 193
Church, Dr. John E. (Joe), 186-7, 188-9, 190, 192, 193
Church Associations, 17, 178
Church of England Zenana Missionary Society, 66, 111, 149-50, 226, 271
church government and organisation, Bishop Selwyn (NZ), 84; Bishop Machray (Canada), 86-7; Bishop Tucker (Uganda), 132-3;

Bishop Copleston (Ceylon), 162; Japan, 153

Church Missionary College, Islington, 18, 33, 52, 59, 97

Church Missionary Review, 171

CMS News-Letter, 231

Church of South India, 214–19

Church of Scotland Mission (CSM), 174

The Church Times, 219

church union, 165, 171–2; in India, 214–19

Clark, Dr. Henry Martyn, 105

Clark, Rev. Robert, 70, 104, 105

Clark, Rev. W., 159

Coates, Dandeson, 16, 98

Cohen, Sir Andrew, 251

Cole, Henry, 124

Coleman, Dr. John and Mrs. Audrey, 292

Commonwealth and Continental Church Society, 87

Conference of British Missionary Societies, 164, 203

Cook, Dr. Albert, 107, 132

Cook, Captain James, 3, 23

Cook, Dr. John, 107, 132

Cook, Mrs. Kathleen (née Timpson), 107, 132

Cooke, Miss M. E. (Mrs. Wilson), 67, 109

Copleston, Rt. Rev. R. S., 98, 123, 158–9, 160, 161

Cornelius, Joseph, 64

Corresponding Committees, 30, 61, 157

Corrie, Rt. Rev. Daniel, 29, 60

Cotton, Rt. Rev. G. E. L., 75

Cowley Fathers (SSJE), 77

Cowper-Temple, William, 101

Crowther, Archdeacon Dandeson, 117

Crowther, Rt. Rev. Samuel Adjai, 52, 53, 54, 55, 56, 57, consecrated bishop, 58; Niger Mission, 98–9; conflict with missionaries and death, 115–17, 167

Crowther Hall, Selly Oak Colleges, 266, 267, 268

Cruickshank, William, 67

Dalhousie, Lord, 69

Darling, Thomas Young, 66–7

David, Christian, 31

David, Rev. George, 120

Davidson, Most Rev. Randall, 237

Dawson, Rev. Thomas, 15

Dealtry, Rt. Rev. Thomas, 76

Dehqani-Tafti, Bahram, 291

Dehqani-Tafti, Rt. Rev. H. B., 290–2

Delamere, Lord, 236

Deng Atong, Rt. Rev. Daniel, 272

Devasagayam, Rev. John, 64

Devonshire Declaration, 237

Dewsbury, Yorkshire, 14

Division of World Mission and Evangelism, 234

Dotiro, Rt. Rev. Jeremaya, 274

Douglas, Rt. Rev. H. A., 77

Drewett, Rev. John, 213

Duff, Alexander, 62, 202

Duncan, William, 88–94, 170

Durham Report (Canada), 40

Düring, Henry, 20

East African Revival Movement, 191–5, 216, 242–3, 244, 245, 250

East India Acts, 26–7, 59

Eastern Equatorial Africa Mission, 94–6, 119–21

Eclectic Society, 4

Eddy, Sherwood, 168

Edinburgh 1910, 167, 178, 203, 215

Edinburgh House, 164

Edmonds, Dr. Elizabeth, 282

educational missions, 62–3, 167, 201–5; in China, 221–2

Edwardes, Major Herbert, 70, 73–4

Egypt, 33, 107, 138–9, 253–6

Elgin, Lord, 145

Elland Society, 22

Elmslie, Margaret (née Duncan), 105, 109–10
Elmslie, Dr. William, 70, 104–5, 109
Ensor, Rev. George, 151
Evangelical Missions Association, 288
Exeter Hall, 73, 103

Female Education Society, 111–12, 146, 147, 149
Female Institution, Lagos, 54
Fenn, Rev. C. C., 156
Fenn, Rev. David, 64
finances and fund-raising, early fund-raising, penny-a-week subscriptions, 14; financial crisis 1841–42, 43–4; financial policies, 48; difficulties in inter-wars period, 177; financial situation in 1980s, 285
Fisher, Most Rev. Geoffrey, 219, 230–1
Fisher, Rev. Leslie, 213
Fort Garry, Manitoba, 85
Fourah Bay Institution, 52
Fowler, Canon John, 283
Fox, Rev. Henry Elliott, 46
Fox, Rev. Henry Watson, 46
Foxbury, 265, 266
Francis, Carey, 246
Frederick IV (of Denmark), 25
Frederick William IV (of Prussia), 136
Freeman, Thomas, 53
French, Rt. Rev. T. V., 73, 137
Frere, Sir Bartle, 120

Gairdner, Rev. Temple, 139
Gambier, Admiral Lord, 13, 263
Garlick, Phyllis, 205
Gell, Rt. Rev. Frederick, 76, 160
Gelsthorpe, Rt. Rev. A. M., 258
German missionaries, 10, 21, 27, 60, 78, 95, 137, 173
Gill, Ken, 283
Gobat, Rt. Rev. Samuel, 18, 136
Gollmer, C. A., 53
Goodall, Marian, 55

Gordon, General, 121, 122
Gossner Mission (Chota Nagpur), 173
Gottlieb, Rev. C. G., 70
Gough, Miss E., 149
Gough, Rev. Frederick, 144
Gowon, General Yakubu, 279–80, 283, 284
Grace, Rev. Thomas, 83
Graf, Archdeacon J. U., 21
Graham, Henry, 104
Grant, Charles, 26
Greenwood, Rev. William, 14, 30
Grey, Sir George, 83
Grimshaw, William, 3
Grogan, Colonel, 236
Growth of the Church in Buganda, 260
Grubb, Sir Kenneth, 264
Guillebaud, Archdeacon Harold, 187
Gutzlaff, Charles, 142
Gwynne, Rt. Rev. L., 173, 256–7

Hadfield, Rt. Rev. Octavius, 82, 119
Haile Selassie, Emperor, 276
Hall, William, 23
Hancock, Sir Keith, 252
Handforth, Rev. Richard, 266
Hau Hau (NZ), 83
Hannington, Rt. Rev. James, 125, 126, 127, 131
Hänsel, Rev. C. L. F., 21
Harding, Rt. Rev. John, 77
Harmar, Mary, 105
Harpur, Dr. F. J., 107, 138, 257
Hartwig, Peter, 9, 12
Hattersley, Charles, 131
Hawkins, Canon David, 282
Heber, Rt. Rev. Reginald, 27, 28, 29, 31, 62
Hehlen, Sophia, 45
Hewitt, Canon Gordon, vii, 264
Heywood, Rt. Rev. R. S. (Bishop of Mombasa), 196, 198
Higgens, Edward, 97, 111
Hill, Rt. Rev. Joseph, 117
Hillman, Jesse, 253–6

Hills, Rt. Rev. G., 92
Hinderer, Anna, 55
Hinderer, Rev. David, 54, 55, 57, 58
Hobson, Rev. John, 144
Hoernle, C. T. and Mrs., 67
Hola Camp (Kenya), 246
Holmes, Geoffrey, 184
Hongi, 23
Hooper, Cyril, 246
Hooper, Rev. Douglas, 133, 175, 244
Hooper, Dr. Elizabeth, 133
Hooper, Canon Handley, 175, 244
Hooper, Jane (Mrs. Low), 109
Horden, Rt. Rev. John, 86
Hough, Rev. James, 29, 68
Hudson Bay Company, 85, 89, 90, 91
Hume, David, 1
Hung Hsiu-ch'uan, 144
Hunter, Archdeacon James, 85

Imad-ud-din, 70
Imam-Shah, 70
Imperial British East African Company, 128, 129
India, 24–30, 34–5, 59–78, 108, 167, 214–19
Indian Female Normal School and Instruction Society (IFNS), 66, 111
Indian Mutiny, 71–4
Inman, Mark, 283
International Missionary Council, 164, 202, 203, 233, 234, 260; IMC Jerusalem meeting, 221
International Review of Missions, 164
Irving, Rev. Edward, 37
Islam, and missions to Muslims, 50, 136, 138, 166, 225, 257, 258, 277

Jackson, Rev. Herbert, 186
Jackson, Dr. Jesse, 204
Jamaica, 10, 35–6
James, Rt. Rev. John Thomas, 28
Japan, 118, 151–5, 163–4, 165, 168–169

Jeremy, Rev. David, 68
The Jerusalem bishopric, 135–7, 138
John, Dr. (Tranquebar), 29
Johnson, Amelia (Baker), 64–5
Johnson, Rt. Rev. E. R. (Calcutta), 77, 160
Johnson, Hannah, 107
Johnson, Rev. James, 115
Johnson, Rev. William, 20, 107
Jones, Rev. Edward, 21
Jones, Rev. William, 120, 125, 126
Journal of an Expedition up the Niger, 52
Jowett, Rev. William, 16, 31–2, 33
Jubilees of CMS 1849, 45–6; 1899, 113, 163

Keble, Rev. John, 38
Kendall, Rev. Eliott, 286
Kendall, Rev. Thomas, 23
Kennaway, Sir John, 264
Kenya, 130, 133–4, 171–2, 174–5, 193, 235–47
Kenya African Union (KAU), 239, 240
Kenya Missionary Council, 172
Kenya – Time for Action, 246
Kenyatta, President Jomo, 124
Keswick, 149, 185, 186, 197
Khurshedji, Rev. Sorabji, 63
Kigozi, Blazio, 186, 188, 189–90
Kikuyu Central Association (KCA), 239, 240, 244
Kikuyu Conference 1913, 165, 170–172
King, John, 23
King, Rev. Thomas, 54
King's College, Budo, 132
King's College, Cambridge, 3
Kinuka, Yosiya, 186–7, 188, 189, 190
Kivebulaya, Canon Apolo, 250
Kivengere, Rt. Rev. Festo, 250
Klein, Rev. Frederick, 136, 138
Kotgurh, 69, 70
Krapf, Rev. Johannes Ludwig, 95, 96, 125, 235

Lagos CMS Grammar School, 54
Lagu, Colonel Joseph, 275, 276
Lamb, Mrs., 55
Lambeth Conferences, 232
Lambeth Quadrilateral, 217
Lankester, Dr. Herbert, 106, 177
Last, Joseph, 124
Lawrence, Sir Henry, 69, 73
Lawrence, John (Lord Lawrence), 69, 73, 122
Lawrence, Miss Matilda, 147
Leasow House, 266
von Lettow-Vorbeck, General, 174
Leupolt, Rev. S. T. and Mrs., 67
Le Zoute Conference, Belgium (1926), 204
Lieder, Rev. J. R. T., 33
Lin, Rev. Timothy, 223
Liskeard Lodge, 265
Livingstone, Dr. David, 96, 121
London Missionary Society, 4, 7, 142
Long, Rev. James, 71
Long Lectures, 71
Lowe, Rev. John and Dr. Dorothy, 266
Lugard, Captain Frederick (Lord Lugard), 128, 204
Luwum, Most Rev. Janani (Archbishop of Uganda), 253

Macaulay, Rev. T. B., 54
Macaulay, Zachary, 36
MacCarthy, Sir Charles, 20
McClatchie, Rev. Thomas, 143
MacDonald, Rev. Robert, 88
Machray, Rt. Rev. Robert, 86, 87
Mackay, Alexander, 122, 123, 124, 127–8
Main, Dr. Duncan, 105, 149
Malaya, 225–8
Malta, 31–2, 33
Malta Mission Press, 135
Manley, Rev. G. T., 183
Mann, Rev. A. and Mrs., 55
Manning, Archdeacon (Cardinal), 46

Mao Tse-tung, 223
Mar Dionysius IV (Metran), 60
Marsden, Rev. Samuel, 11, 12, 22, 23
Martin, Colonel William, 70
Martyn, Rev. Henry, 9, 26, 28, 29, 137, 290
Masih, Rev. Abdul (Sheikh Salih), 28, 29, 68, 104
Masih, Rev. Anand, 68
Maude, Captain the Hon. Francis, 263
Mauritius, 169, 182, 196
May, Rev. Charles, 36
Meadows, Robert, 64
Medical Missionary Auxiliary, 205–206
Medical missions, 103–7, 132, 137, 138–9, 144, 167, 205–6
Mediterranean Missions, 31–3
members' councils, 269–71
Mengo High School, 132
Metlakhatla Mission, 88–94, 170
Middleton, Rt. Rev. T. F., 27, 31
Miller, Miss Katie, 198
Mills, Seymour, 82
Milman, Rt. Rev. Robert, 75, 77
Milne, Robert, 142
"mission partners", vii, 289
The Missionary Register, 14, 15, 16, 66
Moody, D. L., 100, 101, 114; and Sankey, 186
Moravians, 2, 3, 4
Morrison, Robert, 142
Morrison, S. A., 246
Mott, John R., 164, 167, 169
Moule, Archdeacon Arthur, 149
Moule, Rt. Rev. George Evans, 149
Munro, Colonel, 34
Mutesa, Sir Edward Frederick, 248, 252, 253
Mutesa, Kabaka, 121, 123, 125
MRI – Mutual Responsibility and Interdependence, 261–2
Mwanga, Kabaka, 125, 126, 127, 128

Nagenda, William, 192
Nailer, Ann Amelia, 65
Napier, Sir Charles, 69
Nasik, 120, 121
Nasser, President Gamal Abdel, 254
National Christian Council of Kenya, 172
The Native Pastorate and Organisation of Native Churches, 49
Neill, Rt. Rev. Stephen, 3, 215
Neve, Dr. Arthur, 105
Neve, Dr. Ernest, 105
New Metlakhatla, Alaska, 93, 170
New South Wales, 10, 11
New Zealand, 10, 11–12, 22–4, 79–84, 118–19, 169–70
New Zealand CMS, 118–19, 200, 226
Newman, Cardinal John Henry, 46
Newton, Rev. John, 3
Ngalamu, Most Rev. Elinana, 273, 274, 277
Nicholls, Bernard, 213, 246
Niger Expeditions, 52, 56
Niger Mission, 56–8, 98–9, 114–17
Nigeria: the Civil War, 277–84
Nimeri, General, 275, 276
Nippon Sei-Kokwai, 165
Noble, Robert, 65
Noble School, Masulipatam, 63, 65, 72
Noel, Baptist, 46
North-West Pacific Mission, 88–94, 170
Norton, Rev. Thomas, 30, 34
Nova Scotia, 10
Nowroji, Rev. Ruttonji, 77
Nsibambi, Simeon, 188, 190
Nyerere, President Julius, 200
Nyländer, Anne Elizabeth, 22, 110
Nyländer, G. R., 11, 18, 21, 22, 97, 110
Nyländer, Hannah, 22, 110

Oakley, Rev. William, 158, 162
O'Flaherty, Philip, 124

Ojukwu, General, 279–80, 283
Old Cairo Hospital, 228, 253
Oldham, Dr. J. H., 164, 174, 202–3, 204, 237
Oluwole, Rt. Rev. Isaac, 117
Omari, Rt. Rev. Yohana, 199
O'Neill, Thomas, 122
Opium Wars, 141–3, 145–6
ordination of missionaries, 9–10, 18, 27, 61, 80, 81
ordination of nationals, 27, 61, 81, 125, 129–30
the Orphan Press, 67
Owen, Archdeacon W. E., 244
Oxford, 2, 3

Page, Rev. Alan, 246
Palamcotta Seminary, 64
Palestine, 135–6, 137–8, 139
Palmerston, Lord, 47, 101
Parker, Rt. Rev. Henry, 112, 127
Parry, Rev. John and Helena, 266
Partnership for World Mission, 271, 287
Paton, Canon David, 291, 292
Patterson, Most Rev. C. J., 278, 281
Peel, Rt. Rev. William, 133, 171
Pelham, Rt. Rev. J. T., 47
Persia (Iran), 137, 290–2
Peters, Carl, 128
Pettitt, Rev. G., 62, 157
Phelps-Stokes, Canon Anson, 204
Phelps-Stokes Commission, 204
Phillips, Rt. Rev. Charles, 55, 117
Phillips, Miss Helen, 197
Pilkington, George, 129
Poole, Rt. Rev. Arthur, 152
Poulton, Archdeacon, 198
Pratt, Rev. Josiah, 12, 13, 14, 15, 16, 17
Presidents of the CMS, 13, 263–4
Prevost, Captain James, 88, 89
Price, Rev. W. Salter, 120, 121
Protestant Episcopal Church, USA, 142
Provinces of the Anglican Communion, 230–1, 277, 278

Punch, 171
Purvis, John, 131

Ragland, Rev. T. G., 63
Ranjit Singh, 69
Ratnam, Rev. Manchala, 63
Reader Harris, Dame Diana, 264
Rebmann, Dr. Johannes, 95, 96, 119, 120
Red River (Manitoba), 85
"Regionalisation", 228–30
Renner, Melchior, 12
Rhenius, C. T. E., 27, 29, 62
Ridley, Rt. Rev. William, 92, 93, 170
Robert Money School, Bombay, 63, 72
Robertson, James, 122
Robinson, Rev. J. A., 117
Romaine, Rev. William, 3
Romaine, Rev. William (Niger), 56
Roper, Edward, 57
Ruanda-Burundi, 182–5, 185–91, 191–5, 248
Russell, Mrs. Mary Ann, 147
Russell, Rt. Rev. W. A., 145, 146, 147, 148
Ryder, Rt. Rev. Dudley, 13, 16

St. John's College, Auckland, 80
St. John's College, Winnipeg, 87
de St. Jorre, John, 284
St. Stephen's School, Auckland, 81
Salisbury Square, 12–13, 262
Sankey, Ira D., 100, 101, 114
de Saram, Rev. Brian, 282
Sargent, Rt. Rev. Edward, 77
Sass, Julia, 45
Satthianadham, Rev. William Thomas, 64, 67
Saunders, Elizabeth, 118, 149, 150, 197
Saunders, Harriette, 118, 149, 150, 197
Savory, A. F. C., and Marjorie, 282
Schmid, Bernard, 29
Schnarre, J. C., 29

Schön, Annie Catherine, 97, 110–1
Schön, Dr. J. F., 52
Scott, Lord Francis, 236
Scott, Rev. Thomas, 12
Secundra Orphanage, 67–8
Selly Oak Colleges, Birmingham, 265, 267, 268
Selwyn, Rt. Rev. George Augustus, 24, 41, 79–80, 81, 129, 162
Semler, Rev. Ishmael, 120, 125
Shaftesbury, Lord, 47, 101, 136, 143
Shalita, Rt. Rev. Kosiya, 185, 187, 188, 189
Sharkey, Mrs. A., 65
Sharkey, John Edmund, 65, 66
Sharp, Esther (née Macdonald), 183, 184
Sharp, Dr. Leonard, 183, 184, 185
Sierra Leone, 9, 10–11, 12, 13, 19–22, 45, 50, 51
Sierra Leone Company, 10, 11
Simeon, Rev. Charles, 3, 9, 11, 18, 26, 100
Sinclair, Meredith, 255
Singapore, 227
Singh, Rev. Daud, 70
Singhalese Itinerant Mission, 156
Slave trade, West Africa, 10, 11, 19, 35, 36; East Africa, 119–20, 121
Smith, Rt. Rev. George, 143, 146
Smith, Hannah Pearsall, 100, 101, 115
Smith, Dr. John, 122
Smith, Robert Pearsall, 100, 101, 115
Smith, Shergold, 122
Smith, Stanley, 102–3
Society for Promoting Christian Knowledge, 2, 9, 60, 87, 140
Society for the Propagation of the Gospel, 2, 17, 34, 46, 60, 73, 77, 87, 149, 152, 154, 156, 169, 196, 219, 225, 271
Sodeke, 53
Soudan and Niger Mission, 116–17
South American Missionary Society, 272
Squire, Commander Edward, 142

Sri Lanka, *see under* Ceylon
Stanley, Henry Morton, 121, 122
Stanley Smith, Dr. Algernon, 183, 184, 185
Stanley Smith, Zoe (née Sharp), 183, 184
Stanway, Rt. Rev. Alfred, 200
Steele, Very Rev. David, 246
Stewart, Rev. Robert W.. 148, 149, 150. 197
Stock, Dr. Eugene, vii, 46, 112–13, 163, 170, 197
Stokes, Charles, 123, 124
Stokes, Charles Kasaja, 124
Stuart, Rt. Rev. C. E., 192, 253
Stuart, Rt. Rev. E. C., 137
Stubbings, Leslie, 213
Studd, C. T., 101, 102–3
Studd, Edward, 101
Studd, Kynaston, 101
Student Volunteer Movement. 164
Sturton, Dr. S. D., 224
Sudan, 256–8, 272–7
Suez crisis, 253–6
Sun Yat-sen, 220
Symthies, Rt. Rev. C. A., 125
Synge, Dr. Samuel, 106
Syrian Church of south India, 34–5, 60–1

T'aip'ing, 144–5, 146
Tait, Most Rev. Archibald Campbell, 47, 76
Talbot-Rice, Canon W., 198
Tamil Coolie Mission, 156, 158, 159
Tanganyika (Tanzania), 134–5, 196–197, 198–200; Mpwapwa, 124, 125
Taylor, Rev. J. C., 54
Taylor. James Hudson, 102, 147
Taylor, Rt. Rev. John Vernon, Gen. Sec. of CMS 1963–1974, appointed as General Secretary, 259; education and experience, work as secretary, 260–1, 262–3; retirement, 268; on Bishop Tucker, 133
Taylor, Rev. Richard, 82

Taylor Smith, Rt. Rev. John, 173
Te Aute College, NZ, 81, 82
Te Rauparaha, 82
theological education in mission areas, 55, 148, 153, 249, 260, 273
Thomas, Frances, 65, 76
Thomas, Rev. John, 65, 76, 110
Thomas, Mary (née Davies), 65, 76, 110
Thompson, Dr. David Milton and Mrs. Beatrice Milton, 225
Thorton, Rev. Douglas, 139
To apply the gospel, 43, 202
Townsend, Rev. Henry, 21, 53, 54, 57, 58
Tractarians, 7, 38, 41, 46, 178
training of missionaries, 17–18
Tranquebar, 25, 27, 28
Travis, Anne, 282
Trinitarian Bible Society, 37
Trinity College, Dublin, 143
Trinity College, Kandy, 162
Tristram, Katherine, 112, 153
Tucker, Rt. Rev. Alfred, 21, 129, 130, 131, 132, 249
Turner, Rt. Rev. John Matthew, 28

Uganda, 107, 121–35, 183, 192, 247–53, 260
United Society for the Propagation of the Gospel, 271
Universities Mission to Central Africa, 134, 173, 271

Venn, Rev. Henry (the elder), 22, 39
Venn, Rev. Henry, Clerical Secretary of CMS 1846–1872, first attends CMS committees, vii, 3, 16–17; appointed Secretary, as work as an administrator, 38–45, 47–8; *The Native Pastorate*, 49–50; West Africa and Bishop Crowther, 52, 56, 57–8; New Zealand and Bishop Selwyn, 84; last years in office and death, 97–8; as predecessor to Max Warren, 207–8

Venn, Rev. John, 7, 39
Venn, Martha (née Sykes), 39
Victoria (Australia) CMA, 149
Viravagu, Rev. Vedhanayagam, 64
Volkner, Rev. Carl, 82

Waddell, Jean, 291–2
Waddington, Beatrice, 282
Waimate, 80
Waitangi, Treaty of, 25, 40, 79
Wakefield, Edward Gibbon, 24, 79
Warren, Rev. Jack, 188, 208
Warren, Rev. J. A. F., 207–8
Warren, Dr. M. A. C., General Sec-
    retary of CMS 1942–63, appointed
    Gen. Sec., background and work
    as administrator, 207–14; in
    China, 219–20; changes in CMS
    policy, creation of new provinces,
    winding-up of IMC, 228–34;
    retirement, 259, 261; writings, on
    Henry Venn, 43; on Alexander
    Duff, 202; on Bishop Cash, 209–
    210; on Archbishop Fisher, 219–
    230
Warren, Shelagh, 188
Waruhiu, Senior Chief, 240
Waterloo Road, No. 157, 262–3
Webster, Canon Douglas, 213
Weeks, Rt. Rev. John, 21, 22
Wellington, Matthew, 121
Welton, William, 144
Wesley, Rev. Charles, 2, 3
Wesley, Rev. John, 2, 3, 4, 49
West, Rev. John, 85
West Indies, 35–6, 50
Weston, Rt. Rev. Frank, 171
Whitehead, Rt. Rev. Henry, 215
Whitfield, Rev. George, 2, 3
Whitley, Rev. Henry, 157
Wigram, Rev. Edmund, 99
Wigram, Rev. Frederic, 99
Wilberforce, Rt. Rev. Samuel, 41–2,
    45, 46

Wilberforce, William, 8, 26, 35, 36,
    45
Wilhelm, J. G., 21
Wilkinson, Rev. Michael, 69
Williams, Archdeacon Henry, 24,
    80, 82, 83
Williams, Mrs. Jane, 83
Williams, Rt. Rev. Leonard, 82
Williams, Sir Robert, 264
Williams, Rev. Samuel, 82
Williams, Rt. Rev. William, 24, 80,
    81, 82, 84, 118–19
Williams family (NZ), 170
Willis, Rt. Rev. John, 133, 171, 183,
    184, 192
Wilson, Rev. C. T., 122
Wilson, Rt. Rev. Daniel, 18, 28, 40,
    59–62, 68, 71; death of, 73
Wittenbach, Canon Harry, 220
Women in mission, 64–5, 66, 105,
    107–13, 137, 139, 147, 149, 154,
    169
women, work among, 64–5, 146, 147,
    149, 166
Woods, Rt. Rev. Theodore, 178
World Council of Churches, 232,
    233, 234, 260, 275, 276
World War 1914–18, 172–5, 176,
    237
Wright, Rev. Henry, 98, 161
Wycliffe College, Toronto, 201
Wynn Jones, Rt. Rev. William, 198,
    200

Xavier, Francis, 140

Yan Shih-ki, 220
Yoruba Mission, 51, 52–5, 57, 114
Young Men's Christian Associ-
    ation, 167, 168, 215

Zenana Bible and Medical Mission,
    66, 111
Zenker, Rev. Paul, 78, 173